Not in Our Name
War dissent in a Welsh town

Also by Philip Adams:

A Most Industrious Town:
Briton Ferry and its people 1814–2014

Not in Our Name

War Dissent in a Welsh Town

PHILIP ADAMS

This inquiry, I must admit, is a groping in the Dark;
but although I have not brought it into a clear light,
yet I can affirm that I have brought it from
an utter darkness to a thin mist.
John Aubrey

Published by Philip Adams
144 Corve Street, Ludlow, Shropshire SY8 2PG, UK
www.britonferrybooks.uk

First published 2015

British Library Cataloguing in Publication Data. A catalogue record for this book is available from the British Library.

ISBN 978 0 9930671 1 2

Designed by Internet@TSP, Ludlow, Shropshire

Printed in UK by Gomer Press, Llandysul, Ceredigion

Cover photo:
'A No Conscription Fellowship member, about to attend a London Military Service Tribunal to object to his conscription, thumbs his nose at an unwelcome photographer'. (Getty)

Contents

Foreword

Had there existed a Parliamentary Committee on Human Rights in 1916 then the content of wartime legislation and events resulting from that legislation, such as the Defence of the Realm Act and Military Service Acts, may have taken a quite different course.

Today the Parliamentary Committee on Human Rights considers every Government Bill for its compatibility with human rights, including common law fundamental rights and liberties, the Convention Rights protected by the Human Rights Act 1998, and the human rights contained in other international obligations of the United Kingdom.

This book covers both national and local figures who worked together for causes they may not have recognised as human rights in the early Twentieth Century. We can, however, be in no doubt that those who are featured in this book, whether from religious, political or philosophical motivation, were front-runners in the cause of human rights.

One such person was Keir Hardie, and it is with great satisfaction that I have written this foreword to commemorate the 100th Anniversary of Keir Hardie's death on 26 September 1915.

Dr Hywel Francis
Chair Joint Committee on Human Rights
UK Parliament
2015

Author's note

I have decided to limit the scope of this work to Briton Ferry for several reasons. Firstly, due to family interest in two of the town's conscientious objectors: John Adams was my uncle. Another, Tom Thomas was my grandmother's eldest brother. I knew almost nothing about them before undertaking this publication, but had long suspected there was much to tell. Secondly, I feel that the town was very unusual in attracting many very distinguished figures, visiting from Wales itself but also far beyond, so that its history possesses far more than simply local interest. However, although extremely fascinating, the town's story is not entirely unique and, if in slightly different forms, was replicated in what happened in other communities, such as Merthyr, Cwmafan and Taibach can largely be appreciated through Briton Ferry's experiences. My third reason is that I felt that this study, in what is substantially still a very under-explored field, would benefit from my local knowledge, whereas the depth of a more extensive study would be likely to suffer, in terms of both depth and nuancing. Finally, current experts on the subject of opposition to World War One, such as Cyril Pearce, seem clear that local, not national, studies are now required to understand the issues involved.

The author recognises that this book is incomplete in parts. Indeed, it has been written with the intention of eliciting further information from readers, especially with regards Chapters Four, Five, and Six in which the local situation is covered. This is both to complete any gaps in the current work and to confirm (or, more optimistically,) augment the detailed contents of the national Pearce Register of Conscientious objectors. The author welcomes correspondence from anyone with relevant information and assures them that it will be treated sympathetically and confidentially.

Chapter One:

Introduction

'War will exist until that distant day when the conscientious objector enjoys the same reputation that the warrior does today'
(John F. Kennedy)

This, in anyone's view, is a most remarkable story. The context is the transition, within the space of less than a century, of a small hamlet in South Wales celebrated by the first rank of artists and poets for its exceptional beauty, into an industrial melting-pot. Its unusual mixture of favourable terrain, accessible raw materials and readily available labour, favoured the early location here of a variety of metallurgical industries.

The Earl of Jersey, the local, largely absentee, landowner, ceded large tracts of land and presumably harvested concomitant profits – for a while. As his beautiful demesne shrank, its constituent parts were denoted by posh un-Welsh sounding street names – Osterley, Hoo, Rockingham and Vernon – destination indicators for the wealth created by the workers. But, in the early twentieth century, things were starting to change in the western coalfield. In its mining valleys and on the coastal strip from Llanelli to Port Talbot a growing awareness of economic and political exploitation sparked the assertion for that change. Its assertion to resist war led to Briton Ferry becoming an advocate for human rights.

The untold story

For over a century Briton Ferry was 'a most industrious town'[1] and a much-loved community. It no longer is an industrial town but it was during its great period and particularly between the 1900s and

---

[1] *A Most Industrious Town: Briton Ferry and its people 1814-2014* is the title of an earlier book (2014) by the author.

the 1940s that the events described here occurred. It is a substantially an untold story, but the truth concerning which needs to be exhumed and included properly and accurately in the town's history and in the curriculum of its schools. For too many people, what you are about to read has long been an inconvenient truth; one which, until now, has been conveniently buried. Fortunately, there are those who, aware of the truth, believe it should not. The generosity of such people in providing me with valuable, frequently extremely moving documentary material, often having strong personal value for them, has compensated for the mysterious absence of, or gaps in, official records and the equally patchy and generally bigoted reporting of a frequently biased press.

Briton Ferry in the early 19th century

As late as the early 19th century, Briton Ferry could boast of being the most picturesque village in Wales. *Nothing could surpass the beauty of this sequestered spot, embossed in hills skirted by shady woods fertile, vales and luxuriant meadows, the scenery is strikingly diversified.*[2] During the 19th century this scene gradually changed as a result of industrialisation, particularly after the advent of the South Wales Railway in mid-century which accelerated an earlier phase of that industrialisation. Areas such as Briton Ferry that had been renowned for their natural beauty were transformed into urban districts, often shrouded in smoke and dust. Two raw materials, iron ore and coal, were at the root of the great changes that overtook Glamorgan in the 19th century. Once it was discovered that coked coal could be used instead of wood charcoal to smelt iron, a great expansion of industry began. Limestone and water were also needed for the furnaces. These were all found on the northern edge of the coalfield, but when local ores ran out, larger plants for imported ores were built on the coast in such places as Briton Ferry.

Between about 1850 and 1900, the accelerating industrialisation needed to sustain the British Empire resulted in the construction of an ironworks, two steelworks and half a dozen tinplate works

---

[2] An extract from *A History of Wales* published in 1849 quoted by Coun. David Davies, J.P.

Briton Ferry
Glamorgan[3]

around the docks in Briton Ferry. The works required workers and the workers required housing. Many of the workers were agricultural labourers who had moved from west Wales.

Briton Ferry in the second half of the 19th century

As the century, and with it industrialisation, progressed in the town, work depended less on the seasons and more on the regularity of work imposed by production demands. The unequal servant-master relationship gradually gave way in the second half of the century to the *tyranny of the clock*, the specialisation of labour and the receipt of wages wholly in cash. This was the employment pattern into which the town's six tinplate works, two steelworks and other metallurgical-related activities worked. It provided the environment and culture in which organised labour and its resistance to industrial and military conscription would grow. The works can be identified in illustrations on pages 194 and 195. Their geographically close proximity also enabled close ties in terms of political and industrial relations.

The 1894 Parish Councils Act resulted in the formation of Briton Ferry Urban District Council and a strengthening of local identity

[3] Julius Caesar Ibbotson: painting oil on wood 352 x 457 mm; © Tate London, 2015

for the town's 8456 inhabitants until it was absorbed, after 28 years of *independence*, into Neath Borough Council in 1922.

As contemporary photographs show, the many churches and chapels, like the abundant industrial buildings, made a huge impact on the town's physical appearance. Certainly the former also played an equal part in this story and the eighteen chapels indicate the importance of non-conformist Christianity in Wales during the period from 1850 to 1950. In addition to religious worship, they had a clear moral and social role and were the focus of good work, family life and the upbringing of children. Almost every street in Briton Ferry had its *own* church or chapel during the second half of the nineteenth century and, by early in the twentieth century, the town could claim not just eighteen chapels but three Anglican churches. The churches generally supported the war but a hard core of chapels certainly did not.

As the nineteenth century came to a close, working class representation in political office became a great concern for many in Briton Ferry. Some who sought the election of working men and their advocates to Parliament saw the Liberal Party as the way of achieving this aim. A number of so-called 'Lib-Lab' candidates were subsequently elected Members of Parliament by this alliance of trade unions and radical intellectuals working within the Liberal Party. The idea of working with the middle class Liberal Party to achieve working class representation in parliament was not accepted in Briton Ferry, however. Here, socialists rejected the idea of workers making common cause with the petty bourgeois Liberals in exchange for what were perceived as scraps of charity from the legislative table.

In the 1892 General Election, three working men were elected without support from the Liberals. One of these was Keir Hardie, who was to emerge as a national voice of the labour movement. The Independent Labour Party's formation followed in 1893 and Hardie, a pacifist, became its Chairman and Leader. In 1900 he became the first *Labour* MP in Britain and remained the sole Labour MP until World War One.

When war came, most of the members of the Labour Party executive, as well as most of the forty Labour MPs in Parliament lent their support to the recruiting campaign for the War. Only one section held aloof, the Independent Labour Party (ILP). By this time Briton Ferry had become a stronghold for the ILP which insisted on standing by its long-held ethically based objections to militarism.

The lead-up to war

Generally it used to be considered that the assassination of Archduke Franz Ferdinand triggered the First World War. It was, in fact, a final catalyst, succeeding the words and deeds of the politicians that preceded the assassination that led to the catastrophe. Politicians operated within an international system of complicated alliances and antiquated domestic political structures. These alliances and treaties determined which parties would be defended by which. The national political structures determined the amount of democratic control that existed over the armed forces within the alliances. In 1914 Germany, Austria-Hungary and Italy were in a Triple Alliance by which each of the parties would be defended by the others, if attacked. Russia and France had also concluded a pact to resist any aggression by the Triple Alliance. Associated with the Russia-France pact was the Entente Cordiale, an Anglo-French understanding on mutual security.

In their domestic politics all the major regimes were undemocratic in the sense that no executive government was accountable to a legislature elected by universal suffrage. Political power was, therefore, exercised by a small group drawn from the upper middle class and the aristocracy, without a plausible system to check and balance the legislative and executive branches of government. In addition, political leaders were under internal threat from minority nationalities within their borders and from an emerging industrial proletariat dedicated to securing economic, political and social rights for ordinary working people.

The regimes in both pacts had been gradually building up their armaments for at least a decade before the outbreak of war. In particular this had taken the form of a naval arms race between Britain and Germany in which the German Kaiser wanted a navy that could challenge Britain throughout its vast empire. The complexities of the European Alliance system thus converted a localised conflict in the Balkans into a general European war; and subsequently the economic interests of imperialists then converted the European war into a World War. It can be seen that industrialisation facilitated an arms race and also provided the means to make war.

War – the move towards conscription

Records exist for the numbers of both volunteers and conscripts who enlisted in the armed forces throughout the country during World War One. The Cenotaph at Briton Ferry records and commemorates the 120 or so inhabitants of Briton Ferry who died doing military service in that war,[4] and these included three members of my own family.

Britain was the only Great Power without universal military service (conscription) although pressure for its introduction had grown through the early years of the 20th century. The National Service League, which was founded in 1906, was exercised by the fact that in 1914 Germany had 2.2 million soldiers against Britain's 711,000. Consequently, it is not surprising that five consecutive conscription bills were tabled in Parliament in the years preceding 1914.

However, at the beginning of the war political opposition to universal military service also remained strong. The governing Liberal Party opposed the idea, as did large sections of the Labour Party and even some Conservatives. Even after the outbreak of war in August 1914, the Cabinet unanimously dismissed Winston Churchill's proposal for compulsory military service. Foreign Secretary Sir Edward Grey described the British policy should be to pursue a *European policy without keeping up a great army.*

In the absence of conscription between 1914 and 1916, pressure was exerted to enlist voluntarily. The TUC and Labour, but not the ILP, supported recruitment in 1914 and justified it on the basis that it was preferable to conscription. Official pressure came in the form of propaganda such as Kitchener's posters to appeal to men's patriotic duty. Often incentives were offered by employers to keep volunteers' jobs open on their return from service. Women proffered white feathers to men who were not in uniform in order to try to

---

[4] Fourteen only are buried in Ynysymaerdy Cemetery, Briton Ferry

shame them into joining the armed forces. As numbers of dead and wounded grew, this pressure increased.

In order to understand how the country moved towards conscription, it is important to consider the war's course and consequent attitudes to conscription in four distinct phases:

1914 – The Great Illusion

At the outset there was a general belief on both sides that it would be a quick war. In Britain many thought 'it would be over by Christmas' without great loss. This supported the belief that volunteering in the absence of conscription would be sufficient. In Germany the expectation was that the quick invasion of France in 1870 could be repeated. Both were wrong; this was the first occasion on which all the industrialised nations of Europe were at war together and most political and military leaders, as well as their populations, grossly underestimated the time effort and manpower needed to succeed in such a war. This was the 'Great Illusion' which influenced many to enlist. When it became clear that the war would not be over by Christmas 1914, the methods adopted to achieve sufficient conscription became more aggressive.

1915 – Stalemate, stagnation and attestation

As the hoped-for lightning military victory eluded the Germans on the western front, battle lines hardened here – and to a great extent on the eastern front too. However, the high casualty rates on the Western Front and the falling number of voluntary recruits quickly pushed the issue of conscription to the top of the political agenda. After the formation of a coalition government under Asquith in May 1915, the Conservative Party and the Liberal Minister of Munitions, David Lloyd George, orchestrated a powerful media campaign in favour of

Attestation poster

universal military service. In 1915 it introduced the *Derby Scheme* whereby men could attest that they would fight if called upon.

1916 – The Great Slaughter, conscription and arrest

In this phase the combatants' strategies moved from a quick annihilation to a chronic attrition, resulting in two million more casualties—firstly, the French at Verdun in February where the Germans tried to 'bleed the French army white'; then the Somme, in July 1916. Early in 1916, two Military Service acts were passed by Parliament, ensuring that all those eligible to serve were now forced to report for duty. Some categories of men were exempt—among others, those whose work was essential to the war effort, those deemed medically unfit for service and those who could show a 'conscientious objection' to active participation in the war.

Cleaver reported on a typical situation: 'J. Walter Jones, Head of Maesydderwen School, Ystradgynlais, made a number of appearances at tribunals asking for exemption for some of his staff, who he claimed could not be adequately replaced, and he also asked for exemption for some of his pupils who were due to sit examinations or were soon to complete their indentures'. In the summer of 1916 the Military Service Tribunal system became a major operation, as did the growth of anti-conscription organisations. These continued till the war ended.

There were various opinions on the British left about a general anti-war campaign, but it was most expedient to rally around the issue of conscription. From 1915 onwards, this was presented by groups such as the Independent Labour Party (ILP) as a fatal infringement of civil liberties that would allow *Prussian militarism* 'to enter Britain by the back door'. Despite police harassment and the restrictions of the Defence of the Realm Act, the ILP and organisations such as the No Conscription Fellowship distributed leaflets and held meetings which totally condemned the idea of a conscripted British army.

Not only did some see conscription as an infringement of civil liberties, others[5] saw it as ineffective:

---

[5] A. J. P. Taylor: History of England 1914–1945

'Compulsory service did not achieve its alleged purpose of providing more men for the army. On the contrary it kept them out. Munitions workers and coal miners could not be prevented from succumbing to patriotic emotion when enlistment was voluntary. The military authorities had to reject them once conscription went through. Instead of unearthing 650,000 slackers, compulsion produced 748,587 new claims for exemption, most of them valid, on top of the million and a half already "starred" by the Ministry of Munitions.'

1917 – Revolution and peace

After the USA declared war on the Central Powers, the Bolsheviks wanted to take Russia out of the war at any price. Many in the anti-war movement, especially socialists, saw the Socialist Revolution in Russia, and the Bolsheviks desire to quit the war, as an opportunity to secure peace.

Conscientious objectors

> *Thus conscience does make cowards of us all,*
> Hamlet, Act III (i)

The work of historians, journalists, poets and painters has resulted in a wide spectrum of facts, opinion and impressions about the war. There are two stereotypes at the ends of this spectrum. At one end the willing volunteer and conscript may be seen, driven, perhaps, by the collective psychology of patriotic moral duty. At the other end, the individual *conchie*, the shirker, represented by the white feather and a spineless cowardice, is so portrayed. This stereotype implies that the COs were a small and marginal minority comprising isolated individuals who were not part of their communities.

Generally the popular press employed both stereotypes to engender support for the war. The stereotype of the willing volunteer or conscript sought support positively and that of the conscientious objector sought it negatively, showing that the country could engage in a modern war without sacrificing its liberal principles. Together they created an impression that support for the war was widespread, especially as there was little general publicity allowed to support opposition to the war.

In the middle of the spectrum were those with less-absolute positions, for example those who were opposed to combatant duties in the war but who would be prepared to undertake non-combatant ones, or alternative work of national importance. Others changed their views during the war, perhaps when attestation or conscription was introduced, or the war's horrors became increasingly evident.

There is little data on those who opposed the war, but opposition certainly existed before war broke out in August 1914. Trade unionists and socialists in Europe were opposed to war in their belief that war would mean workers of different countries killing one another in the interests of their capitalist bosses. Christian pacifists, Irish Nationalists, Women's Groups and many intellectuals were also against it. With the passing of the Military Service Act of 1916, the attention of many anti-conscription activists turned increasingly from stopping conscription per se to helping its most obvious victims: the conscientious objector. Approximately 20,000 men are recorded as COs during the First World War. My uncle was one of those who refused conscription and it is what I know of his experience which prompted me to study the subject of opposition to the war, and the accuracy, or not, how that opposition has been represented.

Objectors fell into various categories. Roughly seventy-five per cent were socialist objectors who opposed the *imperialist* war on political grounds; others, including many Quakers, opposed it for religious reasons. Some COs felt able to support the war effort as non-combatant, however, *Absolutists* were opposed to undertaking any work whatsoever which they thought aided Britain's prosecution of the war.

The fate of British COs was usually decided by local tribunals, set up under the terms of the Military Service Act to decide whether individuals should be granted exemption from military service. Many of the 748,587 who had appeared before the tribunals before June 1916 offered practical arguments for exemption, such as physical or medical disability. Or their employers did so, claiming that their employees' work was of *national importance*. Family or business situations that could not survive the objector's absence were also cited frequently, rather than principled opposition to the war.

Those who applied for exemption on grounds of conscience were often given short shrift. The No-Conscription Fellowship (NCF) worked tirelessly on such cases. Where possible, the NCF gave advice on how to present applications to the tribunals and always publicising the fate of COs.

Not all who opposed the war were classified as conscientious objectors and some who supported the war were in fact objectors of a particular kind. In the case of the former it was simply because many people fell outside the age parameters for conscription and so their opposition was less obvious. In the latter category many applications were submitted for exemption to conscription which did not indicate opposition either to conscription, or to war.

In Wales others, such as George Lloyd of Wrexham and Robert J. Evans of Brymbo objected because of their Welsh Nationalist beliefs: it was not, they thought, Wales' war.

In general we might say there were three broad reasons for objecting to conscription, with the last two regarded as *conscientious* objection:

1. Practical arguments for exemption
2. Political-philosophical or moral reasons, for example, that the workers in one country should not fight against the workers in another country; nationalist beliefs, or a belief on practical grounds that war in general is simply wasteful and ineffective.
3. Religious reasons, or non-religious belief in the sanctity of life

Of the 20,000 conscientious objectors in Britain during the First World War, more than one-third went to prison at least once, and 1,500 *absolutists*, several of whom were from Briton Ferry, were locked up for the remainder of the conflict. Five from south Wales died as a direct result of the treatment they received in military hands whilst in prison. Many COs accepted non-combatant work or work on various projects of *national importance*.

The objectors, however, were always classified as soldiers and as such constituted a tiny minority of the British army, leading the National Archives to consider conscientious objectors to be a 'relatively minor thorn in the government's side'. Public opinion generally had little sympathy for COs who were treated harshly in prison and stigmatised as 'cowards, peace cranks and pasty faces'; organisations such as the ILP and the No-Conscription Fellowship, too, were stigmatised in the jingoistic sections of the press, possibly because the anti-conscription movement in Britain had no parallels elsewhere in Europe. Fifty years later American conscripts who objected to the Vietnam War were simply called 'draft dodgers'.

The motivation to object was certainly not always on religious grounds. Very often the objection was philosophically or politically based, and the various motivations often became conflated. Fenner Brockway, Clifford Allen, and even Keir Hardie, seem to have had variable views on whether religion was the basis for socialist politics, or the other way around:

> *'There will never be true Christianity without Socialism'*
>   and
> *'. . . the impetus which drove me first into the Labour movement . . . has been derived more from the teachings of Jesus of Nazareth than from all other sources combined.'*

Either way, even though the collective psychology resulted in general support for the war, nevertheless many ordinary, and many distinguished, people did not offer support. So were such people as they were accused of being: shirkers and cowards who pretended they did not want to kill, or were they genuinely pursuing a basic human right to follow their consciences? The conventional wisdom in 1914 was that patriotism was virtuous and that there was a general moral obligation to support the War. Clearly we cannot judge the past by present values but then war meant killing and killing was seen as a necessary evil. Any decision not to support the War through enlistment or conscription was regarded as cowardly unless one had a visible and convincing reason for doing so. Usually, the most acceptable reason for a justifiable objection to enlistment was membership of a recognised religious group or an employer's application for exemption. Unless such membership was demonstrable, it became very difficult to object to conscription on other grounds.

Our main story about conscientious objection starts in 1916 and it is instructive to make a brief note of the situation at that time regarding both support for and opposition to the war in three locations: Cardiff, Huddersfield and Briton Ferry.

Cardiff: meetings for and against conscription

The National Archive's *Spotlight on History* web pages describes events in Cardiff in November 1916, when a peace conference was violently interrupted by a mob of patriots, 'who vividly illustrated the depth of public hostility' towards those who were seen to be hindering the successful prosecution of the war.

Two leaflets, one advertising a patriotic citizens' meeting and another an anti-conscription meeting in Cardiff on 10 and 11 November 1916, provide an insight into the bitterly conflicting emotions aroused by pacifism in wartime Britain. The first advertises 'A Great Patriotic Citizens' Demonstration' to be held in Cardiff on 10 November 1916. It was organised in response to a 'Peace Conference' already planned for the following day by the National Council for Civil Liberties (and advertised in the second leaflet). Briton Ferry was represented at this meeting by its Trades Council and its ILP, NCF and NCCL branches. After failing to get this Peace Conference prohibited under the Defence of the Realm Act, 'patriots' stormed the conference hall, forcing the speakers off the stage and tabling a resolution calling for the war to be prosecuted 'to the bitter end'.

Huddersfield

In his well-known book, *Comrades in Conscience*, Cyril Pearce (2014) analysed the case of Huddersfield and concluded that opposition to war was stronger and was generally tolerated more there than in other towns. This, and other recent work, has questioned the accuracy of both the historical record and modern preconceptions regarding contemporary public opinion. As a result of such current re-evaluation, the orthodox consensus – that the British people's commitment to the war was not seriously questioned – is now shifting. Pearce stresses the importance of recording and analysing local experience, and not just a national picture based on sources generated at the centre. He says:

'we have yet to see a study of COs which sets them properly in their social contexts and attempts to understand them not just as heroic/misguided individuals but also as groups and individuals expressing a broader community consciousness. This is only possible through more careful attention to the detail on the ground and in local communities.'

That is why a study, and particularly of (the exceptional in many ways) Briton Ferry is important.

Briton Ferry

If we change one of Pearce's statements, in which he understates an important point, replacing *Huddersfield* with *Briton Ferry*, it reads: 'although the view from *Briton Ferry* is different, it is nevertheless just as valid as that from Kew, Colindale or the Imperial War Museum'.

We shall see that three key features became apparent in Briton Ferry's case so that one must ask whether or not these were similar to factors that Pearce found maintaining to Huddersfield:

The first dominant feature in Briton Ferry was the energy from the local labour and socialist movement found within the ILP, the NCF and the chapels which substantially led to the town's appellation of 'Little Moscow'.

Secondly, there existed very effective connections between the town and national figures which both articulated and supported that opposition.

Finally, the proposition that the levels of recruitment and conscription were as much due to social and workplace pressures as to patriotism was valid for both Huddersfield and Briton Ferry. This does not suggest that opposition to the war in Briton Ferry was by a majority but that opposition was, nevertheless, not just individual, but collective. From this it would appear that Briton Ferry's experience may have been akin to that of Huddersfield. However, the more compact community of Briton Ferry experienced a rate of objection which was over three times greater than that of Huddersfield, as can be seen from the figures in Appendix 14.

Conclusion to Chapter One

My purpose in this book is to cast as much light as possible on the opposition to the war by the thirty-three conscientious objectors from Briton Ferry who are known to have refused conscription, but it will also consider the influence of those who visited the town, especially during and after World War One, in order to promote peace and international co-operation and assess whether the situation in the Neath-Port Talbot area was typical.

I will consider whether this opposition led to a lasting 'community consciousness' that went beyond opposition to conscription and even pacifism. Indeed, was there a radical philosophical thread in the town which unconsciously stood for human rights across the board? To what extent was the town a place to advocate women's and universal suffrage, equality of opportunity, justice, freedom of expression, racial and religious toleration and world peace?

In order to answer these questions the evidence must now be examined. In the following chapter the use of the records used for this research are explained. Subsequent chapters will then examine the evidence, in order to determine the degree of opposition from both the COs themselves and those who supported them, or their cause.

Chapter Two:
The albums and other evidence

The notion that this minority of people can be dismissed to the margin really needs re-examining. (Pearce)

The records that provided most evidence of Briton Ferry's opposition to war in came from three principal sources:
   1. Albums, photographs and diaries
   2. The 'Pearce Register' of conscientious objectors
   3. Newspapers of the time

Albums, photographs and diaries

Quite unexpectedly, autograph albums provided interesting and convincing evidence of events and the attitudes of those involved in the anti-war and peace movement in Briton Ferry. Originally two such albums were examined, although among my family's papers for many years, they had not been given the attention they proved to merit. The black album at the bottom of the photo was presented to my father on Christmas Eve 1918, and the maroon album on the right of the illustration was presented to my aunt on Christmas Eve 1914.

The albums

Autograph collection was a popular pastime in the early 20th century. Family and friends as well as famous people often added sketches, sayings, proverbs or aphorisms. However the significance of these particular albums is the fact that they feature in their pages the autographs of so many well-known personalities, as well as local, supporters of peace. The black and red albums contained entries made in Briton Ferry during the war. Due to the generosity of a donor, who had read something I had mentioned in an earlier book[6], I was given a third album, one which included several post-war entries. This is the red album to the left. A fourth album was later discovered[7] and it is my belief that more may exist.

Photographs of conscientious objectors in prison or in work centres are rare, but John Adams' papers contained several interesting examples. The source of some the photographs was probably a fellow conscientious objector in Knutsford prison called Wallace Cartwright whose family ran a photographic business in Ystradgynlais. Note the arrow in the top right hand corner of Cartwright's own photograph below.

Allan Colwill's discovery of his grandfather's diary provided a key source directly from a CO.

Wallace Cartwright of Ystradgynlais

---

[6] Adams, as before

[7] Philip Mort, the album's owner, has made its contents and other documents available to me

When conscription was introduced in 1916 John Adams became a twenty-two year-old conscientious objector to conscription and war. Having already lost two young uncles, at the very start of the war[8], we can conclude that he had good reasons to object to conscription in 1916.

The *Pearce Register* of conscientious objectors

The *Pearce Register of British World War One Conscientious Objectors* is projected to appear as part of the Imperial War Museum's 'Lives of the First World War' digital platform. It already contains over 18,000 entries, and brings together data from a wide range of different sources. It is incomplete and is looking to users, such as myself and possibly you, to add new data and suggest corrections so that, over the coming years the Register will become even more extensive and accurate.

Newspapers of the time

For the most part the contemporary newspaper sources were obtained on-line from the remarkable 'Welsh Newspapers Online' source, provided by the National Library of Wales. Sources were: the Cambria Daily Leader, South Wales Weekly Post, The Herald of Wales, Labour Voice/Llais Llafur, Llanelli Star and the Merthyr Pioneer. Additionally occasional reports from the Abergavenny Chronicle and the Hansard official parliamentary record have contributed to this account.

Visiting anti-war support

Many of the political, religious and philosophical leaders of the day visited Briton Ferry for speaking engagements and to discuss the most crucial moral issue of the time: war or peace. Many of the

---

[8] My great-uncle, Lee Adams was a member of the Welsh Regiment. He lived in Hunter Street, Briton Ferry, and was killed at the Battle of the Aisne in September 1914; my great uncle, David Harris Collins, of Giant's Grave, Briton Ferry died in August 1914, in the little-known sea Battle of Coronel; William Adams, my father's cousin of Sand Lane, Briton Ferry was killed at the Battle of Hazebrouck in April 1918.

visitors signed the autograph albums from which it is clear that this tradition of visits continued well after World War One. C. L. R. James, George Padmore, Emma Goldman and Paul Robeson were among later, peacetime, visitors to the town. This suggests that in Briton Ferry, a positive pro-peace internationalist stance existed, as well as anti-war sentiment. But the very interesting question is: why did so many prominent figures single out Briton Ferry to visit?

Perhaps the foremost reason was because Briton Ferry was a place with a great deal of civic pride where things happened: socially, industrially, religiously and politically. It was an active ILP stronghold. The town's opinion leaders in the ILP and the NCF had strong links with some chapels, in particular Jerusalem Baptist Church. The town had a culture of debate and political awareness and particularly appreciated speakers with a wide internationalist outlook. Finally, British Prime Minister, Ramsay MacDonald himself, may have become attracted to become MP for the constituency to which Briton Ferry then belonged as a result of his earlier visits and his admiration of many of its politically active constituents.

Centres of dissent?

Many of the signatures in the albums were obtained at meetings held both at Jerusalem Baptist Church and at other 'centres of dissent' within other chapels, or at regular meetings in places such as Briton Ferry Public Hall or the Crown, (today Jersey) Park.

Jerusalem, was an important, although not the only, focal point for social, political and religious, matters. There the principles of co-operation, pacifism and internationalism were encouraged. Its minister, the Reverend Rees Powell, chaired the Briton Ferry Council against Conscription and his wife the local branch of The Women's Peace Crusade. The chapel promoted the plethora of guest speakers from Parliament, the Trade Unions, Churches and Universities. From August 1917, the Church launched a series of peace meetings and 'chose what was then the very uneasy course of making a stand for peace, Much bitter opposition and hostile abuse was aroused, according to its own Centenary booklet'.[9]

---

[9] Centenary of the Baptist Cause in Briton Ferry 1837–1937

Nonetheless, ILP members found intellectual sanctuary there. 'Jerusalem Baptist Church, since the war, by its determined stand against conscription and for peace by negotiation has earned itself the title of Kaiser's Temple. If Kaiser's Temple is synonymous with Temple of Peace then the title is one for which any church of Christ should be proud. Honour to its pastor and its noble band of workers who exemplify in their actions the great ideals of the Christ, whom they profess and worship.'[10]

Misrepresentation

Certainly a degree of misrepresentation exists today concerning the town's attitude to the war, for example a statement posted on line in 2014 by a south Wales firm[11] that organises educational tours to various battle sites: 'In Briton Ferry every man of eligible age joined the forces'. Many, of course, did join the army, both as volunteers and conscripts; the town also made munitions, but the truth is that many were actively against the war and either refused to join up, or were not required to for reasons of their occupation. What historian Cyril Pearce said of Huddersfield can, therefore, equally be said of Briton Ferry: 'The notion that this minority of people can be dismissed to the margin really needs re-examining'.

Anti-conscription and peace organisations

I will now examine in more detail the main organisations through which anti-conscription, anti-war and pro-peace activities took place in Briton Ferry. Key was the Briton Ferry Council against Conscription. Although it was primarily a national organisation to represent the interests of conscientious objectors, in Briton Ferry its members co-ordinated its activities strongly with the Independent Labour Party (ILP), and more informally with the Union of Democratic Control and the Fellowship of Reconciliation. Of the organisations associated with the Briton Ferry Council against Conscription, only the last was explicitly Christian. The others could

---

[10] *Merthyr Pioneer*
[11] *walesinthefirstworldwar.typepad.com* (Jan 12 2009) accessed September 2014; Stephen and Susan Cocks, of Guided Battlefield Tours, Newport.

Jerusalem Baptist Church, Briton Ferry[12]

be considered to have followed Christian principles in the pursuit and promotion of their goals. Education and propaganda, through public or private meetings, was a means to achieve support for such goals.

The Independent Labour Party

It should be noted here that the word 'independent' indicated independence from the Liberal party, and not, as is often thought, the Labour Party. After the 1892 general election the Trade Union Congress (TUC) proposed the foundation of a new party. A year later the ILP was founded in Bradford, with Keir Hardie as its first Chair. It, along with the TUC, the Social Democratic Federation and the Fabian Society, played a central role in the formation of the Labour Representation Committee. This committee was the forerunner of the Labour Party, which was formed in 1906, and to which the ILP was affiliated from 1906 until 1932.

The Briton Ferry Headquarters of the ILP was at Chequers, 224 Neath Road, next to the Public Hall, built by popular subscription, and close to the Crown Park. The Briton Ferry ILP Branch was

---

[12] Salem, Rehoboth and Jerusalem were the town's three Baptist chapels

Wales' largest with well over 500 members, a fact attributed to its recruitment levels and strong leadership in the steel and tinplate works. Len Williams, a member who worked in the Albion Steelworks, confirmed that membership was drawn from manual trade unions rather than the white collar occupations.

Chequers[13]

He listed its leaders, several of whom were town Councillors, as: Joe Branch, George Gethin, Fred Gwynne, Tom Hughes, Sid Southcott, Edward Richardson and Ivor Thomas. In Briton Ferry ILP it was customary for members to refer to each other as 'comrade'.

Briton Ferry ILP was educational, as well as political, holding debates and literary classes. In November 1918, for example, Messrs J. Kyte (Secretary) and M. Watters (Chair) supported the continuation of the previous winter's Sunday evening literary classes. The new class discussed Henry De Beltgens Gibbins' popular international bestseller *The Industrial History of England*. The ILP's Sunday meetings were timed not to clash with religious services, but the 'churches (were) doing their best to prevent the attendance of youths by prolonging the religious services to an unusual extent.' [14] This alienated many young men from the churches.

The Union of Democratic Control (UDC)

The organisation's purposes were: to campaign to ensure that foreign policy would be under parliamentary, and not militarist

---

[13] This was next to Briton Ferry Public Hall, a wonderful community resource, inexplicably destroyed in favour of a petrol station.

[14] Merthyr Pioneer 8 September 1917.

control; to promote negotiations to take place after 1918 in order to prevent future conflict and to campaign for a peace settlement that would not humiliate defeated nations or result in artificial boundaries which could cause further future friction. Amongst its founders were Charles Trevelyan, Arthur Ponsonby and E. D. Morel; Ramsay MacDonald, Norman Angell, J. A. Hobson, H. N. Brailsford and Lowes Dickinson soon joined them. It is astonishing to record that at least nine of the founder members visited Briton Ferry. The UDC was effectively a coalition of the ILP and Liberal critics of the war. Its policy was adopted entirely by the ILP in 1915 and President Wilson's 14-point post-war Peace Program was based on the UDC's policy. I have seen no evidence of the UDC having any members in Briton Ferry but certainly much sympathy is indicated on the frequency of the visits of such prominent speakers.

The No Conscription Fellowship (NCF)

The NCF had many members in the town. It advised members eligible for conscription to apply for absolute exemption on grounds of conscience. One NCF member who presented himself to the West Glamorgan Appeal Tribunal was told: 'you belong to one of the most pernicious bodies in the country. Its members are going all over the place distilling poison and are greater enemies to Britain than the Germans'.[15] Elsewhere the situation was different: Pearce claimed that 'there was little evidence of its impact in Huddersfield'. There, the NCAC was stronger than in Briton Ferry.

The NCF's founders were Bertrand Russell, Clifford Allen from Newport, and Fenner Brockway. Morgan Jones of Bargoed was a very influential early member. They anticipated the introduction of conscription and its scope. Before it was introduced, he asked men between eighteen and thirty eight whether they were opposed to engaging in combatant activities and those who said 'yes' were its first members. The Fellowship was a confluence of religious and political dissent. It existed from November 1914 until November 1919, before it eventually merged with the Peace Pledge Union and became the No More War movement. It was originally only open to men liable for conscription and had 100,000 members in 1916. The

---

[15] Pioneer

organisation exhibited aspects of both pacifism and civil liberties and was organised as a semi-covert organisation, modelled on Sinn Fein and the Suffragette models.

The movement was well-known for its efficient administrative organisation under Catherine Marshall and its ability to trace and record the whereabouts of its members of conscientious objectors. For this reason more is known about the identities of its member-ship in Briton Ferry than of other organisations, perhaps even of the ILP. The Pearce Register has drawn on the records of Marshall's Conscientious Objectors' Information Bureau to create a national database of conscientious objectors.

The Briton Ferry Council against Conscription preceded the formation of the south Wales branch of the No Conscription Fellowship. Indeed the south Wales branch was formed at Briton Ferry on 19 June 1916, when Morgan Jones was elected as its branch chair.

The Fellowship of Reconciliation (FoR)

The Fellowship was founded in 1914 by Henry Hodgkin, a British

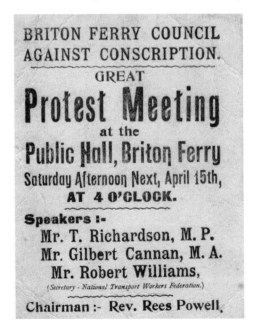

A 1916 NCF Poster
(Ken Donovan)

Quaker, and Friedrich Siegmund-Schultze, a German Lutheran, who was once Chaplin to the Kaiser. By 1917 it had 7,000 members. The Fellowship believes love is the only basis for human society and, as Christians, members were forbidden to wage war. It played a prominent role in acting as a support network for Christian pacifists during World War One, especially concerning the difficult choice of whether or not to become a conscientious objector. It also co-operates with non-Christian faiths. Siegmund-Schultze was arrested and condemned to death for his pacifist involvement and, although the Kaiser intervened to prevent his execution, he was later still badly mistreated.

The new laws

These organisations' activities conflicted with two new laws which came into force during World War One: The Defence of the Realm Act and The Military Service Act.

The Defence of the Realm Act 1914

The Defence of the Realm Act was passed by Parliament on 8 August, 1914 and gave the government wide-ranging powers (for example to enable the requisitioning of buildings and land supposedly essential for the war effort). This act introduced new licensing hours, rationing, censorship, British Standard Time and control of the mines and railways. It also allowed for suspects whose activities discouraged conscription, or that were considered to interfere with military recruitment or training, to be imprisoned without trial. 'No person shall by word of mouth or in writing spread reports likely to cause disaffection or alarm amongst any of His Majesty's forces or among the civilian population'.

Ten persons were executed under the Act for *intent to assist the enemy*. Nothing so drastic happened to anyone from Briton Ferry, but there were several arrests and important court cases involving those men who were found guilty of offences under the act. Whilst the first duty of the state is its defence, its second duty is justice within the realm. It is worth considering whether the Defence of the Realm Act delivered on either count for Briton Ferry's conscientious

Taylor's Foundry made shells for the French Government in 1916[16]

objectors.

The *Munitions of War Act of 1915* was an associated piece of legislation. This enabled the Government to take control of various enterprises as 'controlled establishments' under the auspices of the Ministry of Munitions. One of its effects was to make strikes in munitions factories illegal. Briton Ferry's Taylor's Foundry became the first in Wales to manufacture shells. With Messrs Mullins Ltd, it became a controlled establishment, whilst the Albion Steelworks actually came under French Government control. The munitions crisis of 1915 also led to more intervention by the Government in the workplace in the form of Munitions Tribunals which had the power to punish offenders, even some who had trade union support. As in the case of military tribunals concern was also felt about the role of these, especially, as Bertrand Russell[17] commented: 'Munitions workers, oddly enough, tended to be pacifists'.

The first step towards conscription was the National Registration Act which was put forward in 1915. The reason advanced for national registration was that it would provide the government with

[16] © West Glamorgan Archives
[17] Bertrand Russell: *Autobiography*

the necessary information to establish whether war could be conducted with volunteers. Some five million men were found not to be serving in the Army, of which some 1.8 million were fit and might be available to serve, should it be necessary.

In reality this Act was the thin end of a wedge and one which quickly developed into the *Derby Scheme*, the second step towards conscription. Those deemed to be available by recruiting officers were required to attest to their willingness to serve should they be called upon to do so. The effect of this was to say: 'If you do not join voluntarily now, you'll be forced to join within a few months'. The scheme envisaged calling up conscripts by age group and by placement into occupational categories according to a Board of Trade assessment of the recruits' availability and usefulness. The Derby Scheme introduced the idea of tribunals in order to enable *employers* to appeal for exemption, or against the occupational groups into which those attesting had been placed. The groups were:

1. Essential civilian work
2. Trades and professions from which *a few* could be spared
3. Where a large proportion could be spared
4. Unnecessary occupation – all could be spared

The Military Service Act 1916

As I mentioned in the first chapter, all enlistment prior to this had been voluntary. Prime Minister Asquith had previously said that the National Registration Act was not a prelude to conscription, but it was.

From the first week of February 1916, Recruiting Offices sent Form W3236 to all men of military service age, asking them to enlist, or to provide a certificate of exemption from the Local Tribunals. These had been set up in February. Anyone failing to do either was to be regarded as a deserter.Under the Act, those aged between eighteen and forty-five were obliged to serve in the army unless they were married, widowed with children, serving in the Royal Navy, a Minister of Religion, or working in a reserved occupation. From May 1916, married men became obliged to enlist and, by 1918, this had become the case for all men up to fifty-one

Army Form W. 3236.

NOTICE PAPER to be sent to men who belong to the Army Reserve under the provisions of the Military Service Acts, 1916.

Form W3236 to present oneself for military service at a Recruiting Office

years of age. Men, or employers, who objected to the call-up for any reason had to attend a local Military Service Tribunal, unless they or their employer had previously obtained a certificate of exemption. The grounds for exemption were: already doing work in the national interest, serious hardship, health or infirmity or conscientious objection. Tribunals might grant absolute, conditional or temporary exemption, but rarely did they grant absolute. There were rights of appeal to a County Appeal Tribunal and, finally, to the Central Appeal Tribunal. There were approximately 2000 tribunals in Britain, appointed by Local Authorities.

Clement B. Gardiner of Neath, representing the military authorities, commented on the tribunal workload for Briton Ferry:

'Over 200 cases are to be considered and on Monday twenty-five came up for consideration; fourteen were granted total exemption; for one, six months and eight, three months. Out of this number Mr Gardiner objected to fourteen and he intends laying the names of those he objected to before the military authorities. Lieutenant-Colonel Mansel H. Hunter, OC 7 Welsh Cycle Corps was present.'[18]

This report raises two comments about the tribunal process described here. Firstly the strong presence and influence of the military representatives must be noted. Secondly, the speed at which cases were dealt with is remarkable. The time spent face-to-face on each case in the tribunal room, which, in this case was the Briton Ferry Council chamber could not have averaged more than fifteen minutes.

In April 1917 the *Military Service Act* was tightened in terms of occupational exemptions to get another million men into service and to review the exemptions already given. The Director-General of National Service was given powers to remove all occupational exemptions, but not conscientious objections, in January 1918.

Conclusion to Chapter Two

This chapter has examined the sources of material relating to the conscientious objectors who are portrayed in this book and both the organisations and legal frameworks in which they were involved. The story continues with the administration of the tribunals and the experiences of those individuals who applied to them for exemption from conscription for reasons of conscience. Even though a second Military Service Act gave discretion to tribunals to grant absolute exemption for political (socialist) and other non-religious objectors, this was not followed and it had consequences for many Briton Ferry applicants.

In the next chapters those who came to Briton Ferry from outside Wales to support peace will be outlined (Chapter Three); those from elsewhere in Wales will be considered in Chapter Four; in Chapter Five, the experiences of the conscientious objectors themselves who lived in the town will be examined. Chapter Six reviews the crucial role of women in the cause of conscientious objection and other human rights.

---

[18] *Cambria Daily Leader*, 14 March 1916

Chapter Three:
Support from every quarter

It is not the facts that guide the conduct of men, but their opinions about facts, which may be entirely wrong. We can only make them right by discussion. (Angell)

At the beginning of the twentieth century Briton Ferry began to attract many famous visitors for speaking engagements. This was a phenomenon that increased significantly during World War One and which persisted after the war. It is not possible to establish a particular date when this trend began, but one can explain in general the reasons for it happening. The town was a coherent community, receptive to ideas and a fertile environment for getting things done. It was not averse to change, and especially willing to embrace political change. In particular there was concern about the nature and purpose of industrialisation (except perhaps environmental concern, whose time had not by then arrived) and how it should be used. 'Cometh the hour cometh the man' and if any single person was capable of synthesising and voicing these ideas it was Keir Hardie.

The special peculiarities of local cultures and the altruistic concerns of many of its populace contributed to a fertile environment which attracted him, and numerous others, to Briton Ferry. Their motives for visiting were varied and often such people had interests which overlapped. It is, however, possible to recognise that what motivated all of them and what was such a profound element in the town's intellectual and social make-up, was concern in varying ways, for what we now call human rights. In pursuit of social and political change, there were often strange bed-fellows – those with religious adherence made common cause with those who had none.

This chapter will review the influence of those known to have visited from outside Wales, to oppose military or industrial conscription, support peace through democratic control of foreign policy, or to advocate pacifism. This chapter is in alphabetical order. A chronological list can be found as Appendix Thirteen.

Ernest Bevin

Charles G. Ammon
(1873–1960)

Charles George Ammon attended a
public elementary school in
Bermondsey.
  He was a Methodist and a
conscientious objector and the chief
lobbyist in Parliament for the NCF.
Ammon visited Briton Ferry to speak under the auspices of the ILP
on Sunday 24 June, 1917. That very day the Russian Navy mutinied
at Sevastopol. The following day the 1st US Expeditionary Force
arrived in France.
  Ammon first became Mayor of Camberwell in 1919 and, in the
following year, became Secretary of the Union of Post Office
Workers before, later, becoming Organising Secretary of the Civil
Service Union. In 1922 he was elected MP for Camberwell until
1931, and again from 1935–44. Astonishingly, perhaps, for a World
War One conscientious objector, Ammon became Parliamentary
Secretary to the Admiralty in 1924 and from 1929–1931.
  He was Government Chief Whip in the House of Lords from
1945–49.

William Crawford Anderson
(1877–1919)

Anderson's mother was an ardent radical who
was responsible for his radical education.
Originally he was an apprenticed chemist in
Aberdeen where he attended meetings of the Social Democratic
Federation. After joining the shop assistants' union in Glasgow, he
became Chair after only three months, having strengthened existing
branches and created new. Through joining the Glasgow branch of
the ILP, he gained a strong reputation as a public speaker,
addressing audiences on subjects ranging from Tariff Reform to
National Service.

By 1908 he was elected to the ILP's National Administration
Council. His political position was midway between those of Philip
Snowden and Ramsay MacDonald. Later, Fenner Brockway believed
that his position, together with his warm manner, helped maintain
party unity. Not surprisingly, therefore, Anderson succeeded F. W.
Jowett as ILP Chair in 1910, remaining until 1913. During that time
he wrote *What means this labour unrest?* He also launched the
Daily Citizen with MacDonald in 1912. Anderson aimed to work with
Labour to reassure them that their suspicions of the ILP were ill-
founded. He advocated the nationalising of land, writing *Socialism,
the Dukes and the Land.*

In 1914 he was elected MP for the Sheffield constituency of
Attercliffe. Anderson was, therefore, already an MP and a key
national ILP figure when he visited visit Briton Ferry in March 1916,
but his opposition to the war and support for the Clyde Workers'
Committee cost him his parliamentary seat in 1918. He died of
influenza in 1919, having just completed a further book: *The
Menace of Monopoly: An Argument for Public Ownership.*

The significance of Anderson for Briton Ferry's war resistance
was that, when he chaired Labour's NEC, in August 1914, he gave

an early, reasoned, lead to the ILP to denounce support for the war.
'Each country in turn, largely through the influence of its jingo press
has been stampeded by fear and panic . . . powerful armaments'
interests have played their sinister part, for it is they who reap rich
harvest out of havoc and death'.

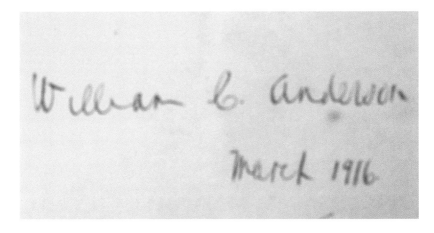

William Crawford Anderson

Norman Angell
(1872–1967)

'It is not the facts that guide the conduct of men, but their opinions about facts, which may be entirely wrong. We can only make them right by discussion'.
(Angell)

Sir Ralph Norman Angell's words appeared over the years on the reading lists of politics students at Swansea University, but few local students who knew Briton Ferry were aware that he had visited the town. He was born in Lincolnshire as Ralph Norman Angell, but later dropped the name *Lane*. He was educated at the Lycée de St Omer in France and at the University of Geneva, whilst meanwhile editing an English newspaper there. By the age of 17 he had migrated to the west coast of the USA, where he carried out various manual jobs, before joining the St Louis Globe-Democrat and San Francisco Chronicle as a reporter. He returned to France to report on matters such as the Dreyfus case for American newspapers and, from 1905 to 1912, he became Paris editor for the *Daily Mail*.

Norman Angell was well known as the author of the 1909 pamphlet, and subsequent book, *The Great Illusion*, the thesis of which was that the integration of the economies of European countries had grown to such a degree that any war between them would be entirely futile, making militarism obsolete and commercial profit from war illusory. This was a different illusion to that referred to in Chapter One, which was that the war would be over by

Christmas 1914 without great loss.

Angell was a principal founder of the Union of Democratic Control, the organisation that campaigned to ensure that foreign policy would be under parliamentary and not militarist control, to promote negotiations to prevent future conflict and to campaign for a peace settlement that would not humiliate defeated nations, or result in artificial boundaries which could lead to further future friction.

He visited Briton Ferry in January 1917. By the time of this visit it had become obvious that the frontal assault on the Somme had failed. Lloyd George had just acceded to power. It was also clear that Lloyd George's policies and authoritarian method of war government offered little immediate prospect of a peace settlement, but only yet further demonstration of the costs and futility of warfare.

Later, Angell served on the Council of the Royal Institute of International Affairs and was an executive member of both the World Committee against War and Fascism as well as the League of Nations Union. He was knighted in 1931 and awarded the Nobel Peace Prize in 1933. From the mid-1930s he actively urged for international opposition to the aggressive policies of Germany, Italy and Japan. In 1940 he visited the USA to lecture in favour of US support for Britain in World War Two. He continued to write and lectured prolifically until the early 1950s. Angell was a towering figure amongst those who sought world peace through transparent, civil, control of foreign policy.

Norman Angell

Ernest Bevin
(1881–1951)

'There never has been a war yet which, if the facts had been put calmly before the ordinary folk, could not have been prevented. The common man is, I think, the greatest protection against war.'

Indisputably, Bevin is considered one of the political giants of twentieth century Britain, and anyone whose working life involved, as Bevin's did, the gradual transition from lorry driver to Foreign Secretary would intrinsically be of very great interest; but that he, too, visited Briton Ferry on 8 January 1911 makes his story in general, and especially his visit, doubly intriguing. One is therefore compelled to ask what his interest was in Briton Ferry and indeed, what was Briton Ferry's interest in him? This is a question to which I will return.

Bevin was orphaned at the age of eight and had to leave school at eleven to work in Bristol Docks. He was a Baptist and learned his oratorical skills as a Lay Preacher before he became a labour activist. By 1905 Bevin had become the unpaid secretary of the Bristol Right-to-Work Committee and joined Bristol Socialist Society. He soon established a carters' branch of the Dockers' union. During the first decade of the twentieth century wages began to stagnate, but retail prices continued to increase. As a consequence trade unions enjoyed increasing support and their membership increased from 1.5 million in 1890 to four million in 1911. This was the national economic background to Bevins' Briton Ferry visit.

Socialism, oratory and the role of the Baptist churches had become three important aspects of life in Briton Ferry by the start of the 20th century. Briton Ferry was therefore an ideal venue for

Bevin, as an up-and-coming trade unionist, to meet with his counterpart Robert Williams, the Swansea Labour Councillor and Secretary of the National Transport Federation. They were the same age and clearly had a great deal to talk about.

Moreover, 1911 was the 'Year of the Great Unrest' throughout the country. Fortunately, Briton Ferry's iron and tinplate industry largely escaped the turmoil that was to follow elsewhere. In the spring, however, 11,000 workers in the Singer Company went on strike in Glasgow and four hundred 'ringleaders' were dismissed. Liverpool had its 'bloody Sunday' in August but Llanelli's August was even bloodier. Events there led to the first ever national rail strike over a seventy-hour working week. Six hundred soldiers were sent to quell the unrest and six people were killed. With Bevin's involvement, by 1922, the Dockers' Union and thirteen others amalgamated to form the TGWU (the Transport and General Workers' Union) and he became its General Secretary from 1922–1945.

What could Bevin have learned from Briton Ferry? Perhaps, like the tinplate workers, he learned that collective organisation and pragmatic trade unionism was of greater benefit than strike action, for example, negotiating the TGWU's withdrawal from the 1926 General Strike. After the strike he began promoting positive benefits, one of which would result in the *Holidays with Pay Act* of 1938.

At the 1935 TUC Conference it was Bevin who spoke out about the Italian invasion of Abyssinia whilst his colleague, George Lansbury, remained silent. Lansbury's stance eventually cost him the Labour Party leadership. After Bevin's appointment as Minister of Labour in 1940, it was he who helped to transform Britain into a total war economy again. He did not baulk at using industrial conscription in the form of directing workers to the coal mines (Bevin Boys), a practice that had been so feared by the ILP and NCF in World War One. Bevin's Emergency Powers (Defence) Act also paralleled the 1916 Defence of the Realm Act which the ILP had so hated.

After World War Two, Bevin was appointed Foreign Secretary. He was a staunch ally of the USA in the ensuing Cold War, and perhaps took advantage of this relationship to support the Marshall Plan, a scheme for revitalising war-battered Western Europe. He also encouraged the formation of NATO and the development of Britain's nuclear weapons programme. Britain's influence after World War Two had diminished and the country effectively became dependent on the USA for defence.

The latter position was at odds with his position on colonialism and the Empire. He realised that the working class had never benefitted from either, a sentiment with which many in Briton Ferry would undoubtedly have agreed. It was in 1947, during Bevin's tenure at the Foreign Office, that Indian Independence was granted. Perhaps it was through his visiting places such as Briton Ferry, which were also visited by anti-colonialists such as Bipin Chandra Pal, Brockway and Morel, that Bevin was influenced in his recognition that the working classes, whether those of Britain or the colonies, had never benefitted from the Empire.

Ernest Bevin *(Philip Mort)*

A. Fenner Brockway
(1888–1988)

Another extremely important and well-known personality, who first came to Briton Ferry in 1912, was Archibald Fenner Brockway. The son of nonconformist missionary parents, he was born in India and lived there until the age of four. During the Boer War he developed an early fascination with politics and assisted the Liberals in the 1905 election before becoming an early member of the ILP. Professionally he was a journalist and edited the ILP's newspaper, the *Labour Elector*. After the *Labour Elector's* editorial offices were raided by the police in 1915, he was prosecuted for seditious libel but won his case. The paper committed the ILP to oppose the war and Brockway himself opposed conscription; he also resolved not to enlist in any capacity to serve in the war effort. Brockway's anti-war activities continued into 1916 when, with Clifford Allen as Chairman and himself as Secretary, the No Conscription Fellowship was founded. They faced government opposition and sanctions; their eventual refusal to pay a fine led to imprisonment in Pentonville Prison. Further refusal to be conscripted led to Brockway's incarceration in the Tower of London, where he was subjected to harsh treatment, including a bread-and-water diet with solitary confinement.

He was also among the first members of the Fellowship of Reconciliation. As Chair of the Central Board of Conscientious Objectors, he frequently received white feathers[19] but was particularly pleased that he was able to convince the authorities to recognise political motives as valid reasons for objection. However, like several of Briton Ferry's absolutists, he was not released from prison until six months after the Armistice.

---

[19] White feathers were intended as a symbol of cowardice given to men who did not join up in order to shame them into doing so.

In January 1920, six months after his release, he visited Briton Ferry. He returned to political affairs with the India League to campaign for Indian Independence. No doubt he was an influence in persuading Dil Thomas[20] and his colleagues to read the works of Gandhi and Nehru. During the 1926 General Strike he edited *The British Worker*, the TUC's journal. After his first election to Parliament for Leyton East in 1928, he was subsequently re-elected in 1931, but refused to support the National Government and broke off his Labour party ties.

Later he campaigned for Indian Independence and was suspended from Parliament for protesting against the imprisonment of Gandhi and Nehru. He did not oppose British participation against fascism in World War Two: 'I could no longer justify pacifism when there was a fascist threat'. At the end of the war he became reconciled with the Labour Party. During his time as MP for Eton and Slough, from 1950-1964, he became known as the 'MP for Africa', because of his leadership of the anti-colonial movement in Britain. By the late 1950s he had become a national figure, having founded the Campaign for Nuclear Disarmament (CND) and in 1980 he became Chair of the World Disarmament Campaign. He was six months short of his 100th birthday when he died.

He knew most of the colonial leaders seeking independence from Britain and played a leading role in the change from British Empire to Commonwealth. His visits to Briton Ferry so soon after his release from prison are indicative of the town's importance and the strength of its belief in peace.It is significant that Brockway spent time in Briton Ferry before, during and after the First World War. Before the war, it was his ILP role which brought him to the town, whilst during the war, the reason for his visit was undoubtedly to work with Morgan Jones and Joe Branch to create a formidable NCF branch in the town.

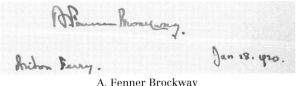

A. Fenner Brockway

----

[20] See Chapter Five.

Charles Roden Buxton
(1875–1942)

Buxton visited Briton Ferry on 12
November 1916, during the most frenzied
period of activity for the Military Service
Tribunals. At a public meeting, which
attracted an audience of nine hundred
people, he addressed the matter of *Peace
by Negotiation*. He was soon to be
followed over the next six months by others speaking on a similar
theme: Snowden, C. P. Trevelyan, Angell, Dunnico and, last but not
least, Henry Davies of Cwmafan.

Buxton grew up on his family's estate in Essex and was educated
at Harrow School and Cambridge University, where he was
President of the Union. After University he left for Australia, where
his father was Governor of South Australia, to become his Private

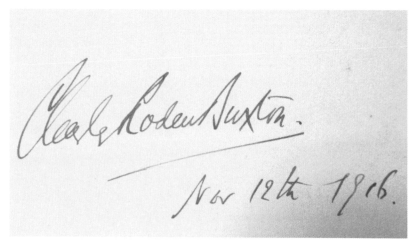

Charles Roden Buxton

Secretary. Later he spent time in the Far East, North America and in France.

He took up law and was called to the bar in 1902, but from that time until 1910 he was Principal of Morley College, an adult education college in Westminster, London.

Buxton married Dorothy Frances Jebb in 1904. The Jebbs were an affluent family with a social conscience. The family founded the *Save the Children* movement. They first lived in Kennington, then an overwhelmingly working-class area of London. Their lifestyle was frugal and this continued during their travels throughout Britain, so much so, that, although great philanthropists, and they were often thought to be tramps.

Buxton contested East Hertfordshire and was elected at the second attempt as a radical Liberal MP for Ashburton, Devon, in 1910. He was a member of Lloyd George's Land Enquiry Committee before losing his seat in the second 1910 election.

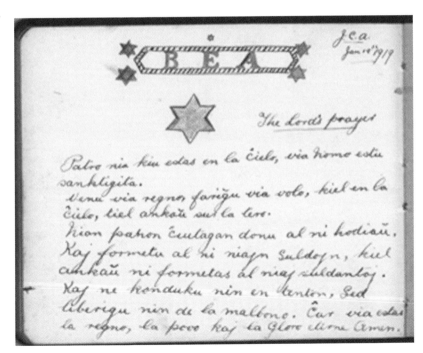

The Lord's Prayer in Esperanto

Afterwards, when he went to the Balkans with his brother, Noel, to stop the drift to war he was shot through the lung by a Turkish assassin, but survived. Buxton argued for a negotiated peace and joined with Ramsay MacDonald, Charles Trevelyan and E. D. Morel in founding the Union of Democratic Control in November 1914.

Buxton was still a Liberal Party member when he first visited Briton Ferry, but he left it and joined the ILP in 1917. The war in the Russian sector of the eastern front had come to an end and the Provisional Government, which had refused to abandon the war, was destroyed. One of Buxton's first engagements as an ILP member was to attend a public peace meeting, chaired by George Jones, at Jerusalem Chapel, Briton Ferry, on Tuesday 6 November, 1917. Not surprisingly perhaps, he delivered 'a most statesmanlike address' but in Russia the moderates, who had been trying for a peace settlement which would be welcomed by European socialist parties such as the ILP, had failed. That same day Bolshevik Red Guards captured the Winter Palace and the Bolshevik Revolution had begun. Peace, it seems, would have to wait.

Buxton was Secretary to a Labour Party's delegation to the Soviet Union in 1920 and wrote about the visit in a later book. He worked unremittingly for peace and the equal distribution of the world's land and resources, both from his position as MP for Accrington in 1927 and Elland in 1929. He was also President of the British Esperanto Society and a Quaker.

Earlier I mentioned John Adams' translation in his autograph album of the Lord's Prayer into Esperanto and this alone would serve to indicate Buxton's influence on Briton Ferry, Jerusalem Church and certainly my uncle. However, the opposite may well be equally true, for it was after Buxton's earlier visit to the town that he joined the ILP and it is perhaps also significant that, soon after joining the ILP, he again returned to Briton Ferry.

Gilbert Cannan MA
(1884–1955)

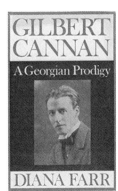

Cannan came originally from a Salford family of
nine children. He was a pacifist, a conscientious
objector and a member of the National Council
against Conscription. He attended Manchester Grammar School
where he was a sufficiently talented as a linguist to win a
scholarship to King's College, Cambridge. He abandoned his early
thoughts of a legal career in order to write, becoming best-known
as a novelist and dramatist.

After he joined the *Society for the Abolition of Censorship* he
fought censorship together with J. M. Barrie, the famous author of,
among other things, Peter Pan. His opposition to it in any form was
very topical in south Wales at the time of his visit.

In April 1916, Cannan undoubtedly visited Briton Ferry in his role
as a strong opponent of censorship. His presence indicated there
being national support for public distribution of anti-war literature.
Not long afterwards the 'Briton Ferry Ten'[21] were to be charged for
the distribution of the *Everett and Early Conscientious Objector*
leaflets. On May 11, 1916 the police raided the ILP Headquarters at
Briton Ferry when Joe Branch and nine others were prosecuted
under Section 27 of the Defence of the Realm Act and were fined
heavily. (Garnet Waters and William Meyrick Davies were similarly
prosecuted for distributing leaflets against recruiting on Neath
Road, Briton Ferry, as a result of which they were both imprisoned.)

Cannon's visit to the area was timely: in Port Talbot, a No
Conscription Fellowship rally, also in May, saw four local councillors
charged with obstruction in Bethany Square. This was a pattern of
events that continued throughout the war: in 1918 the magistrates
were given powers to seize 25,000 leaflets from Councillor Tal
Mainwaring's home. They did not find any.

---

[21] These will be explained in Chapter Five

Hugh Dalton
(1887–1962)

Hugh Dalton was born in
Neath, the son of an
Anglican Clergyman. He was
educated at Eton, where he was friendly with Rupert Brooke, and at
Kings College, Cambridge where he became a socialist and joined
the Fabian Society. He was influenced by Sidney Webb to take a
Doctorate at the London School of Economics, before becoming, for
a brief time, a barrister.

During World War One he served in the army. One must,
therefore, ask what business Dalton, an opponent of pacifism, could
have had in Briton Ferry in 1924 and how his visit might have been
received. One reason perhaps is that it was a response to Herbert
Dunnico's recent visit (see below) during which Dunnico had spoken
out against the Government's naval programme. By the time Dalton
had visited he had written *Principles of Public Finance*, but his
autograph album inscription does not particularly refer to finance:

> *'No matter how entrenched the wrong*
> *The fight now hard, the day how long*
> *Fight on, fight on!*
> *Tomorrow comes the song'.*

One can only guess at what Dalton may have been alluding to:
was the 'wrong' the Great War itself, or the post-war peace settlement at Versailles; was it the fact that insufficient homes and jobs
had been provided for the returning heroes of the war, or was it to
the imminent Dawes Plan[22] to which he was referring? Of course it
may have meant that the 'fight' was his personal struggle for

---

[22] A staggered payment plan for Germany to pay reparations after World War
One

election, but might it have referred to minority Prime Minister MacDonald's current fight to hold his government together with Liberal support? In the October 1924 election later that year, he fought to be elected Labour MP for Camberwell. That may have been the fight he was thinking of and when, a year later, he joined the shadow cabinet, came the song. In 1929 he was singing another song because he then succeeded his wife as MP for Bishop Auckland.

This was happening against the background of the country's growing economic and unemployment problems which resulted in the May Report's recommendation for the Government to cut unemployment benefits. MacDonald and Chancellor of the Exchequer, Philip Snowden, accepted the report, but the majority of the cabinet voted against. This forced MacDonald into a coalition government and in turn forced Dalton to for the expulsion of MacDonald from the Labour Party. Dalton did not join the National Government with MacDonald and he eventually lost his seat in the disastrous-for-labour 1931 election.

During the 1930s Dalton taught at the London School of Economics before re-entering Parliament after the 1935 election; he shaped Labour Party foreign policy, which opposed pacifism and the appeasement of Neville Chamberlain. On the domestic front he wrote *Practical Socialism for Britain* which emphasised how the state could be used as a national planning agency. This influenced the new Labour Leader, Clement Attlee.

As a result he was an appropriate Minister of Economic Warfare in World War Two: a role in which he established the SOE (Special Operations Executive). In 1945, although he was offered the position of Foreign Secretary in the Attlee Government, he declined and instead was offered Chancellorship of the Exchequer. After having nationalised the Bank of England in 1946, he was forced to resign following a budget leak to be replaced by Stafford Cripps.
Dalton's close friend, Mary Agnes Hamilton, said of him . . . 'he has forthright convictions of a robust kind . . . he loves the rough and tumble, the shouting and the fight.'

Dalton's service in the forces in World War One makes his visit to such a peace-loving town as Briton Ferry in 1924 difficult to explain. Before and after his visit, both Emrys Hughes and Minnie

Pallister were to be seen and heard there, so did Dalton come to the town for a 'rough and tumble'? If he did it was unlikely to be about war and peace. More likely it was to support the new Prime Minister in his own constituency on other important matters of the day such as housing and employment. Curiously, it was the Prime Minister and MP for Briton Ferry, Ramsay MacDonald, that he would later vote to expel from the Labour Party.

> "No matter how entrenched the Wrong,
> "The fight how hard, the Day how long,
> "Faint not, fight on!
> "Tomorrow comes the song!"
>
> Hugh Dalton.
> January 13th 1924.

(Cheryl Clement)

Rev Sir James Herbert Dunnico, LL.D, JP
(1876–1953)

Herbert Dunnico (left)

From Gresford, near Wrexham, Herbert Dunnico was Welsh, but when he came to Briton Ferry in 1916, it was because of his pacifist activities, not his Welsh connections. He started work in a factory aged ten, studied in his spare time and won a scholarship to Nottingham University. He was then ordained as a Baptist Minister in Warrington and Liverpool and chaired Liverpool Free Church Council.

On the 6 March 1916 he was the special preacher at the Sunday morning service in Jerusalem Church and he filled the 750 seats. At the evening service the building was even more packed, despite wretched weather. His sermon *Dare to be a Daniel* lasted an hour and was described as 'a magnificent stand of conscience'. The dare was to challenge those who may have hesitated to object to conscription.

In 1916 he formed the Peace Negotiation Committee to call for a truce with Germany and was Director of the Peace Society. Today, Dunnico's name can be seen on the plaque at Neath Abbey to commemorate the work of Joseph Tregelles Price, the Quaker founder of the Society.

Elected Labour MP for Consett in 1922, Dunnico held the seat until 1931. In 1924 he became the first Labour MP to vote against the Labour Government because of their programme to build light cruisers; he feared another arms race. He was Deputy Speaker of the House of Commons from 1929-31. He supported the National Government of 1935 on the grounds that party political partisanship was damaging to the national interest. Dunnico was knighted in 1938.

A freemason, he created the unusual New Welcome Lodge in 1929 in order to attempt to link Freemasonry and the Labour Party, whose left wing had been against it. The lodge later became open to all men working in the House of Commons and Lords.

Dunnico paid several visits to Briton Ferry from 1916 until after the war. Along with Dick Wallhead, he was a most frequent and influential visitor.

Herbert Dunnico

JOSEPH TREGELLES PRICE
FOUNDER OF
THE PEACE SOCIETY
LIVED IN THIS HOUSE.
THE PEACE SOCIETY FORMED JUNE 14TH 1816, IS THE OLDEST IN THE WORLD. IT IS THE PARENT OF THE ORGANISED PEACE MOVEMENT.

"HE WAS NOT DISOBEDIENT TO THE HEAVENLY VISION"

PRESIDENT:
PRINCIPAL PHILLIPS, B.A., D.D.

DIRECTOR:
HERBERT DUNNICO, J.P.

Peace Society plaque showing Dunnico's involvement

John Bruce Glasier
(1859–1920)

During his Briton Ferry visit in 1911, lecturer and journalist, J. Bruce Glasier was a guest of Joe Branch's family at 6 Osterley Street. The latter was Chair of Briton Ferry's ILP and the visit was on its business. It is reasonable to assume that the prospect of war and the consequential risk of military and industrial conscription, would also have been among the topics discussed.

Glasier was one of the four ILP leaders and his wife, Katharine, had been a founder member. He was one of eight children brought up in extreme poverty in the Ayrshire Hills. Following the Glasgow Bank crash in 1878, a thousand firms went into liquidation and Glasier found it hard to get work for twelve years. During this time he read and came to see capitalism as a cause of poverty. He considered the prospect of becoming a church minister until he read Charles Darwin and T. H. Huxley. After hearing H. H. Hyndman of the Social Democratic Federation he became an SDF activist. Also influenced by William Morris and Peter Kropotkin, Glasier preached an ethical and utopian socialism.

In the 1880s Keir Hardie, another Ayrshire man, got to know Glasier and said of him: 'He is still an idealist but he has come to recognise that the way by which the ideal may be reached is more prosaic than his fresh enthusiasm at the time imagined'. Glasier had succeeded Keir Hardie as party leader in 1900 and led the party until 1903, when he, in turn, was succeeded by Philip Snowden. After his 1902 visit to Aberdare, many south Wales visits followed over the years. Abercrave, Bargoed, Barry, Mountain Ash, Cardiff and Ystradgynlais made him welcome during the period of his editorship of the *Labour Leader* between 1905 to 1909, and afterwards.

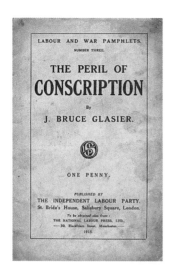

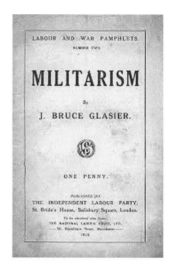

Glasier wrote the ILP pamphlets entitled *The Perils of Conscription* and *Militarism*. These referred to military conscription, but Glasier also foresaw a conscript army being used to break strikes, in a similar way to that which Hardie had envisaged in the threat of compulsory conscription of munitions workers. His fear had some justification, both when the Lancashire and Yorkshire Railway Company was found to be employing blackleg labour, and in Briton Ferry.

The Lancashire and Yorkshire Railway Company had attracted scab labour with the incentive of avoiding conscription on the pretext of doing essential war work on the railway in the Liverpool area. This situation eventually came to have ramifications in Briton Ferry during the case of Garnet Waters and William Meyrick Davies. The pair had been charged, under the Defence of the Realm Act, with serious industrial implications. I will expand on this later.

Glasier was opposed to World War One, and although from 1915 he suffered from cancer, he continued to write until his death in 1920. His influence on Briton Ferry was primarily to give guidance and support to the labour leaders in their political objections to military conscription, to counsel them to be on guard against industrial conscription, and to remind them that the ILP included members who were also religious. The religious members also needed its political support.

Keir Hardie
(1856–1915)

Militarism and democracy cannot be blended
Capitalism . . . . knows no country, has no patriotism

Hardie was invited to Briton Ferry by the Trades and Labour
Council and his topic, when he spoke at the Villiers Recreation
Ground, on Saturday 17 July 1903, was Religion. He was an
inspiring speaker and Bill Gregory[23], recalled fondly that Keir
Hardie was the first political speaker he ever heard. Hardie's
pacifism and Christian Socialism sometimes brought him back to
Briton Ferry to speak under the auspices of the ILP on a number of
occasions, for example, he spoke at the English Congregational
Church in Ritson Street in 1905.

An ILP Conference in Scotland during the 1900s *(Allan Colwill)*

---

[23] Gregory was a barber in the town. The account of his interview with Dr Hywel
Francis of Swansea University can be read in Appendix Five.

Hardie was brought up in extreme poverty in Lanarkshire. At the age of eight, working as a baker's delivery boy, his was the only income in the family. By the age of eleven he was a coal miner, working a twelve-hour day. However, by the time he was seventeen he had taught himself to read and write. He established a trade union at his workplace and by the age of thirty had become Secretary of the Ayrshire Miners.

Soon afterwards he met the Pankhursts, who converted him to the cause of women's suffrage: he was also a supporter of the Temperance movement. Politically he was disillusioned with the Liberals and, consequently, worked with fellow Scot, Robert Smillie, in order to form a workers' party. In 1888, when he unsuccessfully stood as the Independent Labour candidate for mid-Lanark, Tom Mann helped with his election campaign, but he was eventually successful in 1892 with his election at West Ham.

Keir Hardie

The Independent Labour Party's formation followed in 1893 and Hardie became its Chairman and Leader. He was defeated in the 1895 election following a speech in which he had castigated the House of Commons for not adding condolences to the families of the 251 victims of the 1894 Pontypridd pit disaster to the congratulations on the birth of Edward, the heir to Queen Victoria.

When fifty thousand people turned out to hear him speak at an

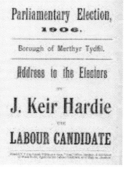

Parliamentary Election,
1906.

Borough of Merthyr Tydfil.

Address to the Electors

J. Keir Hardie

LABOUR CANDIDATE

Keir Hardie's written address to Merthyr electors (1906)

open-air meeting, organised by Emmeline Pankhurst in Manchester, he was arrested because the local authority had declared these meetings illegal. It is not clear what authority they had to do this but, in any case, the Home Secretary was so concerned at the amount of publicity Hardie was getting that he ordered his release.

Hardie was also an advocate for the disestablishment of the Church of England and his own religion could be considered to be a type of Christian Socialism. These views appealed to the people of Merthyr Tydfil, whose ILP branches (founded in the late 1890s) supported his nomination to become the second member for the parliamentary borough. In 1900 he became the first *Labour* MP in Britain and, in fact, was the only Labour MP until World War One. At that time Hardie encouraged the idea of a Labour Representation Committee to get seats in the House of Commons. At that time, too, his interest in the WPSU (Women's Social and Political Union) resulted in the development of a relationship with Sylvia Pankhurst. By 1906 Labour had won twenty nine seats and by 1910, when he became party leader again, forty seats, but the government was still, as yet, Liberal.

Hardie's pacifism was at odds with the jingoism of 1914. When war was declared he reminded the people that they had not been consulted about it and tried to organise a national strike against the War and to encourage international workers' resistance to it. 'The Church will not lead in this holy war against crime and bloodshed, so the task is left to the workers'.

His health suffered and it is possible that the horrors of the war and the loss of his dream of international brotherhood, broke his heart. The party – which was to have taken the war as an

Keir Hardie at the outbreak of war
(Allan Colwill)

J. KEIR HARDIE, 1914

opportunity to overthrow the capitalist class – became represented in a capitalist war government. Keir Hardie died in Glasgow 1915: his successor as MP for Merthyr was Charles Stanton, a man active in the pro-war Socialist National Defence Committee. However, by 1922, Richard Wallhead, the ILP candidate, managed to win Merthyr back.

Philip Snowden said of Hardie: 'The moving impulse of (his) work was a profound belief in the common people. His socialism was a great human conception of the equal right of all men and women to the wealth of the world and to the enjoyment of the fullness of life.'

After his death, the ILP and the chapels of Briton Ferry held annual remembrance services for Hardie, but today little remains physically to remind us of him. Number forty-one Victoria Street in Briton Ferry was named *Hardie House* after him when the Kyte family lived there. The house name has unfortunately been obliterated since, but perhaps the present owners might consider 2015 as the right time to reinstate its famous name. In Baglan the name lives on, but not as Keir Hardie Road; now it is simply known as Keir Hardie. Perhaps dropping the words *Road* or *Heol* is a reflection of his humanity which was recognised in many other languages not just English. Others have said there is a more prosaic reason for omitting the words!

Keir Hardie at an outdoor rally

Keir Hardie road sign.

Bernard Noel Langdon-Davies MA

(1877–1952)

Langdon-Davies was the first Secretary of the NCAC at the time when Bob Smillie was its first President and George Lansbury sat on its executive committee. Langdon-Davies once visited Briton Ferry in September 1916 under the auspices of the NCCL – the organisation having been formed from the NCAC. At the time of that visit Military Service Tribunal Appeals were ubiquitous and the operation of the Military Service Act was raising many concerns about civil liberties. On Sunday 18 August 1917 he returned to the Crown Park '(where) the usual ILP meeting was held'. At the end of the war, when the NCF's mission was diminishing, Langdon Davies served as a member of the Committee to oppose military training in schools. He was author of *Democracy and the Press* (1920), an ILP publication. He also wrote an *ABC of the Union of Democratic Control.*

J. Langdon-Davies, Bernard Langdon's nephew also visited Briton Ferry in July 1919 where he spoke on *Militarism in Education*, no doubt closely following his uncle's theme. Military training in schools and the implications of press ownership for democracy remain current concerns in this country.

Bernard Noel Langdon-Davies MA

George Lansbury
(1859–1940)

George Lansbury, who grew up in poverty
and hardship in the east end of London,
was one of a family of nine children.
During his political career he was
determined to alleviate deprivation and to
improve opportunities for working people, to promote social justice,
women's rights and world disarmament. He was a Liberal party
member but quit the party in 1886 when it refused to support a
shorter working week. Lansbury became a Christian Socialist, but
he left the Social Democratic Federation, which was being led by an
over-autocratic HM Hyndman, in order to join the ILP. Lansbury was
involved in many other activities, too. In 1900 he stood in the *Khaki
Election* as an anti-Boer War candidate. However he was not elected
to parliament until ten years later, when he became member for
Bow and Bromley, at the time he was involved in the *Don't shoot*
leaflet distribution to soldiers who had been called to deal with
strikers.

When he visited Briton Ferry on 21 January 1912, Lansbury made
two entries in Philip Mort's family autograph album. The first
outlined his position on women's suffrage: 'Women and men should,
and one day will be, comrades and still lovers, each helping the
other to a fuller and nobler realisation of true motherhood and
fatherhood'.

The second demonstrates his general, and misplaced, optimism
for the immediate future:

> *'All before you is the way.*
> *Give the past unto the wind*
> *All before you is the day.*
> *Night and darkness are behind.'*

Lansbury's resignation from the ILP came in 1912 when he instead stood as a *Votes for Women* candidate. In the event he lost because many Labour party members were still against votes for women until all men obtained suffrage. He publicly supported militant action in support of votes for women. This resulted in six months in Pentonville, during which time he went on hunger strike until his sentence was partly remitted.

Lansbury in the east end of London

In August 1916, Lansbury was permitted by the town council to use Neath Town Hall in order to speak on *High Food Prices*. But the same Council meeting refused its use to Philip Snowden to speak for a planned speech on *Current Politics*. Lansbury had helped to establish the *Daily Herald* newspaper in 1912 and became its editor. The paper maintained a strong pacifist stance throughout World War One and also gave support to the 1917 Russian Revolution, but the latter activities contributed to Lansbury's failure in his 1918 attempt to be elected to Parliament. Subsequently, he devoted himself to local politics, became Mayor of Poplar and led the Council in its fight against the levying of rates from the poor in order to subsidise the rich elsewhere. Thirty councillors were imprisoned in Brixton for contempt of court, in refusing to implement its order to levy the rate. Eventually success resulted, when a Bill went through Parliament to equalise the levying of rates.

When Lansbury visited Briton Ferry in 1921, he had much in common with those who had been prosecuted in 1916, under the Defence of the Realm Act, for leaflet distribution, and also with those like my great uncle Tom Thomas, a hunger striker whilst he was imprisoned for his conscientious objection. Lansbury's inscription in the *White/Clement* album reads: 'The whole wide world and all that therein is for the service of all.'

Lansbury returned to Parliament in 1922, holding no office in the 1924 government but he became First Commissioner of Works in the 1929–31 Labour government. After the electoral defeat of 1931, he did not follow MacDonald into the National Government but became Labour Party leader and Leader of the Opposition from 1932–1935. His pacifism and opposition to re-armament in the face of rising European fascism led him to resign the leadership in 1935. He spent his final years travelling through the USA and Europe in the cause of peace and dis-armament, becoming President of the PPU.

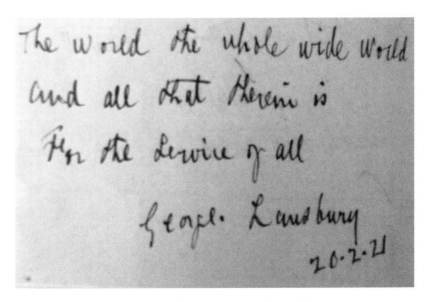

Lansbury's 1921 album inscription *(Cheryl Clement)*

Ramsay MacDonald
(1866–1937)

MacDonald's introduction to Briton Ferry and Aberafan 'was subtly contrived, the constituency being first nursed with a series of cultural lectures'[24] before the constituency elected Britain's first Labour prime minister. MacDonald's advent was to provide the town 'with the most exciting political experiences that the town ever knew or is likely to know . . . every hall was packed, enthusiasm was electrifying. Every ruse was adopted by his opponents to defeat Ramsay MacDonald but . . . it made no difference, MacDonald winning every time.'

Ramsay MacDonald was the son of an unmarried maidservant from a Scottish working class family from Lossiemouth and ended his elementary education at eleven, though he continued for six more years as a pupil-teacher in the local Board School he had attended. He then become a clergyman's assistant and also an assistant to a Liberal candidate in Bristol. There he joined the Social Democratic Federation, followed by the Fabian Society and, in 1900, he became the first Secretary of the Labour Representation Committee, before joining the ILP in 1903. Whilst working as a journalist, he had stood unsuccessfully as a parliamentary candidate, but was elected in 1906 for Leicester. His wife died in 1911, the year that MacDonald became Leader of the Parliamentary Labour Party, leaving him with four children.

MacDonald had been against the Boer War, which he regarded as imperialistic. After he condemned it at a meeting of the Fabian Society, he resigning from it. He was, also, totally against Britain's involvement in the First World War and resigned his chairmanship of the parliamentary Labour party when it voted for war credits.

---

[24] J. Ivor Hansen

Five days later he met with Philip Morel, Norman Angell, E. D. Morel, Charles Trevelyan and Arthur Ponsonby to found the Union of Democratic Control. Historian A. J. P. Taylor described the organisation as 'the most formidable radical body ever to influence British foreign policy.'

MacDonald said in Parliament that Grey was wrong in declaring war: he wanted Britain to stay neutral, but Boulton's[25] view is that MacDonald does not deserve his reputation as a pacifist because he equivocated. Three days after advocating neutrality he told his Leicester constituents: 'Whatever our view may be on the origin of the war, we must go through with it.'

MacDonald was MP for Leicester when, on 12 March 1916, he visited Swansea and Briton Ferry under the auspices of the ILP. At the Elysium Hall in Swansea he spoke of peace, saying one would not crush militarism by war and that 'one could not crush and humiliate people and then make peace'. Peace was not possible until Belgium was no longer occupied by Germany.

The *Labour Voice* reported on an all-ticket event at Briton Ferry Public Hall: 'a huge crowd was kept outside and several attempts were made to rush the door but a strong force was able to resist these attempts.' Some persons interfered with the electricity supply, but not the gas supply, so the meeting was held in semi-darkness with gas lighting.

When war came the ILP stood by its long-held objections to militarism. It refused to support the war effort and many of its MPs broke ranks to support it. MacDonald and others, such as Philip Snowden, Keir Hardie and W. C. Anderson, did not do so. MacDonald was forced to resign as Labour Party chairman in 1914, having failed to convince the Labour party that Britain should stay out of the war. He was defeated in 1918 because of his anti-war stance, but during the 1920s his pacifism earned him great respect and he was back in Parliament in 1922 when Labour replaced the Liberals as the 'second party'. MacDonald became the first Labour Prime Minister of the United Kingdom, for a nine month period in 1924, albeit with Liberal support, and again from 1929-1931. In the days before television, political campaigning was conducted differently, as Hanson described:

---

[25] In 'Objection Overruled'

'One night when MacDonald, as Britain's prime Minister, was due to return to Aberafan to fight another election, I awaited on the main road near St Theodore's Church, amidst the biggest crowd I had ever seen in the town. There were occasions when we were so tightly packed that we could have lifted up our feet and be carried along'.

Hanson stated that MacDonald left his limousine at Pyle to travel to Aberafan in a taxi. In Briton Ferry I was told a different story: that after MacDonald had finished in Port Talbot, his supporters from Briton Ferry showed their support by manually towing his vehicle from Baglan to Briton Ferry.

MacDonald appointed Margaret Bonfield as Minister of Labour; she also became the first female government Minister, Privy Councillor and visitor to Briton Ferry. The Great Depression then forced him to lead a national Government but the result of this was his expulsion from the Labour Party.

Ramsay MacDonald – outside Briton Ferry Public Hall

Thomas Mann
(1856–1941)

Thomas Mann
(Socialist Party)

Mann was from Coventry, where he first worked in a local colliery. During that time he witnessed a serious pit explosion and consequently left for Birmingham. After a seven year apprenticeship there he moved to London, where he became a strong Christian Socialist. Sam Mainwaring (senior), once of Neath, was his foreman. Mann joined the Amalgamated Society of Engineers and the Social Democratic Federation and in 1886 and wrote *What a compulsory 8-hour day means to the workers*. This influenced the trade union movement to accept the eight-hour working day as its policy.

As a result of having read the *Communist Manifesto*, he came to see the main purpose of trade unionism as the overthrow of the capitalist system. Mann was successful in getting Keir Hardie elected as MP and, from 1891-93 Mann, was a member of the Royal Commission on Labour. He was one of the main leaders of the 1889 London Docks strike during which the employers tried to starve the dockers into submission. With the support of organisations like the Salvation Army, the employers met all the strikers' demands after five weeks. Mann became secretary of the ILP in 1894 and afterwards President of the newly created General Labourers' Union. During the successful Liverpool rail strike of 1911 he was arrested and charged with sedition, for issuing leaflets attempting to persuade the soldiers not to fire on the striking workers. He was sentenced to a six-month jail sentence but was released early as a result of public pressure.

Mann was opposed to World War One so he joined the British Socialist Party which opposed the war. He wrote this in Briton Ferry in the White/Clement autograph album: 'Our little lives are kept in equipoise by opposite attractions and desires. The struggle of the instinct that enjoys and the more noble instinct that aspires'. No doubt his Liverpool experience had enabled him, in May 1916, to advise Joe Branch and his Briton Ferry co-defendants on their strategy for defending themselves against alleged contraventions of the Defence of the Realm Act.

After the war, in 1919, Mann was elected Secretary of the Amalgamated Engineering Union and, in 1920, became a founder member of Communist Party of Great Britain, together with Arthur Cook and Sylvia Pankhurst. After he was acquitted at a trial in Cardiff for sedition, in 1934, he went on to join the International Brigade in the Spanish Civil War.

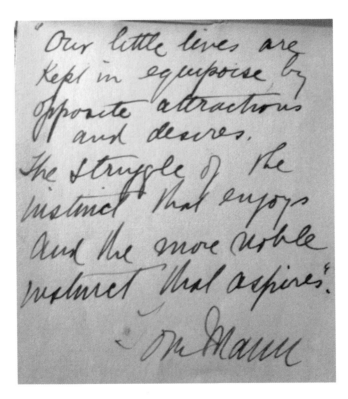

Thomas Mann's inscription *(Cheryl Clement)*

James Maxton
(1885–1946)

James Maxton was born in Glasgow. Both his parents were teachers and he was expected to have an academic career after graduating with an M.A. from Glasgow University in 1909.

Maxton joined Barrhead ILP in Glasgow as a result both of the influence of speakers (such as Philip Snowden, Ramsay MacDonald and Keir Hardie) and the grinding poverty he witnessed amongst the children he taught. However, it was his friendship with John Maclean of the Social Democratic Federation that moved him away from being a conventional product of a lower middle-class background. He became active in the Schoolmasters' Union from 1906-1910 and taught evening school with Maclean at Pollokshaws, devising a course entitled *Citizenship and the social sciences*. By 1912 he had become the leading figure in the ILP in Scotland.

Maxton's socialism influenced his view of education. He saw the child as a living organism, whose mental and physical growth was dependent on the correct amount of nourishment, and not merely as a piece of malleable plastic. Education, he thought, ought not to be divorced from other social problems and the teacher's role was not to teach but 'to assist the child to learn'.

In the early years of World War One he worked on barges and then, as a conscientious objector and member of Clyde Workers' committee, strongly opposed the war. He organised anti-war strikes in the shipyards, calling on munitions workers to down tools and not support the war effort. In 1915 the munitions industry had been disorganised, resulting in a shortage of shells and a row between Lloyd George and General Kitchener. The former antagonised the Unions by suggesting that workers' excessive alcohol consumption, and the resultant absence from work, caused disruption. However, Maxton knew the true cause to be due to mismanagement and said so forcibly. As a result of his activities Maxton was dismissed as a teacher and, after his arrest in 1916, was imprisoned for a year, having been found guilty of sedition. The significance of the Clyde events was that it increased the call for *industrial* conscription, thereby antagonising Labour even further against military conscription.

After his release from prison, Maxton visited Briton Ferry in December 1917 to participate in a well-attended Peace Meeting at Jerusalem Church with Theodora Wilson-Wilson. Following defeat as a parliamentary candidate in the 1918 election, he was eventually elected as MP for Bridgeton in 1922. He led a *Socialism in our Time* campaign in 1925 and became ILP leader the following year. He chaired the ILP for two periods: from 1926–31 and from 1934–39. Maxton opposed re-armament in the 1930s. The ILP broke from the Labour Party in 1932 and Maxton became its symbol until his death in 1946. Afterwards the ILP lost its vitality and viability.

Maxton was well-respected and was regarded as having the potential Prime Ministerial material. He was considered one of the greatest orators of his time, both inside and outside the House of Commons. Even his opponent, Winston Churchill, described him as 'the greatest parliamentarian of his day'. Gordon Brown, Prime Minister from 2007–2010, centred his PhD thesis on Maxton and eventually wrote his biography.

E. D. Morel
(1873–1924)

Morel established himself
early in the 20th century
as the greatest investi-
gative journalist of his
time. His outstanding
characteristic was the truly international scope to his interests.
Morel was born Georges Edmond Morel-de-Ville in Paris, the son of
a French civil servant and English Quaker mother, but he became a
British subject and anglicised his name.

Morel, whilst he had been working as a shipping clerk in
Liverpool and Belgium, had studied the cargoes entering and
leaving Antwerp and had deduced that something terrible was
happening in the Congo, from which vast profits were being made
by Belgian interests. The Congo Reform Association was formed to
change the exploitative trading system between Belgium and the
Congo which included forced labour. His campaign to expose slavery
and corruption earned Morel international renown and the respect
of the British authorities. He is remembered in the Liverpool Slavery
Museum.

The next campaign in which he immersed himself engendered a
very different reaction. Although he was not a pacifist, he believed
from the outset that the World War One represented unnecessary
human slaughter, that no principle was at stake, and that the British
public was not being told the truth about why they were fighting. He
thought it was cant for Britain to claim to be fighting for freedom
and democracy whilst it was allied with Russia, and he suspected
that the real explanation might lay in secret treaties. His wartime
essay *Ten Years of Secret Diplomacy* was later acknowledged by A.
J. P. Taylor as the foundation for all subsequent research into the
causes of the war.

Morel's controversial views brought him to Briton Ferry on 5 September 1916, presumably under the auspices of the UDC, because he had not yet joined the ILP. One wonders whether the *Content, De Belder, Mahe* and other families, the Belgian war refugees who were then living with local families in the town, attended Morel's speaking event. If so they might have received some re-assurance about events in Belgium and Germany. At that time Morel was publicising *The Truth about German Internment Camps* and wrote to various newspaper about them (such as *The Pioneer* on 25 September). He said that the impression created by the press in Britain was that 'our prisoners are abominably ill-used in Germany. That it is a part of the campaign of hate, waged in this respect with no regard for the feelings of the unfortunate relations of these men at home'. The truth, said Morel, was to be found in the *White Books*, published as Cmnd 8235 and Cmnd 829 by the British Government. The books were based on official reports from the staff of the American Embassy in Berlin. They reported on conditions in between sixty and seventy internment camps, and none gave cause for complaint. He felt it regrettable that these too had been 'studiously withheld by the Newspapers.' Morel also pointed out that official German reports about the invasion of Belgium painted a different picture from that of the British press, and it was a pity that they had been withheld by British newspapers.

In addition to being a prolific writer, Morel had another quality– he was a skilful organiser. As disparate anti-war groups, ranging from the Quakers to the left of the Labour Party, came together to form the Union of Democratic Control, Morel was the natural choice for secretary. Under his guidance, the UDC focused its attack on the causes of war, and on preventing the anticipated next one, rather than campaigning directly against the contemporary slaughter. In that way, Morel made the job of the authorities more difficult, as they failed to find a plausible pretext on which to proscribe the organisation and so continued their struggle in working out how they might silence Morel.

Evidently harassment did not work. Scotland Yard opened his mail and tapped his telephone. UDC meetings were attacked by mobs which tore down banners, threw stink bombs, and assaulted participants and soon it had been made impossible for them to rent a hall in London. Morel became so used to being shunned by old friends that when a former journalist colleague in military uniform greeted him in the street, he was so surprised and grateful that he burst into tears.

In Whitehall, meanwhile, the search continued for an excuse to prosecute the nation's most effective anti-war campaigner. Eventually, a letter Morel had written to Ethel Sedgwick (niece by marriage of Arthur Balfour the former Prime Minister) was seized upon in which he asked her to sneak a copy of his pamphlet *The Truth of War* into Switzerland to be given to the French anti-war writer, Romain Rolland.

This was deemed to be an offence under the Defence of the Realm Act, and Morel was sentenced to six months in prison. Despite a petition to the Home Secretary, he was categorised as a *second division prisoner,* which meant he was allowed to write and receive just one letter and have one 15-minute visit at the end of each full calendar month he was in prison. During daylight, he was allowed an hour's exercise in the cell yard, and was required to sew canvas mailbags and weave rope into hammocks and mats for the navy. From four in the afternoon until eight o' clock in the morning, he was held in solitary confinement. His cell was extremely cold, next to that of a prisoner who had raped a child.

His wife and other sympathisers became concerned about the 44-year-old man's physical and mental health. The Home Secretary, Sir George Cave, was bombarded with appeals from Morel's small but dedicated band of supporters, which he ignored until the prisoner had almost completed his sentence. Then Cave magnanimously ruled that he could be released three days early.

An additional concern of Morel's was British policy towards Ireland generally. He was linked to Roger Casement and as a result labelled a traitor by the *Daily Express*. Of course now we know that Casement was actually framed by government and wrongly executed.

The 'beloved voice' that Edmund Morel heard as he left Pentonville prison, at the end of January 1918, was that of his wife Mary, who stood by him steadfastly through the worst ordeal of his life, as he fell in popular esteem from being hero to public enemy. There were some who thought he had not suffered enough. In the

Commons, on 14 February, Colonel Walter Faber, a Conservative MP, furiously asked why Morel had been let free at all. Another Tory, William Joynson-Hicks, wanted him stripped of his citizenship. Bertrand Russell saw Morel two months after his release, and noted that 'his hair was completely white (there was hardly a tinge of white before). When he first came out, he collapsed completely, physically and mentally'.

After joining the ILP in 1918, Morel had criticised the Versailles Peace settlement and was expected to become Ramsay MacDonald's Foreign Secretary, but MacDonald held the post himself. President Wilson's fourteen point peace programme at the Versailles Peace Conference reflected much of Morel's work. To the Labour Party, he was a hero. In 1922, he had the immense satisfaction of contesting the parliamentary seat of Dundee against Winston Churchill, whom he heartily despised, and winning. Two years later, he was walking in woodland when he felt tired, sat down by a tree, and died, a death hastened by his prison ordeal.

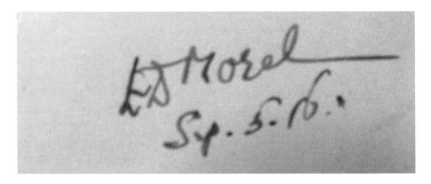

Edmund Dene Morel

J. Turner Walton Newbold
(1888–1943)

John Turner Walter Newbold
(1888–1943)
*(National Portrait Gallery
photograph)*

Born at Culcheth in Lancashire, Walton
Newbold was educated at Manchester
University where he later lectured in
history and politics and engaged in
industrial and economic research. He was
a born Quaker and joined the ILP in 1910
and later the NCF. Before the war he had
also worked as an investigative journalist,
his aim in writing *The War Trust Exposed*
being the exposure of the threatening
dual influence of the private armaments
industry and capitalist militarism. In March 1914 he wrote a book
entitled *How Asquith helped the Armour Ring* to express his view
that there existed a gang of international capitalists who wanted the
profits that war would bring.

Newbold arrived in Briton Ferry on 28 May 1915 to speak about
the *Kultur of Krupps* following the 1915 ILP conference which he
attended as a Buxton delegate. He also gave an 'engrossing lecture'
at Merthyr on the same subject. This visit took place when the
'Shells Crisis' was at its very peak and Lloyd George was about to
become Minister of Munitions. With the strength of the ILP in Briton
Ferry's steelworks and tinplate mills, influential visits such as that
of Newbold, which postulated the existence of self-serving
armaments cartels, were not well-received by the authorities.

After joining the NCF in 1916, Newbold was to become a
conscientious objector, but a Manchester Tribunal rejected him as
physically unfit for service. This enabled Newbold to spend much
time writing such articles as *The class struggle in Wales* and visiting
the south Wales valleys during the rest of the war. That year he
wrote *How Europe armed for war*. At Llwynypia, in December, he

spoke on *The economic causes of war*, and, in June 1917, he spent a full week at Aberaman giving a series of nightly lectures.

At Newport, in November 1917, he saw 'This combination of employers and the elimination of skilled workers by machines, the unified control and system of manufacturing, the standardisation of all possible products and the introduction of women workers brought about by the contingency of the war' as something the ILP had to be aware of and prepared for. *Capitalism in south Wales* was the subject at Trealaw in 1918. In 1919 he regarded Woodrow Wilson as 'the man who would halt the spread of socialism and save the world for private enterprise'. In 1921 he resigned from the ILP to be, elected for Motherwell in 1922 and become the first Communist Party of Great Britain MP in the United Kingdom. He lost his seat in 1923 and then abandoned the Communist Party in 1925 to rejoin the Labour Party.

Bipin Chandra Pal
(1858–1932)

It is astonishing to realise that, over thirty years before India gained Independence from Britain, the groundwork was being laid in Briton Ferry. Yet that is exactly the case when one considers that freedom fighter Bipin Chandra Pal visited the town on 5 March 1911.

Pal was one of three of the Congress Party's extremists, with Lala Laipat Rai and Bal Gangadhar Tilak. Pal preached that independence could only be won by sacrifice and suffering. To get the message to the foreign rulers of India he also espoused such extremist measures as the boycotting of British-made goods, lockouts in British-owned businesses and industrial concerns, and the burning of Western clothing as ways for Indians to achieve that goal.

'When I look upon myself as an isolated individual, I feel how weak I am, and yet at war perpetually with the universe. When I realise my self as part of that universe, I feel I am as mighty as He who made it and rules it: I and God are one'.

Bipin Chandra Pal was born into a wealthy Hindu family in 1858, in a village in Sylhet (in present-day Bangladesh). At twenty-one, he became the headmaster of a high school for several years before he worked as a librarian and secretary for the Calcutta Public Library. Pal became attracted to the Brahma movement after coming into contact with prominent Brahma leaders. He soon became a convert to the ideas of the extremist wing of the Indian National Congress. At the 1886 and 1887 sessions, he forced the Congress to take up the cause of Assam tea garden labourers who were being cruelly treated by the planters.

In 1898, Pal went to study comparative theology in England, but returned to India after a year. After his return, he began preaching the ideal of *Swaraj* (complete independence) through his weekly journal, *New India*.

Pal's notoriety grew as a result of the upsurge he encouraged against British policy regarding Bengal. He claimed that partition was a British move to split the Bengalis and thus break their growing political influence. In response to the partition he started the daily paper *Bande Mataram* and became its chief editor. He also organized a propaganda tour in various parts of Bengal, Assam, Utter Pradash, and Madras. It was during this tour that he became known throughout India for his oratorical skills, and people often travelled great distances to hear him speak.

In 1907, Pal was imprisoned for refusing to give evidence against Aurovinda Ghosh in the Bande Mataram Sedition Case. Ghose was a poet, scholar and freedom fighter who wrote fearlessly and pointedly in the English daily newspaper, *Bande Mataram*. He asked people to prepare themselves for passive resistance, spending a year on remand in solitary confinement. Ghose was acquitted. Perhaps Pal and Ghose had much in common with Briton Ferry's conscientious objectors and 'seditionists'.

Upon Pal's release in 1908, he went to Britain to 'lead the life of an enforced exile', and remained here for three years, returning for the final time in 1919, as a member of the Home Rule League deputation led by Tilak. Pal's open criticism of the non-cooperation movement led by Mahatma Gandhi caused him to lose popularity amongst the Indian population, and he retired from active politics in 1925. He died in May, 1932.

Ernest Bevin had visited Briton Ferry at the time of Pal's visit to the town. Thirty-six years later it was to be Bevin, as British Foreign Secretary, who would grant India its independence.

Pal made this entry in the Mort family album.

Thomas Richardson
(1868–1928)

Richardson was born at Little Usworth, Chester-le Street, in County Durham. At the age of thirteen he was a trapper in a local coal mine earning about a shilling a day. A trapper's job was to open and the close the air circulation doors to allow the trams to pass. He worked a twelve-hour shift. His brother, Robert, was killed, along with forty-one others, in a mining explosion at Usworth in 1885. The death of his younger brother may well have been a factor in his decision to join the NCF and to prevent further, unnecessary, deaths in war. His upbringing in the industrial environment of County Durham was undoubtedly an influence on his decision to become an ILP member.

Richardson became MP for Whitehaven from 1910–1918. On 7 August, 1914, days after the outbreak of war, he spoke with Keir Hardie at a peace rally in Merthyr's Shiloh Chapel. After eighteen months of war, when he spoke at an NCF protest meeting on 16 April, 1916, at the Public Hall in Briton Ferry, the subject was more focussed on military and industrial conscription and censorship. The meeting was addressed by a very strong trio: Gilbert Cannan (anti-censorship activist) and Bob Williams (trade union leader) who joined forces with Richardson. The meeting was chaired by the Rev. Rees Powell of Jerusalem Chapel.

The Richardson family in 1885 (Thomas is second from left in the back row. His brother, Robert, is to the far right in the front row)

Bertrand Russell
(1872–1970)

Bertrand Russell

Russell was one of the foremost philosophers of the twentieth century, but to the general public he was best known as a campaigner for peace and as a popular writer on social, political and moral subjects. The Encyclopaedia Britannica said of him: 'During a long, productive and often turbulent life, he published more than seventy books and about 2,000 articles, married four times, became involved in innumerable public controversies, and was honoured and reviled in almost equal measure throughout the world'.

And he was Welsh, born at Trellech, near Cwmbran, in Monmouthshire. His early life was tragic and sad. Before he was six, his parents, sister and grandfather all died and he and his brother were brought up by his grandmother, with Bertrand being educated at home and studying mathematics joyfully. His isolation came to an end when he entered Trinity College in Cambridge. Before World War One, Russell was a Lecturer at Cambridge University, having written the *Principles of Mathematics* in 1903 with A. N. Whitehead, and having become a Fellow of the Royal Society. During the War he took an active part in the NCF. He was dismissed by Trinity College and was fined a hundred pounds for writing a leaflet criticising a sentence of two years imprisonment for a CO. The war had a profound effect on his political views in which he abandoned his inherited liberalism in favour of a thorough-going socialism.

In July 1916 Russell delivered public speeches on his Welsh tour, after meeting NCF, ILP and NCAC members in London. The first speech was outdoors on 2 July at Port Talbot. That afternoon he told the crowd in Gallipoli Square, Taibach: 'the prolongation of war . . . is due to our unwillingness to enter into peace negotiations, is due

The Banning of Bertie *(Emily Johns/Peace News)*

to our jealousy of German trade, and our accumulation of hatred'. Councillor Henry Davies of Cwmafan later reported that, when Russell addressed his audience, seven police officers and a shorthand reporter, acting for the police, were present. Russell said of his visit: 'the men are not suffering from the war in any way but they all seem to be against it.'

At the second meeting, in the evening at the NCF, Briton Ferry, 'without meeting any local obstruction'. Russell referred to Briton Ferry in his work *Prophesy and Dissent*, expressing concern at the prosecutions of 30 April and 18 May, 1916. He wrote the following to Ottoline Morell from the Grand Hotel, Port Talbot, on 4 July:

'Sunday evening I spoke at Briton Ferry – a really wonderful meeting – the hall was packed, they were all at the highest point of enthusiasm – they inspired me, and I spoke as I have never spoken before. We put a resolution in favour of immediate peace negotiations, which was carried unanimously. (I did not notice any abstentions, though presumably the two plain clothes men who had come to take notes must have abstained). Those who had not already signed the peace petition signed it in large numbers – one needs no prudent reticences – no humbug of any sort – one can just speak out one's whole mind. I thought the Great Offensive would have excited them but it hasn't.'

Following Russell's speeches at Port Talbot and Briton Ferry, he made a further speech in Cardiff which is depicted in the poster on the previous page. The text reads:

'Britain's greatest leading philosopher Bertrand Russell was banned under the Defence of the Realm Act from a third of the country for an anti-war speech he made in Cardiff on 6 July 1916'.

Russell's own description[26] of this event was:

'My speeches to munitions workers in south Wales, all of which were accurately reported by detectives, caused the War Office to issue an order that I should not be allowed in any prohibited area. . . . At the War Office General Cockerill

---

[26] Bertrand Russell: Autobiography

had beside him a report of my speeches in south Wales and drew special attention to a speech I made in Cardiff saying there was no good reason this war should continue for another day . . . such a sentiment made to miners or munition workers was calculated to diminish their ardour. . . . I was encouraging men to refuse to fight for their country.'

Russell spent much time in south Wales that year. He later visited Merthyr and attended the *Peace Conference*, and an anti-conscription meeting organised by the National Council for Civil Liberties in Cardiff on 10 November. When offered a post at Harvard, his Majesty's Government, in August 1916, did 'not consider it to be in the public interest to issue a passport to enable Mr Russell to leave the United Kingdom at the present time'.

In 1918 Russell spent six months in Brixton prison for writing a pacifist article in the NCF journal *Tribunal*, suggesting that the American Army might be used as strike breakers. This was a continuation of Newbold's theme and indicated how widely the Defence of the Realm Act was being interpreted. Russell was initially sympathetic to the Russian Revolution in 1917, but a visit to the Soviet Union in 1920 left him with a deep distaste for Soviet communism. He ceased to be a pacifist in the 1930s with the rise of Hitler. In 1950 he received the Nobel Prize in literature for 'championing humanitarian ideals and freedom of thought'; he became a founder member of the CND in 1958 and was imprisoned again in 1961 for his part in a CND (Campaign for Nuclear Disarmament) demonstration. He also became Chair of the World Disarmament Campaign.

Bertrand Russell

Robert Smillie
(1857-1940)

Smillie was a trade unionist and politician. Born in Belfast, he was a self-educated, penniless orphan who moved to Glasgow at fourteen to work in boiler shops and the mines. There, amid talk of socialism and revolution, his interest in politics was sparked. Smillie set up classes in mine management and got free school books for children. Through the 1880s and 1890s, he helped form the Scottish Miners' Federation, the Scottish Trades Union Congress, the Labour Party in Scotland and the Independent Labour Party. His attempts to stand for Parliament failed at this time, possibly because his views were too advanced for the electorates.

He was a friend and close associate of Keir Hardie and President of the Miners Federation of Great Britain from 1912–1921, and between 1922 and 1928, and President of both the NCAC and the Triple Alliance of miners, transport and rail workers. He became president during the first national strike and was involved in tense talks with the Liberal government, wishing to keep the miners out of the restrictions of the Munitions Act. As President he played a key role in moving the miners' support from the Liberal Party to Labour. Smillie once caused Prime Minister Asquith to break down and cry in Parliament. He condemned conscription vigorously.

Smillie came to Cardiff's Cory Hall and to Taibach in October 1906 as a guest of the ILP branch to speak 'about social reform'. His visits to south Wales increased in number because of his roles in the Miners' Federation. At Abertillery, in April 1914, conscription had not yet become the furore to be discussed that it would later. On 15

January, 1916, Smillie told a *Western Mail* reporter that conscription was 'the biggest mistake of all which would lead to the 'enslavement of industry under militarism'. A week later he wrote to Bargoed ILP to suggest it was a fait accompli.

Smillie visited Briton Ferry on 7 July, 1917 through the ILP and the Miners' Federation. This was just a week before the soldiers and industrial workers of Russia began their demonstrations against the Provisional Government in Petrograd. No doubt Smillie spoke of these matters in addition to specific conscription issues in his role of President of the National Council against Conscription. He later welcomed the Russian Revolution in a speech at Leeds. It was at the time when control over occupational exemptions from military conscription was being tightened and anxiety was being expressed about its implications for industrial conscription and labour dilution. Briton Ferry was concerned.

Robert Smillie had a twenty-two year old son. On 9 August, 1918, he was court martialled at Sandwich Bay in Kent following his refusal to obey orders in line with his conscientious objection to military service. As late as April 1919, questions were raised in the House of Commons about the speeches and writings made by Smillie and Swansea's Robert Williams, of the Transport Federation, which urged the workers to emulate the Bolsheviks and bring about a revolution

Lloyd George, therefore, saw Smillie as a dangerous man and offered him a government job in an attempt to control him, but he refused. After the war ended Smillie was one of the first to call for the Labour Party to pull out of his coalition government. Nonetheless Smillie pushed the Government, which had taken control of the mines for the war's duration, to give the miners improved wages and a seven-hour day. The cost of the improvements was labelled the 'Smillie Tax', with the *Chronicle* suggesting the rise in the price of coal was 'not down to the coal owners' but to Smillie and Williams: 'the whole country has to be victimised to pay blackmail to the triple alliance – to the Smillies and the Williamses – who think they have a stranglehold upon us'.

When peace returned, he was appointed to the Sankey Commission, to decide whether to re-privatise the mines. Its leader, Sir John Sankey, supported Smillie's demand for national ownership, but Lloyd George betrayed him and returned the mines to their aristocratic masters. The overall situation, when Smillie visited Briton Ferry on 4 June 1922, was normalising, but unemployment was high and the coalition government was decaying with internal dissentions. After the coalition collapsed at the end of 1922, Smillie attempted to enter Parliament once again. This time he was successful, being elected MP for Morpeth at the 1923 election.

The significance of Smillie's visits to Briton Ferry was not only in terms of the anti-*military* conscription effort, his presence was also important for the support he gave to the town's rail, transport and munitions workers. The 'Waters and Davies case', an inflammable mixture of industrial relations and conscription issues, was still ongoing and *Industrial* conscription remained a threat. Smillie was aware of Lloyd George's methods and it was Smillie's awareness of what went on, and the support that was returned to him from Briton Ferry and elsewhere, that motivated Lloyd George's attempts to control him.

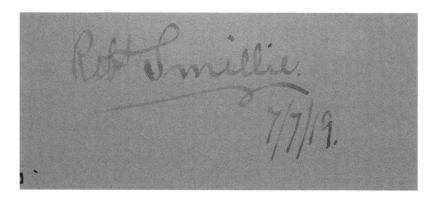

Robert Smillie

Philip Snowden
(1864–1937)

Philip Snowden was one of the most
prominent people to campaign
against the war and to argue for an
early peace. In Parliament he
defended the principles of
conscientious objection and took up
matters concerning individual objectors.

He first visited Briton Ferry in peacetime. In May 1906 he
attended as the ILP's national chair with his wife, Ethel, for both of
them to speak at the fourth Briton Ferry Annual Labour
Demonstration. *The Cambrian* reported that: 'two hundred
stalwarts braved the elements and paraded the streets, carrying
banners, led by the Briton Ferry Brass Band, with Mr Philip
Snowden MP and Mrs Snowden bringing up the rear in a hansom
cab'.

The march over, a crowded meeting gathered at the Assembly
Rooms. Henry Davies of Cwmafan presided, with the support of
Councillors Gethin and James Thomas, Evan Evans, the town's ILP
Chair, and Ivor Thomas, its Secretary. The event was aimed at
fostering support for trade unions and the Labour party, with
Snowden saying that the party is 'leading human souls to what is
best and getting what is best out of them'.

The Snowdens did not stint in their endeavours. On the Saturday
evening proceedings continued with a double act in Rehoboth
Chapel to promote the ILP, followed on Sunday evening by a similar
event at Zoar Chapel in Giant's Grave. A further visit took place in
November, 1911, the year of great industrial unrest throughout
Britain, after trade union membership had more than doubled to
four million in the last two decades. This was a consolidation visit
for the Snowdens. By the time of their next visit their minds would

be turned to other matters. Indeed that visit came on 25 September 1916, with both again in attendance. This time, however, conscription and women's suffrage took up the headlines on the agenda.

Now it is time to examine Philip Snowden's background. He was a weaver's son from west Yorkshire where his father was a Methodist Sunday school superintendent. It was his father's tenacity that enabled him to continue his education to become an insurance and civil service clerk, until he became crippled by a spinal disease. When researching a speech he had been asked to deliver by his local Liberal Party on *The Dangers of Socialism* he instead became convinced of the ILP's ideology. After a partial recovery in the 1890s, during which time he was able to attend political meetings in nearby Nelson, he was able to write and lecture for the ILP in Keighley. He lost his first election in Burnley in 1900 but won Blackburn for the Labour Party in 1905 and the Parliamentary Labour Party was born. Soon he turned to the ILP, becoming Chair for the first time, from 1903 to 1906, and becoming prominent in national politics.

From 1912 to 1914 the ILP gave much publicity to the growth of the private arms industry and the growth of overlapping directorships, with Snowden contributing books, including one entitled *Dreadnoughts* and *Dividends: Disarmament and the Arms Race.* He correctly predicted that general conscription would follow once the conscription of single men was conceded. Snowden also moved an additional clause in the Military Service Bill to safeguard the persistent objector from the death penalty.

He visited Briton Ferry in September 1916 when MP for Blackburn, having been denied the use of Neath Town Hall to speak on *Current Politics*, the previous month. Councillor John Morris of Neath said 'Why, the name of Philip Snowden stinks in the nostrils of every patriot'. George Lansbury, however, was permitted the use of the Hall to speak on *High Food Prices* (Cambria Daily Leader: 4 August, 1916).

Snowden was in Australia when World War One started, retuning to Britain in 1915. He was not a pacifist but he was against conscription and was regarded as the ILP's shrewdest foreign affairs spokesperson. He also shrewdly exposed in Parliament the inconsistencies, unfairness and irregularities of many Military

Service Tribunals and the treatment of conscientious objectors. He was effective at local level because the NCF's nationwide intelligence organisation was able to feed him with information about local injustices on which he could question the authorities. For example, he asked the President of the Local Government Board if he would have a Special Enquiry made into the action of the Gower Rural Tribunal in respect of the treatment of Mr H. V. Waters. Waters was both a conscientious objector and considered to be doing work of national importance but, in October 1916, Snowden claimed that he was denied a fair hearing because the Tribunal Chair, Colonel Pearson, had a grudge against the Waters family. (H. V. Waters was the brother of Cecil and M Waters of Briton Ferry). Colonel Pearson was removed.

Snowden ensured that a clause was inserted into the Military Service Act to safeguard persistent objectors from receiving the death penalty under its provisions. Another example of Snowden's Parliamentary persistence was his question to the President of the Local Government Board: he asked whether all exemptions granted by Neath Tribunal Chair, William Burrows Trick (an auctioneer by profession) were being granted on condition that those exempted joined the Local Volunteer Corps. (Of which Trick was Honorary Commandant holding the rank of Major). He also asked 'whether the local corps have paraded at the Drill Hall and marched through town on Sunday with spades, forks, hoes etc to work on Mr Trick's Penylan Farm and whether his son-in-law and prospective . . . have been exempted?' Snowden knew the answers before he asked the questions. The whole point was to put the answer on public record. On 25 July, 1917, he asked whether Thomas Henry Williams of Cwmafan was being force fed at Shrewsbury Prison, and whether this had led to the goitre in his neck.

Snowden's stance during the war was unpopular with his constituents and he lost his seat in 1918, but in 1922 he was back in the Commons as MP for Colne Valley. After MacDonald's appointment as Prime Minister, in January 1924, Snowden was appointed Labour's first Chancellor of the Exchequer. In his budget he reduced duties on some foodstuffs; reduced spending on armaments and provided money for council housing. He did not realise how serious unemployment had become however and criticised the Liberals' Keynesian ideas expressed in its 1929 election manifesto *We can conquer unemployment*.

In 1927 he repudiated the ILP, in favour of the Labour Party proper, for its increasing militancy in drifting 'from evolutionary socialism to revolutionary socialism' but Labour emerged as the largest party in the 1929 general election and Snowden became Chancellor. His policy was considered by many to be an obstacle to tackling unemployment and the Great Depression. When he and MacDonald broke with Labour policy in 1931 by joining the National Government, they were expelled from the Labour Party.

Disappointing though Snowden's economic policies were for most people in Briton Ferry, there were still many (as I suspect my first name attests) who saw his stance against conscription and his parliamentary techniques as brilliantly conducted, thus making him an especially significant person in the eyes of many Briton Ferry people.

Philip Snowden

Reginald Sorensen
(1891–1971)

Sorensen's autograph album entry, signed on his visit to Briton Ferry in 1921, simply said:

'When shall we learn to bring the mountain top glory to the valley? When we awake and will it.'

Was this a general quotation from his repertoire, or was it a specific reference to Briton Ferry? Was he merely attempting to describe people's situation in 1921 and prescribing a course of action to improve that situation? He certainly was not referring to the glory of war because he was an NCF member; a pacifist who founded the Peace Pledge Union and anti-militarist. Perhaps the reference to mountain top glory was a description of the time when women's suffrage was to be achieved, for he was a member of the Men's League for Women's Suffrage.

Reginald Sorensen was born in Islington and worked as an errand boy and did factory work in his youth. On one occasion he was sent home from Sunday school due to his questioning attitude. He was Fenner Brockway's brother-in-law and a colleague of Sylvia Pankhurst. Not surprisingly, perhaps, he joined Finsbury ILP branch in 1908 and the NCF in 1914. That was through his membership of the Men's League for Women's Suffrage. As a Minister of Religion (Unitarian) he was exempted from military service, but he nonetheless declared himself a pacifist and anti-militarist, working with the Workers' Educational Association. In 1929 he was elected to parliament as a Labour MP to Leyton but lost his seat between 1931 and 1935. He established the Peace Pledge Union with Richard Shepherd and Arthur Ponsonby, but in 1936 he declared his support for re-armament, saying that 'there are worse things than war'. Sorensen was a staunch supporter of Indian Independence. 'We are appalled by what is happening to the Jews in Germany, but what has been happening in India is just as bad'.

On his return visit to Briton Ferry in October 1958, fifty years after he had joined the ILP, he was again Labour MP for Leyton, but his position had changed as he moved to the right. Nevertheless, he still strongly supported the movements for colonial liberation, causing Aneurin Bevan to tell him: 'Your trouble, Reg, is that you believe in liberation in every country but your own.' India had gained independence by the time of Sorensen's second visit, suggesting that Bevan's remark was a compliment rather than a criticism.

From the 1920s until his death he published extensively.

Reg Sorensen *(Cheryl Clement)*

Ben Tillett
(1860–1943)

Tillett was a Bristolian who was a
founding member of both the ILP and
Labour Party. He created the first trade
union for unskilled workers. With Tom
Mann and John Burns, he led the
successful 1889 London dock strike
which guaranteed four hours continuous work for dockers and
became President and General Secretary of the International
Transport Workers' Federation in 1904. He fought four general
elections unsuccessfully, including Bradford in 1892 and Swansea in
January 1910. He was followed as President of the International
Workers' Federation by Swansea's Bob Williams from 1920-1925.

In June, 1910, he gave a lecture at Rehoboth Baptist Chapel,
under ILP auspices, on his visit to Australia, chaired by Dr W. B.
Harry. (The Australian Trade unions had donated £30,000 to
support the National Transport Workers Federation). Tillett was a
co-founder of the *Daily Herald* with Lansbury and Dyson.

Tillett supported Britain's involvement in World War One. He
wanted pacifists severely punished and split the Labour Party by
supporting the war. It is noteworthy that Tillett spoke at Rehoboth –
a chapel that gained a pro-war reputation. Possibly as a result of
this, he never became prominent in the Transport and General
Workers' Union and his role diminished in the 1920s. Nevertheless
he was elected as MP for Salford North 1917–24 and 1929–31.
Ernest Bevin was his deputy when President of the TUC in 1929.

Charles Trevelyan
(1870–1958)

Charles Trevelyan, (not to be confused with his brother G. M. Trevelyan, the distinguished historian) was educated at Harrow and Trinity College, Cambridge. His family politics were Liberal, but in 1895 he joined the Fabian Society and developed his views on social reform. This led to him winning the Elland seat in 1899 at a bye-election for the Liberals and becoming Parliamentary Secretary for the Board of Education from 1908 to 1914. He advocated a completely secular system of education. In the House of commons he advocated the taxation of land values, Liberal-Labour co-operation on social legislation and, forcibly, the abolition of the House of Lords.

At the beginning of the war Trevelyan resigned his post as Parliamentary Secretary to the Board Of Education. He was one of four senior members of the government opposed to the war, but only he, John Burns and John Morley resigned; Prime Minister Asquith persuaded Lloyd George against it. Trevelyan was vilified by the press and his Constituency Association and estranged from most of his family, but his mind was turning to other matters.

Shortly afterwards, Trevelyan joined with Angell, MacDonald, Morel and Rowntree in forming the Union of Democratic Control (its purposes are described in Chapter Two). Some regard the UDC as Trevelyan's brainchild and an organisation whose necessity arose because, in Trevelyan's words: 'the rulers, the diplomats, the militarists have failed.' The *Herald* reported on his visit, not as an NCF member but under the auspices of the ILP, to Briton Ferry on 16 May 1916. Joe Branch presided at a meeting before a large audience at the Public Hall. Trevelyan outlined the various phases the war had taken, arguing it could have been prevented had more peace conferences been held.

Everyone wanted to hear from Trevelyan on another issue, one which was causing an enormous stir in the town. At the time Davies and Waters, Briton Ferry's NCF Chair, were in prison for an offence under the Defence of the Realm Act, namely the seditious distribution of anti-conscription literature. It was no surprise that the hall was so packed. By December of that year the Public Hall management committee had decided that no further meetings of that kind might be held at the hall. As a consequence when Trevelyan spoke on behalf of the Council for Civil Liberties, of *People's Rights* On Friday 15 December, the meeting had to be held elsewhere.

At the war's end Trevelyan joined the ILP, winning Newcastle Central for Labour in 1922. He became President of the Board of Education in 1924, serving again, between 1929–31, in MacDonald's Labour Governments. He was expelled from the Labour Party in 1939 for opposing the National Government.

Richard C. Wallhead

(1870–1934)

Richard C. Wallhead (L)
with Keir Hardie

Dick Wallhead was as a lecturer, socialist and journalist who visited Briton Ferry many times and was well-liked by many in the town. Before World War One he was organising secretary for the ILP and Labour candidate for Coventry. He came to Briton Ferry in this national ILP capacity on 16 January 1916 and retained his connection with Briton Ferry and south Wales between the wars. He was opposed to the war.

He visited the town again in May 1916 under the auspices of Briton Ferry Trades Council. A vote at Jerusalem Baptist Church's Sunday evening service was held on a motion against conscription and was declared carried with four dissentients. The mover was Mr George Jones and the seconder, Mr Chris Way, while the pastor, the Reverend Rees Powell, also spoke against the measure.

On the weekend of 15–16 July 1916 two open air meetings were held, with a third at the Public Hall which was packed with an enthusiastic audience to hear him give 'a great address on *Peace Negotiation*'. He spoke again on 28 December 1917, this time at another outdoor event Briton Ferry and was subsequently fined £50 at Neath, and, in default, four months imprisonment under the Defence of the Realm Act.

'for false statements likely to prejudice the recruitment, training, discipline and administration of His Majesty's forces in speeches at Briton Ferry and at Cwmdu (Maesteg) on 12 September. Amongst other utterances it was alleged he said

that boys of eighteen did not join for the duration of the war, but that they would be the Regular Army of the future'.
(*Aberdeen Evening Express*)
His exact words were:

'There are a lot of women in the field. You mothers take warning: you who have sons of eighteen years are under the impression that your sons are joining for the duration of the war. But that is not so. Every lad of eighteen years joins, but for the regular army of the future. I know there is posted up in every barrack room notices to the effect that boys of eighteen years will be kept for the regular army in the future. Commanding Officers have also told them on parade and therefore we have also got conscription in the worst form.'

Considerable interest was evinced at Neath one Friday in connection with the presentation of the case against him. There were four summonses. The defendant was legally advised by Mr Edward Roberts (Dowlais) and the prosecution for the Home Office was taken by Mr Edward Powell, Neath. The cases had been adjourned two weeks to allow Mr Wallhead to prepare his defence.

Sergeant Williams was cross-examined by the defendant and admitted not having taken a verbatim report of the speech, but the passages in question so impressed him, he said, that he went straight to the police station and reported them. PC Lisk said he distinctly heard the defendant say that boys of eighteen would be the army of the future. Captain Hamilton Kerby Shore, of the Adjutant-General's Department at the War Office, said the Defendant's statements were absolutely untrue: no such notices were posted up in barrack rooms.

Mr Wallhead argued on legal grounds that the proceedings were irregular and that there was no written record of what he had said. He only spoke about permanent militarism. He pleaded guilty to the second charge regarding the notices and was fined £25 in each of the two Briton Ferry cases, or in default four months imprisonment. He was ordered to pay costs in the Maesteg cases. Advocate's fee of five guineas was allowed.

He was sent to Swansea Prison for four months, but was released after two. In March, 1918, he related some of his recent prison experiences to a big meeting of the Briton Ferry ILP, presided over by Mr Joe Branch. Two years later he became Chair of the ILP nationally for two years. Nevertheless, he again came to Briton Ferry on 20 February 1922, before winning Merthyr from the Liberals and holding the seat until his death in 1934. Indeed Richard Collingham Wallhead was one of only five ILP MPs to retain their seats after the 1931 election – a fine tribute to his Merthyr predecessor, Keir Hardie.

Richard C. Wallhead

Conclusion to Chapter Three

This chapter considered the influence of speakers from outside Wales who were invited to Briton Ferry to express their views. They had overlapping interests, experience and ideas which were of great interest for the townspeople. Categorising their ideas narrowly may not do full justice to the breadth of each individual's interests but it is useful to highlight the main topics that they represented. The visits of the female speakers listed below are covered in Chapter Six.

Anti-militarism: Newbold, Philip Snowden, Wallhead
Internationalism: Angell, Buxton, MacDonald, Morel, Pal, Trevelyan
Militarism: Dalton; Emmeline and Christabel Pankhurst, Tillett
Pacifism: Brockway: Dunnico, Hardie and Russell
Press freedom: Cannan, Langdon-Davies, Emrys Hughes
Socialism: Glasier, Goldman and Hardie
Suffragism: Hardie, Lansbury; Pankhursts, Ethel Snowden
Trade Unionism: Bevin, Mann, Maxton, Richardson, Smillie

What must have been extremely difficult for the authorities was the fact that these activists were generally sober, respected and mature members of their communities. It was difficult to depict them as rabble-rousers. In addition,there also existed in Briton Ferry a political-religious axis involving educated people and those whose self-improvement created added challenges for the authorities. It is difficult today to imagine the combined moral force of the strengthening trade unions, non-conformist churches and other sources of pressure, such as Briton Ferry's powerful Co-operative movement and the WEA.

In combination with local circumstances, these speakers helped to produce a lasting culture in the community which was not just anti-war, or pro-peace: it was almost a composite statement of how human beings should be treated and how they should live. There was also a significant religious element in many of the ideas expressed but the more local religious and political speakers will be reviewed in Chapter Four.

Chapter Four:
Welsh support for the resistance

They were all at the highest point of enthusiasm – they inspired me,
and I spoke as I have never spoken before.
(Bertrand Russell)

This chapter considers a selection of those who came to Briton
Ferry from elsewhere in Wales to attend organised indoor and
outdoor meetings in which they offered their support and opinions
on the issues of the day.

Yr Alltudion Cymraeg/The Welsh Exiles at Knutsford Prison
Photographer Wallace Cartwright of Ystradgynlais
is in view front row second left

Henry Davies – Cwmafan

(1883–1953)

Henry (Harry) Davies was the leading ILP figure in Cwmafan and a frequent official at Briton Ferry events. As in Briton Ferry, Cwmafan's NCF Branch was closely associated with the ILP and Davies was a prominent member of both in Cwmafan.

An early attempt to hold an anti-conscription meeting took place in December 1915, when the meeting to be held at the Grand Hotel, Port Talbot, was thwarted when members arrived to find the doors locked. The event was transferred outdoors to a much colder Bethany Square. That was not the last time it was necessary to hold meetings outdoors, or at secret venues. During one such meeting Davies made allegations that Councillor Percy Jacobs, the Mayor of Aberafan, had gone through the district advising the adoption of conscription. Jacobs denied the allegations and Davies' feelings on the war were expressed in a verse that he wrote in Briton Ferry on 27 February 1916:

> Blessed are the peacemakers, so Christ said,
> But men have lost the message;
> The world is strewn with sick and dead
> For nothing-but a mess of potage.

It seems that Davies was to Cwmafan what Joe Branch was to Briton Ferry: a leader with charisma. The charisma was apparent when both represented their members at important legal proceedings. In Davies' case the Glamorgan Gazette, of 31 March, 1916, reported on a tribunal at which he represented no fewer than thirteen conscientious objectors who had refused non-combatant status. No wonder he was often also referred to as the *Welsh Keir Hardie*!

Those he represented were:

Joseph N. Davies, Albert Rankin Evans, William Grane, Edward Haycock, John Haycock, Joseph Llewelyn, Arthur Millington, David Mort, William Mainwaring, Daniel H. Phillips, Christopher R. Scott, William Arthur Thomas and Lancelot Thomas Waters.

Later, in May 1916, he was charged by Superintendent Ben Evans at Aberafan with obstruction at an NCF rally in Bethany Square. Charges were also laid against three other local councillors who had spoken at the meeting: ILP Councillor Harry Davies of Taibach, ILP Councillor Tal Mainwaring of Margam and James Price, a miner and member of Aberafan Town Council, who had chaired the meeting.

A week previously the police had raided the ILP centre in Cwmafan and confiscated all the branch's literature, including the *Everett* and *Repeal the Act* leaflets. A subsequent court case resulted in charges against Tal Mainwaring, Dan Morris (Cwmafan ILP's Secretary) and ILP members Jenkin and William Williams for distributing circulars likely to prejudice recruiting. A parallel tribunal was held at Neath early in June 1916 in which Joe Branch was the principal defendant in a class action against him and nine others from Briton Ferry, one of whom was my grandfather. This is reported in Chapter Five.

A further meeting, chaired by Davies, was the cause of much trouble. It was held under the auspices of the NCCL at Gallipoli Square in Taibach on 18 June. Fred Bramley, the TUC General Secretary, called for the repeal of the Military Service Act. This resulted in four members being charged, with imprisonment for Morris and Mainwaring because they refused to pay their fines. A fuller description of their committal can be read later under the heading of *Tal Mainwaring*.

None of this deterred Davies. In July he chaired more public anti-war meetings in Cwmafan and Taibach. One involved Richard Wallhead and another in which Bertrand Russell spoke 'to a large and appreciative audience near Cwmafan police station'. Despite all this, later that year Davies was at Briton Ferry Public Hall supporting Ethel Snowden in her call for peace negotiations.

'Harry Davies' work on behalf of the bottom dog has been purely disinterested. His labours have sprung from a desire to benefit his fellow man, and his steadfast adherence to principles in face of the vilest abuse, and sacrifice of his own personal interests place him in the forefront of trustworthy men to whom the workers can relegate their cause'.

That would have made a fitting epitaph for Davies, but events in his life took a sharp turn. In 1917, in the course of doing work for the local Poor Law Board, he was prosecuted for fraud and received a jail sentence after some of the money he had to distribute was mis-used. This might have ended all Davies' hopes of furthering his political ambitions, but it did not do so altogether. Although he lost his place, from being the front runner, for selection as a Parliamentary candidate, before his death in June, 1953, he had become the Mayor of Swansea.

James Ewart Edmunds – Cardiff
(1883–1962)

Jimmy Edmunds was born the son of a teacher at Llanelli Hill, but during his school days he lived at his parents' home at School House, Cardiff Road, Pontypridd. After qualifying at Cardiff University he became an assistant master at Lansdowne road School from 1903 to 1920 and married in 1911. As a teacher he became Secretary of Cardiff Trades Council and, during the war, a No Conscription Fellowship official. He was granted non-combatant status as a conscientious objector and was placed in army reserve class W. He was one of four Cardiff teachers whose resignation was demanded by Cardiff Council in May, 1917, because of the Council's objection to conscientious objectors' engagement in teaching. Others, however, who declared conscientious objection were allowed to continue teaching. Consequently Edmunds' case for exemption, and a demand for a Public Enquiry about it, was officially backed by both the NUT Executive Committee and Cardiff Trades Council.

At this time, Sir Clement Kinloch-Cooke, Unionist MP for Cardiff East, alleged that conscientious objectors were having too easy a time in Home Office Camps.[27] Two witnesses were forthcoming to destroy Kinloch-Cooke's allegations. The first was an Ernest E. Hunter, who described his assertions as 'unjustified calumnies' on the basis that he had just completed an inspection visit to four camps. At Broxburn camp, for example, COs were hired out to work for a private contractor (called Rough and Sons) at a chemical manure works. The Home Office were paid full standard wages for the COs' services. There, a second witness, Dr J. C. McCallum, a

---

[27] Llanddeusant, Llanon, Ballachulish and Broxburn – *Pioneer* 19 May 1917

previous Medical Officer of Health for Argyllshire and a CO at the camp, confirmed that no COs had left Broxburn despite the atrocious working conditions: they endured them.

Edmunds continued to expound his views after the war. He was at Porthcawl in June 1919, with J. A. Kelly, Dan Griffiths, and Minnie Pallister. During several visits to Briton Ferry, for example in July and December 1919, he spoke of *Education and Democracy*. Such activities increased his popularity, and when Edmunds stood in the 1929 election as Labour candidate for Cardiff East he dislodged the incumbent of five years. The dislodged incumbent was none other than Sir Clement Kinloch-Cooke.

The dismissal of teachers from their employment because of their objection to conscription was a major problem for local authorities, as we shall see in the cases of Emrys Hughes, Dan Griffiths, Morgan Jones and others. One implication of dismissal was that teachers' opposition to conscription would affect their professional standards. Edmunds fought his case against dismissal and won. He was assigned to do work of national importance as a school-teacher!

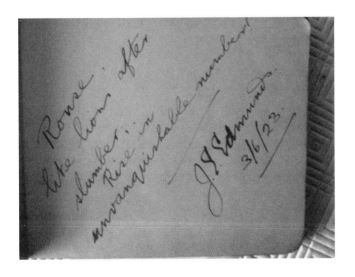

Daniel F. Griffiths – Llanelli
(1881–1968)

Griffiths was a single, 36 year-old teacher and playwright from Myrtle Terrace, Llanelli. He was a Congregationalist, NCF member and conscientious objector. His case was described as 'peculiar' in a number of ways.

Ivor Thomas of Briton Ferry accompanied Samuel James of Llanelli, (Secretary of the Dan Griffiths Committee) as leaders of a deputation to represent Griffiths' case with the President of the Board of Education and the Brace Committee chairman. *(Llanelli Star 21 July 1917)*. One must ask oneself: what was so peculiar about this case that it required such a deputation?

First of all, Griffiths had based his case on the unusual grounds of capability to be conscripted, rather than religious or political objection, even though his arguments were political. Secondly, there were allegations that his application for exemption from military service on grounds of conscience was not dealt with fairly and that Griffiths was persecuted during the tribunal proceedings for his socialist ideas. Thirdly the Military Representative, former Labour Alderman Nathan Griffiths, said that Dan Griffiths was the only teacher who had not attested and accused him of bringing J Walton Newbold to the town after Newbold had been prosecuted and fined under the Defence of the Realm Act. Griffiths' supporters retorted that it was actually Nathan Griffiths who invited him. The Tribunal was postponed for nine weeks.

In May 1917, Dan Griffiths' application for absolute exemption by the Llanelli tribunal[28] had been granted on the grounds of his work and physical condition, but the Military representative, Alderman Nathan Griffiths, appealed. As a result, the Carmarthen Appeal Tribunal quashed the absolute exemption and placed Dan Griffiths into a non-combatant category. At that stage Griffiths claimed that

---

[28] Tribunal procedures are explained in Chapter Five

the Appeal Tribunal proceedings were irregular and leave was granted for him to appeal to the Central Tribunal.

From this point events became even more bizarre: Griffiths was asked to attend a medical so that the Committee for Work of National Importance would know what medical category he would have been assigned had he not been exempted. With assurances in August that his attendance for medical examination would not prejudice his work as a teacher (which was deemed to be of national importance, he attended the medical and was put into class C3. (Circular 983 from the Army Council exempted teachers in this grade from military service.)

By November, the Central Tribunal ruled that under no circumstances would Griffiths be permitted to teach, but was permitted to find *work of a clerical nature in a government-controlled establishment.* In January he was asked to attend Llanelli Recruiting office to join non-combatant service. In February a warrant for his arrest was issued and, on 7 March, Carmarthen magistrates handed him over to a military escort to be taken to Cardiff Barracks and thence Aldershot. There he was court-martialled on 3 April 1917 and given six months' imprisonment with hard labour. After spending nearly three months at Wormwood Scrubs he was despatched to Dartmoor.

Griffiths, 'our old friend from Llanelli', was in Briton Ferry on 19 January 1919, at a Trades and Labour Council Meeting. He spent an hour and a half recounting his experiences as a conscientious objector to a packed hall. He related that he had been purposely placed in a hospital ward among wounded soldiers just returned from Salonika. The intention to humiliate him by placing him with injured soldiers was unsuccessful because he claimed that he had 'just about converted the ward to an ILP branch before he left'.

The Llanelli Star had reported the proceedings on 11 March 1916. When Griffiths said:

'A person of my mental make-up, who views the question of war like myself, historically, economically and politically, is simply incapable of any military service. . . . I have what is probably an exceptional moral conscientious objection to taking part in any war. For 15 years I have done my best to (describe) a world-wide economic system that leads us inevitably to war as it leads us to riches and poverty and to industrial wealth. My political and social philosophy renders me entirely useless as a soldier.'

Griffiths' views were ably expressed in his book: *The Real Enemy and other Socialist Essays.* It comprised essays which he had written for *The Daily Herald, The Labour Leader, The Socialist Review* and *The Swansea Labour News.* The book had a foreword by Ramsay MacDonald.

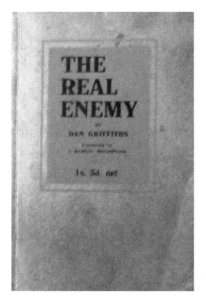

Book The Real Enemy

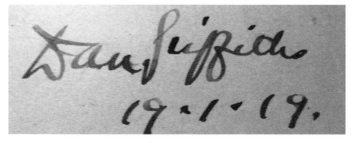

Courtesy Cheryl Clement

Emrys Hughes
(1894–1969)

Emrys Hughes
(Cheryl Clement)

Emrys Daniel Hughes was a Tonypandy man who was educated at Mountain Ash and Leeds before becoming, first, a teacher and, then, a local journalist. At Leeds, the College at which he studied was partly used for wounded soldiers and this pointed him towards pacifism. In turn, his opposition to war quite possibly resulted in his being turned down for a post as a teacher. After becoming an enthusiastic Labour supporter he came into close contact with Keir Hardie and joined the PPU. He also became Secretary of Aberdare NCF.

By March 1916 he was before Mountain Ash Military Service Tribunal, as both an applicant for exemption and as a newspaper reporter, but he was not granted exemption from service. The County Tribunal at Pontypridd upheld the Mountain Ash Tribunal's decision, saying that they found Hughes had neither any moral nor religious objections. From there he followed the usual conscientious objector's route of being declared an absentee, appearing before Mountain Ash Magistrates and then being taken to Cardiff Recruitment Office. A year in Caernarfon Jail followed, but Hughes still managed to visit Briton Ferry's ILP branch during the war.

Hughes visited Neath in July 1919 to speak on Cimla Common, where his audience 'listened with marked attention.' He again visited Briton Ferry on 3 June 1921. An unsuccessful attempt to become MP for Bosworth in 1923 followed, and a year later he married Nan Hardie thus becoming son-in law to Keir Hardie.

Between 1931 and 1946 he edited *Forward*, the newspaper of the Socialist movement in Scotland and also gained a wide experience of the activities of local government. In the late 1930s, *Forward* was one of the few left-wing publications to criticise the Moscow Trials. (The trials were an excuse by Stalin to purge potential opposition to him based on his failed economic policies.)

The journalistic experience proved of great benefit to him and he was elected as Labour MP for south Ayrshire at a by-election in 1946. He was re-elected in the next six general elections and edited a Scottish edition of *Tribune* after World War Two. Hughes often criticized the leadership of the Labour Party and had the whip withdrawn twice, for substantial periods, over his stance against nuclear weapons. Hughes was a constant opponent of the activities of NATO. Throughout the rest of his career he stood on the left wing of the Labour Party, he remained on the back benches of the House of Commons, and generally considered a fiery rebel.

The Plaid Cymru leader, Gwynfor Evans, was a fellow pacifist and member of the Peace Pledge Union who won Carmarthen from Labour in a 1966 by-election. When Hughes was showing him around the House of Commons, he pointed out the Welsh table in the tea room, and warned him: 'You'd better not sit there, your name's mud among that lot.' Hughes published a large number of biographies and other works, among them *Keir Hardie, Churchill, Macmillan,* and *Sir Alec Douglas-Home.* His biography of Sidney Silverman, also a World War One conscientious objector, was particularly important as it was the success of Silverman's private member's bill which resulted in the ending of the death penalty in the UK.

Hughes also recorded his experiences of his visits to Briton Ferry:

'It had a little hall, which had formerly been a nonconformist chapel, where regular Sunday night meetings were held in wintertime and which were always well attended. They sang hymns from a Socialist hymn book and it was as much like a religious service as a political meeting. . . .'

These meetings had been going on all throughout the war when Briton Ferry had been known in the surrounding district as 'little Moscow'.

Emrys Hughes
(Cheryl Clement)

Morgan Jones – Bargoed
(1885–1939)

Morgan Jones – Bargoed
Independent Labour

Jones was at Briton Ferry on 19 June 1916 for a most important event: the formation of the south Wales Branch of the NCF. In the circumstances his attendance was quite remarkable.

Morgan Jones was a miner's son from Gelligaer who won a scholarship to Lewis School, Pengam, and then Reading University. His brother Eddie, ten years younger was also a CO. He joined the ILP in 1908 and started up the Rhymney Valley's first ILP branch. By 1911 he was elected to Gelligaer Urban District Council and from there directed his attention to municipal house-building, especially for the Bargoed area. In 1913 he became President of the Glamorgan Federation of Teachers. War was approaching. It 'proved to be one of the most traumatic periods in his life and speeded up his transition from a provincial to a national one', according to Dylan Rees[29].

As well as being a Baptist lay preacher, Jones was also a conscientious objector, an NCF founder member, and member of the NCF national committee. His objection to conscription was on religious grounds, but it was his activities in denouncing conscription that led to his imprisonment under the Defence of the Realm Act. He saw conscription as a block on world peace. He found the jingoism of the south Wales Miners' Federation distasteful; he argued for diplomacy, not armed conflict.

Jones was both a Gelligaer Councillor and a conscientious objector when he had to appear before Gelligaer's Military Tribunal. This meant that the Council had, effectively, to consider the case of one of its own members. It decided in February 1916, by 10 votes to 8, to uphold the law. Afterwards, Bertrand Russell met Jones and wrote to Ottoline Morrell about the encounter:

---

[29] Morgan Jones; Educationist and Politician (1987).

'Today I had lunch with the Rev. Morgan Jones, a prominent pacifist here (in south Wales) and a real saint . . . it is wonderful what the COs have done for the cause of peace – heroism is no longer all on the side of war. I ought to have gone into the more hostile districts . . . here it is merely a picnic.'[30]

Jones took an absolutist stance and was kept in solitary confinement, despite the tribunal's offer of alternative service under the Home Office Scheme. He was arrested at his parents' home on 28 May 1916 and put into military hands at Caerphilly as an absentee. He lost his teaching post and received a sentence of 61 days for not paying his fine. It is this that makes his visit to Briton Ferry in June 1916 so remarkable. When Jones later served his sentence it included three weeks solitary confinement and detention until the end of 1917.

The formation of the south Wales Branch of the NCF was concluded effectively. Morgan Jones became chair of the branch which comprised four groups: Monmouth, Cardiff, Mid-Glamorgan and Swansea. Briton Ferry's Council against Conscription came within the Swansea group. It had H. Morris of Gorseinon as Treasurer, with Mansel Grenfell of Gorseinon and Tom Evans of Ynysmeudw as Committee. Evans, who later became a senior lecturer at Aberystwyth University, typifies the calibre of many of the NCF's members.

Jones was imprisoned several times between April 1916 and August 1919, appearing as a deserter at Bridgend Police court as late as April 1919. He was also one of the defendants but tried in *absentia* at the Mansion House trial of eight NCF members[31]. The charges, supported by Lord Derby as a witness, were that the Committee of the NCF made statements in the *Repeal the Act* leaflet that would prejudice recruiting. The trial caused widespread interest in south Wales.

The leaflet stated:

'We cannot assist in warfare; War which to us is wrong; war which the people do not seek, will only be made impossible when men who so believe remain steadfast to their convictions.

---

[30] The Autobiography of Bertrand Russell
[31] See following and illustration on page 126

We strongly condemn the monstrous assumption by Parliament that a man is "deemed" to be bound by an oath that he has never taken and forced under an authority he will never acknowledge. Admit the principle (of compulsion) and who can stay the march of militarism? Repeal the Act. That is your only safeguard. What shall it profit the nation, if it shall win the war and lose its soul.'

Mr Bodkin, who appeared at the Mansion House trial for the Director of Public Prosecutions, said:

'There are times when thought and tongue are to be curbed, and at no time is it more essential that there should be wholesale restraint upon expression of views which are mischievous and against the interests of the country.'

Bodkin adduced that there had been no military dictating, nor curbing of the civil liberties of the public, because it was the highest form of freedom to fight for their country. The hearing was lengthy and each defendant was fined £100 with £10 costs.

Jones was granted a seventeen month furlough on health grounds after two successive terms of hard labour. From Kinmel he was moved to Wormwood Scrubs and Warwick Work Centre. He was court-martialled as a deserter five months after the war had ended and remained in detention until August 1919. After returning to his Council work he was eventually to become the first conscientious objector MP to be returned to the House of Commons, this after the war when he became MP for Caerphilly from 1921–1939. He was succeeded as MP by Ness Edwards, also a conscientious objector.

During his furlough in December 1918 Morgan Jones had visited Briton Ferry from Bargoed. His interest in providing municipal house-building was a likely subject of discussion with fellow Briton Ferry conscientious objector, Dil Thomas. Jones came back to Briton Ferry in April 1919, no doubt to encourage Briton Ferry Council to do what was being done for house-building in Bargoed. Dil Thomas finally succeeded in the 1920s to persuade Neath Council to build such houses in the Brynhyfryd area of Briton Ferry.

After the war Morgan Jones also campaigned for a Secretary of State for Wales and fought against cuts in education: 'you cannot bring the ethics and practice of the counting house into the elementary schools or into the secondary schools either.'

Tal Mainwaring
(1890–1968)

Noah Mandry was Tal Mainwaring's great-great grandfather. He came from Llanguick Parish in his twenties to work in Taibach copper works around 1830. His family settled in Cwm Brombil where five of the seventeen cottages became, at one time, occupied by Mainwarings. 'Noah was born as Mandry but was buried as Mainwaring'[32].

Tal was the son of colliery blacksmith/farrier Samuel Mainwaring, who worked at Morfa pit. Tal's father was born in 1864 and he and his wife Catherine became a coal mining family of nine. Tal was baptised at Beulah Chapel, Groes on 2 March 1890. Ten days later disaster was to befall the family. Five minutes after Sam descended the pit, a huge explosion occurred beneath him. His two uncles, Noah and Thomas, were on duty in the bowels of the pit. Both died, along with 85 others, including thirty-three year old next-door neighbour, William Barras, the pit manager. The village became the scene of utter confusion and the school, which Tal's brother William attended, closed for a week.

Tal and his brothers, William, David and John nevertheless became underground workers. His youngest brother, Harold Noah, was named after his uncle. Tal also had two sisters, Janet Edith and Gwendoline May. In later years they, too, would no doubt have fully understood Keir Hardie's castigation of the House of Commons in 1895 for not adding condolences to the families of the 257 victims of the Pontypridd pit disaster to their congratulations on the birth of Edward as royal heir to the throne.

After leaving school Tal joined his father at Morfa pit, at first as a surface worker, and later as a tram driver. By the age of eighteen he was a committeeman at his pit lodge and by the time he was twenty-three he was chairman.

---

[32] Allen Blethyn – personal correspondence

122

'About this time there were emerging two men, both working in the coal industry, who dedicated their lives to socialism and to the affairs of the town. They were Alderman Harry Davies and Tal Mainwaring. They spread their political gospel at every opportunity and often in the open air.'[33]

Tal Mainwaring became interested in politics in his early twenties and by his late twenties was active in local politics, as a Margam District Councillor. As an ILP and NCF member his interest widened into more national politics, as he worked alongside ILP Secretary, Daniel Morris of Cwmavon. When conscription came in 1916, Mainwaring was an early supporter for exemption from military service on political grounds, but he was not a conscientious objector, as many imagined. Several other Mainwarings from the area were conscientious objectors: Richard Mainwaring of Taibach, the brother of another Tal Mainwaring, and his brother, William J of Margam. Thomas A Mainwaring of Brombil was yet another. Tal's activities in the NCF continued. After a No Conscription Fellowship rally at Bethany Square, Port Talbot, in May 1916, Mainwaring was charged with obstruction, along with fellow Margam District Councillor Harry Davies, James Price of Aberavon Town Council and Henry Davies, of Cwmavon. Harry Davies of Margam had been a member of Glamorgan County Council.

'Tal Mainwaring spoke with a pleasanter tenor voice (than Harry Davies), with his head thrown back defiantly, and with his hands grasping the lapels of his coat. Although I heard both men speak many times in public, I never heard them employ much humour, but Tal could lampoon opponents occasionally with dry humour. During one of Ramsay MacDonald's first general election campaigns locally, Tal devoted much of one speech to the columns of hostile press, and he caused many grins by referring to two newspapers as "The Daily Wail" and the "Western Mule".'[34]

---

[33] J. Ivor Hansen: Profile of a Welsh Town
[34] J. Ivor Hansen: Profile of a Welsh Town

Fred Bramley
(TUC collection)

On Sunday 18 June, an anti-conscription meeting was held in the afternoon, under the auspices of the National Council for Civil Liberties at Gallipoli Square, Taibach. It was chaired by Alderman Harry Davies. The speaker was Fred Bramley and its purpose was to demand the repeal of the Military Service Act. The reason given for holding it in that particular spot was reported: 'to avoid attention from the authorities because of their recent activity which unfortunately resulted in four of their comrades finding themselves in the police court'[35].

Following the fines imposed on Mainwaring and others, which they had refused to pay, Mainwaring was imprisoned for three months; Morris for two months.

'Great waves of enthusiasm witnessed the departure of Councillor Tal Mainwaring and Dan Morris en route to Swansea Gaol from Aberavon station last Saturday evening (24 June)'.

'The police endeavoured to persuade them to pay, and showed their willingness to serve distress warrants on them but the two comrades refused their offer. . . . Eventually the authorities sent for them at 5.30 pm and this time they were followed to the railway station by hundreds of enthusiastic people to see them off. Some of the crowds climbed the platform palings; women wept; and the men sang themselves hoarse and waved their headgear. Their attention was now diverted by the arrival of the train packed up with its Saturday night load of visitors to town. These people never left the platform, but were caught up in the well of enthusiasm and again the Red Flag was sung – this time with renewed vigour and joined in by the Aberavon Male Voice Party, who were leaving by the same train. It was impressive scene. The singing having ceased a voice shouted out Are we downhearted? "No" responded a thousand voices. Again and again this cry went up. And now silence reigned.

---

[35] *Pioneer*, 24 June 1916.

Councillor Harry Davies had suddenly risen to speak and the few remarks he was able to make were generously punctuated with applause and "hear, hear". Movements on the platform indicated the departure of the train. Porters bawled out warnings and the guard hurried along the platform as best he could to close the doors. A green flag was waved, a shrill whistle sounded from the engine, and thus departed, the Comrades were gone – but the spirit remained.'[36]

After the first fortnight in Swansea jail Tal Mainwaring was already able to speak of his prison experiences and repeat Madame de Stael's pronouncement: 'I never knew what freedom was until I went to jail'.

By October 1916 Mainwaring did speak of his prison experiences at an NCF fund-raising social event in Briton Ferry. In his speech he spoke of 'political prisoners', the result of which was his prosecution. However, the ILP members of the British Steelsmelters' Union had ensured that it was Union policy to welcome back COs (and those serving sentences for sedition it seems) on the same basis as soldiers from the front. This was a precedent which the mining union also seemed to follow in Tal's case.

The ILP branch at Taibach had no meeting rooms so that it was the private homes of members or officers such as Tal Mainwaring and Councillor Davies which were raided. This was the equivalent of raiding the offices of a major political party today. On 13 January, 1918 the Pioneer reported that the Magistrates Bench gave permission for Inspector Ben Evans to seize 25,000 leaflets from Mainwaring's home under S.51 of the Defence of the Realm Act. This, it should be noted was *before* there had been any evidence of public distribution and was given in his absence whilst he was in prison.

On another occasion: 'At Tal Mainwaring's house they were less successful, finding only the current number of the "Tribune" together with a number of pamphlets entitled "British Prussianism". And here again it reflects no great honour on the methods adopted by the civil authorities in raiding a man's house in his enforced absence'.

---

[36] *Pioneer,* 1 July 1916.

After the war, Tal married Dorothy M. Evans (Dora) in 1919 and had five children (Ken, Rufus, Frederick Samuel, Cathy and Dorothy. Frederick Samuel was Dai Mainwaring's father).

Tal Mainwaring's grandson, Dai Mainwaring, said he was not close to his grandfather, which was possibly because Dai's parents had moved to Birmingham. However, as a boy he did sometimes meet his grandfather . . . Dai remembers one occasion, at Villa Park in Birmingham, when they attended an England v Wales soccer match in 1958. Tal not only related the tale of his imprisonment in Swansea, but he also told of a visit to the USSR in the 1920s (with TUC General Secretary, Fred Bramley, and Bob Williams, Secretary of the National Transport Workers' Federation). The purpose of the visit, which coincided with the Labour Day celebrations, was to discuss the formation of a new, international, group of trade unions. Bernard Mainwaring, a nephew of Tal, claimed that Tal spoke over the radio to Britain to describe the march-past. The schedule also involved visiting the Kremlin and each member of the delegation was presented to the General Secretary of the Central Committee of the Communist Party of the Soviet Union: Tal had whispered to Dai that he could not forget Josef Stalin's eyes, as they seemed to be so full of cruelty. Fred Bramley died in office the following year.

In his working life Tal went on to become a check-weigher at Bryn colliery, then a miners' agent. He went on, too, to become Mayor of Port Talbot, not just once, in 1924–25, but again in 1952–53, when he also became a freeman of Port Talbot Borough. He had, after all, been instrumental, with Harry Davies, in the local government amalgamation which led to the creation in 1921–22 of the borough.

Daniel Watters – Cwmafan
(1865–)

Donald Watters was a Cwmafan man who often visited Briton Ferry and expressed his views on topical issues in the form of illustrations in family autograph albums. Sometimes the cartoons were of politicians: he drew several of Lloyd George, showing his harsh attitude. Watters also supported the conscientious objectors by drawing cartoons which highlighted their cause. The cartoon below is his riposte to Lloyd George's determination to 'make their path as hard as I can'.

Watters' depiction of Lloyd George
as a militarist

He was also graphically eloquent on the role that women were playing politically during the war, particularly the schism that was emerging amongst them as to whether they should or should not support the war.

Watters' cartoon[37] entitled 'Evolution or devolution of women' is interesting for a number of reasons. The images show a progression of female figures towards a headless image. This could be likened to a weapon of war; a bayonet on a rifle. The topic

[37] The cartoon may be a reversal of an idea of Sarah M. Severance, the American women's suffrage advocate. She wrote on the *Devolution and Evolution of Women* in order to express her views on the inequality experienced by women in historic European and Asian cultures, women's employment and responsibilities to family and church.

of evolution, following the themes of Darwin and others was still a divisive issue whilst devolution had not yet gained its modern meaning and was defined as *degeneration*.[38] Was Watters saying that support for the war by some of the suffragette movement would damage their cause? Given his membership of the ILP and NCF in Cwmafan, it seems likely that Watters would have supported women's suffrage and been bitterly disappointed by those who supported the war, which had led to a *devolution* of women. There may be other explanations linked to press comments at the time, but this hypothesis seems to be the most likely.

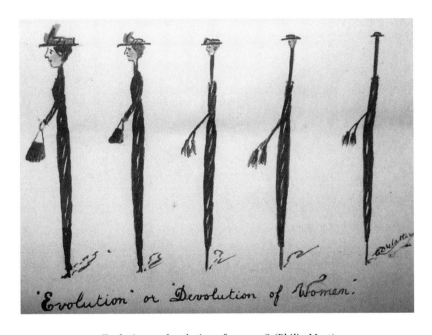

Evolution or devolution of women? *(Philip Mort)*

---

[38] Oxford English Dictionary

Robert (Bob) Williams
(1881–1936)

MR. ROBERT WILLIAMS, SECRE-
TARY OF THE TRANSPORT
WORKERS' FEDERATION

Bob Williams.
(Dr Harold Lewis/Sam Dawson of the International Transport Federation (UK))

Williams was born in Swansea and worked as a coal trimmer at the docks, becoming a Labour Councillor from 1910–12. During that time he became the first Secretary of the National Transport Federation and a leading member of the Union of Democratic Control. In July, 1914, he assured the Parliamentary Labour Party of full support in the country for any anti-war activity in the House of Commons. When he spoke, under the auspices of the No Conscription Fellowship, at Briton Ferry Public Hall in 1916, it was to explain how he believed that democratic control of foreign policies could be the achieved through international trade unionism. He repeated these ideas with H. J. Harford of the Herald in August 1917 (at a full-to-overflowing) Ebby's Olympic Cinema in Cwmafan.

His candidature for Aberavon constituency, in the election of 1918, was on behalf of the October Revolution (Labour) Party, but he failed. Major John Edwards won the seat for the Liberals with 62.8% of the vote, with Williams realising 35.7% on a 71.4% turnout.

Nevertheless he had other important things to attend to which he dealt with most successfully. The first was to re-establish links with German transport unions after the war. Johann Doring, of the German dockers recalled an encounter in Amsterdam in 1919: 'We saw the British comrades, Robert Williams, Harry Gosling and Ernest Bevin . . . when comrade Williams saw us, he took three or four great strides and stretched out his hand. Bevin was also affected, saying it was 'A very happy meeting which will ever live in one's memory.' Williams went on to consolidate this rapprochement at the ITF Congresses at Vienna and Hamburg in 1922 and 1924. At the latter he castigated both German financiers and Allied militarists for coercing the Germans into impossible reparations. Perhaps this was his finest hour and perhaps, accounts for his five years' presidency of the International Transport Federation (from 1920 to 1925).

Williams joined the Communist Party in 1920 and visited Moscow with a deputation of British trade union officials to discuss the formation of a new, international group of Trade Unions – the Red International of Trade Unions.

Williams was a potential Labour party leader, but he was not everyone's preference.

'I had heard (Bob Williams) recently in the Grand theatre address a mass meeting with an inflammatory speech which ended with the scorching peroration; "I believe in revolution; peaceful if possible, but revolution".'[39]

Although the transport workers were a signatory to the Triple Alliance with the National Union of Railwaymen and the Miners Federation of Great Britain, Williams' union failed to support the miners when their wages were cut as a result of de-control of the mines in 1921. That was *Black Friday* but, in 1925, the government agreed to grant a temporary subsidy to the mining industry to avoid wage reductions. That was *Red Friday*.

In the meantime, Ramsay MacDonald had won the Aberavon seat for Labour in 1924 with a 28.2% swing and, soon afterwards, in 1925–6 Bob Williams became chair of the Labour Party.

After criticising the miners during the 1926 strike, Williams (having become General Manager of the Daily Herald, a job he held from 1922-30) was deselected as a Labour candidate, After supporting Ramsay MacDonald's apostasy to the National Government, Williams could find no work, a factor that was a likely contribution to his suicide in 1936.

---

[39] J. Ivor Hanson, as before

Conclusion to Chapter Four

The common characteristic of those supporters described in this Chapter was their ILP and NCF membership and the strength in which they expressed those organisations' policies regarding the right to conscientious objection either orally or via the printed word. In some cases their values were expressed through their membership of other organisation such as the National Council for Civil Liberties, or their Trade Union. These supporters' names were known throughout Wales and, in the cases of Morgan Jones and Robert Williams, known throughout the country.

Each bullet in the table below shows membership of the organisations concerned and whether or not the individuals concerned were imprisoned under the Defence of the Realm Act, or detained at a prison or work centre as a conscientious objector.

	NCF	ILP	UDC	Other	Imprisoned/ work centre
Harry Davies	•	•		•	•
Jimmy Edmunds	•			•	
Dan Griffiths	•	•		•	•
Emrys Hughes	•	•		•	•
Morgan Jones	•	•		•	•
Tal Mainwaring	•	•			•
Robert Williams	•	•	•		

Postal Censorship.

The communication returned in this cover constitutes a breach of the Defence of the Realm Regulations. The writer is warned to be more careful in future.

N.B.—The communication will be allowed to proceed if the passage or passages referring to *Jeppelin raids die* are omitted, and if it is re-posted to the addressee in the usual way.

W 14215—235   5,000   12/15   H W V (P 1934/4)
18855—29   10,000   3/16

An example of censorship under the Defence of the Realm Act

The authorities frowned upon certain peace meetings by resisters

Chapter Five:
The Briton Ferry Resisters

*'It was not till we came here that we realised the debt of gratitude
we owe to those who have gone before us.'*
(Tom Thomas, Conscientious Objector).

Introduction

This chapter examines the experiences of some of those men from
Briton Ferry who resisted conscription on grounds of conscience,
and those who supported their resistance. Resistance commonly
took one of three forms.

Firstly, there was direct resistance from the conscientious
objectors themselves. At the time of writing thirty-three objectors
have been definitely identified from Briton Ferry, even though there
is much more known about some than others. It is possible that
others may yet be identified. The grounds for resistance and the
degree of resistance varied. There was much political and religious
resistance and these grounds were often combined. The degree of
resistance, however, was generally very strong, with the spectrum
of resistance comprising absolutists at one end and a sole objector,
who accepted work in the Non-Combatant Corps, at the other.

Secondly, as well as direct resistance, there were supporting
activities that were provided in the main by local politicians, trades
union leaders and some non-conformist churchmen.

Finally, support was evident from many members of the public,
whose affiliation to organisations (such as the ILP) manifested itself
through their activism – for example, the distribution of anti-
conscription literature, or attendance at educational, non-
conscription and other anti-war meetings.

The flow chart that follows explains the process that many
objectors followed when they sought exemption from military

service. The application process had developed from the original tribunals held under the Derby scheme. Controversial from its inception, it was modified in August, 1916, following pressure in Parliament from organisations such as the NCF, after physical mistreatment and unjust legal processing of objectors had been made public. It is important to remember that *all* eligible men were sent Form W3236, offering the choice of enlisting, or to provide proof of exemption, meaning that hundreds of thousands of applicants sought exemption from conscription on grounds other than that of conscientious objection. These objectors generally left the application process before the appeal stage.

The total number of applicants who appeared before the Briton Ferry local tribunal for exemption is unknown. However, something of its membership and workings is known.[40]

'Each evening twenty-five applicants appealed and, on Thursday, twelve were exempted on the grounds of certified trades and one on conscientious grounds. At the Briton Ferry Council Chamber on Thursday evening such a large number was present that many were asked to leave, including some women. There were interruptions by some present over questions put by the military authority – saying that he was abusive and immoral in refusing to recognise a question about conscientious objection.'

The military representative had refused to define, or was unable to say what constituted a conscientious objection. Another newspaper[41], reporting on a West Glamorgan Appeal Tribunal, heard the disclosure from a steelworks bar dragger that 'I was told by a member of the Briton Ferry Tribunal that God never gave me a conscience'.

The tribunal comprised the following members:

---

[40] *Bombshell at Briton Ferry: South Wales Weekly Post*, 25 March 1916.
[41] *Herald of Wales*, 22 April 1916

- James Thomas (Chair), 37, Elementary school head-teacher
- William Morris, 56, Tinplate works manager of Middleton Villas, Neath Road.
- Sidney Herbert Colwill, 58, Accountant, 9 Cwrt Sart Terrace.
- H. Alexander Clarke, Surveyor, 43, Brynsiriol, Neath Road.
- C. S. Gardner (Military Representative), Neath

Further examples showing the conduct of tribunals can be found in the appendices.

The conscientious objectors will be dealt with in alphabetical order, ranked by surname. The amount of information about them varies, and to ensure that everything known of each individual is recorded here, those who read each individual record in sequence, will find repetition. Where details have been obtained from the Pearce Register, or from local sources, whether in the form of documents or the memories of descendants, the information is reasonably comprehensive, but biographical and anecdotal information is far less complete where it has been extracted solely from national records. It is anticipated that the publication of this work might provide the necessary impetus that will reveal previously undiscovered names and further detail about individual histories.

Exemption from military service

Prospective conscript takes Form W3236 to attend recruiting office

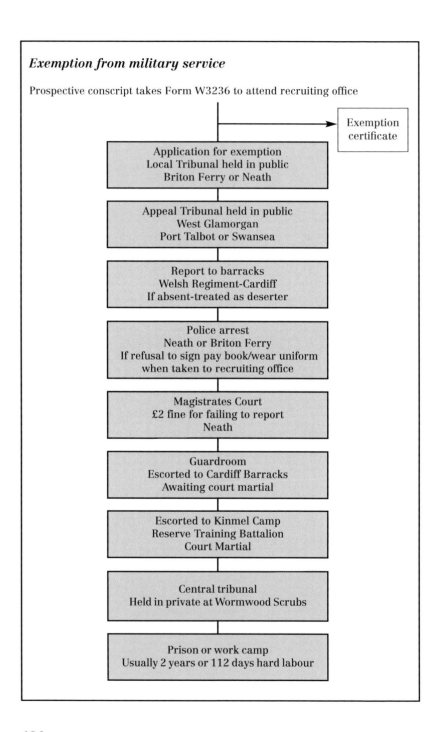

Exemption certificate

Application for exemption
Local Tribunal held in public
Briton Ferry or Neath

Appeal Tribunal held in public
West Glamorgan
Port Talbot or Swansea

Report to barracks
Welsh Regiment-Cardiff
If absent-treated as deserter

Police arrest
Neath or Briton Ferry
If refusal to sign pay book/wear uniform
when taken to recruiting office

Magistrates Court
£2 fine for failing to report
Neath

Guardroom
Escorted to Cardiff Barracks
Awaiting court martial

Escorted to Kinmel Camp
Reserve Training Battalion
Court Martial

Central tribunal
Held in private at Wormwood Scrubs

Prison or work camp
Usually 2 years or 112 days hard labour

Local tribunals for military exemption applications were held in Briton Ferry's
Council chamber above the library

Kinmel Park

Kinmel Park Military Training Camp is near Rhyl in north Wales. Its
main purpose was to train soldiers for military service. It was also
used for injured soldiers to convalesce and to detain conscientious
objectors temporarily. The conscientious objectors were sent there
from an area west of a line from Blackburn, Lancashire, to
Newport, Monmouthshire. The camp was known in the locality of
Rhyl as 'Kill'em Park'. Kinmel Camp was actually twenty camps,
with approximately twenty huts in each, on a site which had no
physical barriers to separate it from the surrounding countryside. It
housed some 15,000 soldiers and at any one time catered for some
seventy conscientious objectors. Robert Graves and J. B. Priestley
were two notables who were sent there. However, the full history of
the Camp went largely neglected until the publication in 2014 of
Robert H. Griffiths' *The Story of Kinmel Park*.

Prior to publication, attention on the Camp's history had mainly
focused on descriptions of the riots that had occurred there in
March, 1919. The Camp was then being used to repatriate Canadian
soldiers but delays in doing so, coupled with deficient conditions, led

Kinmel Park Camp

to riots in which five people were killed, twenty-three wounded and seventy-eight arrested. Griffiths has rectified this and devoted a chapter to the Camp's use for accommodating conscientious objectors. Many young soldiers and conscientious objectors lived in insanitary and over-crowded conditions at the Camp. There were many deaths and suicides: the Camp had been built when the prospect of a short war seemed realistic and, given this aspiration, the wooden barracks unsurprisingly provided only rudimentary facilities.

In April, 1916, newspaper reports appeared of non-combatant soldiers being court-martialled and sentenced to two years' imprisonment with hard labour at Kinmel. These were men who had lost their appeals at local Military Service Tribunals. Several from Briton Ferry, as well as elsewhere in Wales, arrived at Kinmel Camp during the summer of 1916. Conscientious objectors were considered to be soldiers and expected to obey military orders at the camp. If they did not wear army uniform, refused to parade, or sign an enlistment form they would be referred to a Central Tribunal at Wormwood Scrubs and then – almost certainly – be sent to a prison.

In May, 1916, a batch of seven Newport conscientious objectors arrived. Amongst them was Albert Rudall, an ILP and NCF member. Rudall died in 1918, aged 30, as a result of the sustained harsh treatment and deprivation he received in Kinmel, the civilian prisons of Warwick and Dartmoor, and the work centre at Keddington. He was one of five Welsh conscientious objectors to die in the work centres: H. Benyon of Swansea; G. H. Dardis of Risca, and Messrs J. Evans and Statton of Cardiff were the others.

Not all of Briton Ferry's conscientious objectors were sent to Kinmel: Edgar Elias was an early Briton Ferry conscientious objector who seems to have avoided Kinmel, perhaps because he accepted non-combatant service at his tribunal at Briton Ferry on 8 May. However, after Ernest Gething and Hwyrnos Jones' appeals were refused on 5 May, both resisters were sent there. They found the conditions in Kinmel so bad that they absconded, but they were forced to return for a second court-martial.

A batch of COs, similar to the Newport cadre, of nine Briton Ferry men, arrived on 13 and 14 November, 1916, having been arrested as absentees. *The Pioneer* reported on 2 December, 1916, that:

'Nine local men in Briton Ferry were arrested as conscientious objectors. Some of these young men will be missed as members of the ILP; others will be missed as workers in the churches to which they belonged, while all will be missed at meetings of the (no conscription) fellowship. Of their sincerity we are convinced, and they will inspire us in this fight for the principles for which we stand.'

The nine were: Brynley Griffiths; Tom Thomas; Edgar Treharne; William John; Jack Johns; Ivor Johns; C. T. T. Jones; Arthur Thomas, and James Mort. The Tribunal at Briton Ferry had denied them exemption, as did the Regional Tribunal. After attending the local magistrates' court they were escorted to Kinmel to join 60 Training Reserve Battalion on 23 November to be court-martialled. The Courts-Martial resulted in sentences of two years' hard labour, commuted to 112 days. Similarly, John Adams, Richard Gethin and Daniel T Davies were escorted to 58 Training Reserve Battalion, Kinmel in March, 1917, and court-martialled there. Cleaver quoted the case of William Isaac Thomas, a Gorseinon man who was with John Adams at Wakefield and Talgarth, whose sentence was pronounced in front of hundreds of soldiers on parade.

Wormwood Scrubs

Wormwood Scrubs prison in west London was completed as a permanent prison in 1891 with its bricks being made in situ by some of the prisoners. In World War One 'the Scrubs' was where the Central Military Tribunals took place. Tribunals were perfunctory – often lasting for only three minutes, a derisory amount of time in which to determine the future of a man's life. The prison acted as a feeder location from where most unsuccessful appellants against conscription were re-allocated to other prisons or work centres as members of Army Reserve Class W. The first work centre was opened at Dyce near Aberdeen in August 1916. Some were retained at Wormwood Scrubs, in its capacity as a civil prison for various sentences. A list of prisons and work camps indicating those to which Briton Ferry men were assigned can be seen on pages 142-143.

Two exercise periods were timetabled in prison

Daily life in prison

The typical daily routine for conscientious objectors has been described by Boulton:[42]

Time	Activity	Detail
5.30–6.00	Paraded to lavatories	Wash and empty cell pails. Scrub walls and furniture. Fold bedding to regulation pattern
6.00–6.30	Breakfast	One pint of porridge without milk
6.30-7.15	45 minutes controlled exercise	
7.15-12.00	Work	
12.00-13.00	Lunch	Typical: half pound potatoes; six ounces of bread; ten ounces haricots; two ounces crude fat bacon
13.00-16.15	Work	
	Supper	One pint porridge; a half a pound of bread. Cocoa was offered after four months of sentence had been served or for good work, until 1918.

During the evenings reading was permitted and on Sundays the men were allowed to attend a religious service within the prison. In 1917 a number of concessions were granted to those men who had served over twelve months of their sentence. They were allowed to associate and communicate during exercise and walk in groups of two or three of their own choosing. Two exercise periods were timetabled. Prisoners could borrow four library books at a time and were allowed to wear their own, civilian clothes. Should they have so wished, they could have hired a fellow prisoner to clean their cell, but they never embraced this option.

---

[42] A more detailed dietary schedule is shown in Appendix Eleven.

Prison and work camp destinations

The nineteen destinations, after the Central Tribunal at Wormwood Scrubs, of Briton Ferry's conscientious objectors, are known and are listed below. The list is alphabetical by surname, not by date of sentencing. A fuller list of prisons and work centres in which conscientious objectors were incarcerated is listed below.

	Name	Prison/Work Centre	Category
1	*Adams, J. C.*	Knutsford; Talgarth; Wakefield	Home Office
2	*Ball, W. James*	Unknown	
3	*Davies, Arthur Emlyn*	Carmarthen; Pembroke Dock	Absolutist
4	*Davies, Dan T.*	Dartmoor; Talgarth; Wakefield	Home Office
5	*Davies, R. J.*	Unknown	
6	*Davies, William Meyrick*	Dartmoor	Home Office
7	*Elias, Edgar*	Unknown	Non-combatant service
8	*Gething, Ernest*	Caernarfon; Wakefield; Dartmoor	Absolutist
9	*Gethin, Richard*	Wakefield; Talgarth;	Home Office
10	*Griffiths, Bransby*	Penderyn	Home Office
11	*Griffiths, Brynley T. J.*	Crai	Home Office
12	*James, G.*	Unknown	
13	*Jenkins, S.*	Unknown	
14	*Johns, Ivor*	Unknown	
15	*Johns, Jack*	Wandsworth	Absolutist
16	*Johns, William*	Unknown	
17	*Jones, Cyn T.*	Wormwood Scrubs	
18	*Jones, Hwyrnos B.*	Dartmoor	Absolutist
19	*Lord, W. J.*	Unknown	
20	*Mort, Jim*	Unknown	
21	*Parry, Emlyn*	Pembroke Dock	Absolutist
22	*Pearson, John H.*	Unknown	

23	*Phillips, Cyril James J.*	Unknown	
24	*Polley, Edward A. B.*	Cardiff C. P.	
25	*Thomas, A. E.*	Blackdown; Wandsworth	Absolutist
26	*Thomas, E. Dil*	Wormwood Scrubs; Dartmoor	Absolutist
27	*Thomas, Herbert J.*	Unknown	
28	*Thomas, Ivor Owen*	Carmarthen	Absolutist
29	*Thomas, Thomas*	Dartmoor; Wandsworth	Home Office
30	*Thompson, L. J.*	Wakefield;	Home Office
31	*Treharne, Edgar*	Wandsworth	Absolutist
32	*Walters, A. L.*	Unknown	Absolutist
33	*Williams, Samuel*	Wormwood Scrubs	

Briton Ferry Council Chamber: Local Tribunals were held here in
1916 and 1917. *(Trustees of Briton Ferry Resource Centre)*

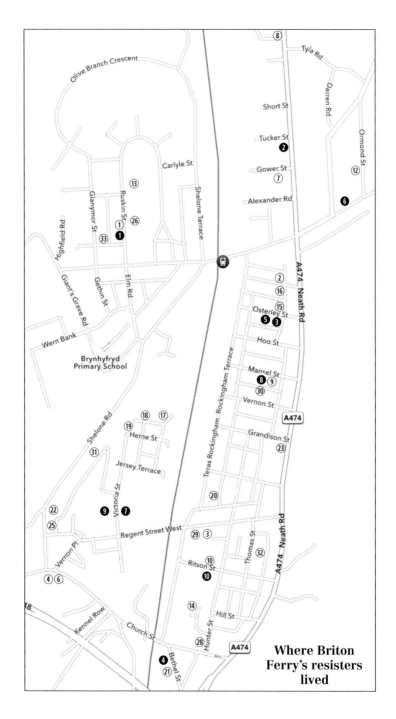

Where Briton
Ferry's resisters
lived

Where Briton Ferry's resisters and conscientious objectors lived
(see map opposite)

The locations of conscientious objectors and the DoRA defendants are indicated. The addresses are as shown on today's map and the area shown is approximately one mile by a half-mile. R. J. Davies lived just off the map to the south (bottom of map).

Conscientious Objectors (numbers correspond with the list on pages 142–143). COs not shown on map: R. J. Davies; Brynley Griffiths; Polley; Herbert Thomas

THE 'BRITON FERRY TEN' RESISTERS

❶ James Adams
❷ Arthur Armstrong
❸ Harry Evans
❹ William Davies
❺ Joe Branch

❻ John Jefferies
❼ Henry John Kyte
❽ Robert Poley
❾ James Rees
❿ Bert Tudor

THE RESISTERS

John Adams (1894–1962)

John Adams

John Charles (Jack) Adams was the oldest of three children from a family of Briton Ferry tin-workers. For a time the family were next-door neighbours of Joe Branch, the Chair of Briton Ferry's ILP, in Lowther Street. John attended Vernon Place School and Jerusalem Baptist Church. On leaving school he worked with his father, in the Gwalia tinworks. Two of John's uncles, one of whom was a regular soldier, had already been killed early in the war, so we can conclude that John had good reasons to object to conscription. He was twenty-two when it was introduced in 1916 and was mature enough to assess the significance of his relatives' deaths, not as a war against militarism but a war *between* militarisms. He joined both the ILP and the NCF.

The grounds for his application for exemption in 1917 were, most likely, a mixture of the religious and the political. His case followed the procedure shown on page 136. The Local Tribunal denied him exemption; he appealed, with Dan Davies and Richard Gethin, at the Appeal Tribunal at Port Talbot, with Alderman Hopkin Morgan presiding. *The Cambria Daily Leader* reported on 21 February, 1917:

'All three were single (22, 29 and 32 years of age), two being tinplate workers and the third a grocery manager. They refused combatant and non-combatant service, or anything to do with the military machine. One, who had a defect in his speech, produced a letter from his father in the course of which he wrote: "Owing to the treatment I received by the military at Llanelli which rendered me hors de combat for two years by being bayoneted in the street while going to catch a train, he believes if he becomes a soldier he would, if ordered by a superior officer, have to do the same as those soldiers did and his conscience would not allow it". Another, who went to the Baptist Chapel every Sunday said he was not bound to any religious body and the third said he was baptised at 15 years of age and could not reconcile militarism with the teaching of the New Testament. All were refused'.

John Adams was then ordered to report to Cardiff Barracks. He refused to comply, was arrested at Briton Ferry and required to appear before the court at Neath to answer a charge of desertion. 'Adams was fined forty shillings on Wednesday and remanded to await escort with Richard Gethin (29), behinder tinworks, and Daniel T Davies aged 31, grocery manager, all of Briton Ferry. They were absentees from HM Forces.'[43] The transfer to Cardiff Barracks took place on Sunday 4 March, 1917. There, three days later, Adams refused to sign the Welsh Regiment pay book and to wear a uniform. This act of defiance resulted in his transfer to the 58 Training Reserve Battalion (TRB) at Kinmel Park on Friday 9 March, and his subsequent court-martial a week later. He was sentenced to two years' hard labour, commuted to one year and 253

---

[43] Herald of Wales, 10 March 1917.

days, before being taken, three days later, to Wormwood Scrubs to attend the Central Tribunal on 28 April.

The Tribunal considered him to be a genuine conscientious objector, class A, who should be referred to the Brace Committee. He accepted the offer of joining the Home Office scheme (HOS); under its terms he would submit to civilian control in an under-used prison or work centre. Such an expedient course of action had been contrived by the authorities to sidestep the brutality that COs had previously been experiencing in the Army and prison. The designation of this category of objector meant that from 4 May he was classified as a member of *Army Reserve Class W.* Consequently, he was taken to Wakefield Work Centre on 7 May, 1917. After five months there he was transferred to Talgarth Work Centre for several months, before further transfers to Knutsford and, finally, Wakefield in April, 1918.

This acceptance of alternative work by conscientious objectors was not uncommon where they would not join the Non-Combatant Corps; however, a significant proportion of Briton Ferry's objectors were *Absolutists*, who declined to work in prison or work camp, on the grounds that this would still be of assistance to the war effort.

Wakefield Prison

John Adams sent this postcard home, with his cell marked by an X.

Wakefield 1

The absolutists had sound reason to suspect that alternative work might aid the war effort. One of the Wakefield practices that COs found especially repugnant was that of being hired out to private employers, rather than performing their usual internal tasks of making mailbags, mats or baskets in the prison itself. Other Briton Ferry COs reported similar arrangements at Penderyn Work Centre. They considered such practices would displace the incumbent workers, thereby freeing them up to serve in the army. One hundred and forty of the six hundred Wakefield inmates refused to co-operate with this practice, a principled stance that resulted in forty arrests and seven objectors being returned to prison under military escort.

Inmates of Talgarth Work Centre: Talgarth Navvies
(John Adams is second from left, front row)

Talgarth

Whilst John Adams was in custody at Talgarth Work Centre, near Brecon, his parents sheltered a family of Belgian refugees, with whom John was permitted to correspond. He worked there from September, 1917, in a group of sixty objectors whose task was to lay the pipes for a water supply to the sanatorium. Each worker received eight (old) pence a day for his labour, plus board and lodging and a work suit. William Isaac Thomas was a fellow inmate, an English Baptist and local businessman from Gorseinon. He had been arrested on 3 March, 1917, but soon realised that discipline at Talgarth was lax. Deciding that, as there was no Saturday evening roll-call, he would exploit this omission as an opportunity to abscond and head for home. As ill-luck would have it, however, that night chosen for his enterprise did have a roll-call. Thomas was caught out and the reward for his efforts was that he was sent to Dartmoor where the prevailing regime was decidedly stricter and less accommodating to escapees.

Knutsford

On completion of the work at Talgarth, Adams was transferred to Knutsford, where one of his tasks was to resume sewing mailbags. As relief from this repetitive drudgery he learned Esperanto and expressed his feelings through drawing and writing, including in Esperanto. The cartoon on page 152 is an example of his work; the target of this particular piece of satire is David Lloyd George whose perception of pacifists and socialist conscientious objectors was that they were merely Bolsheviks, marching under a different banner.

At Knutsford there were instances in which the conscientious objectors were the subject of derision, harassment and thuggery by local inhabitants and the press. After several disturbances Governor Hunt – by reputation an intelligent and humane authority figure – decided to intervene in order to protect his charges. Cleaver's opinion is that at 'Wakefield the Government was more concerned with isolating COs from the public than punishing them . . . (and) clearly wished to deny the COs, many of whom were articulate and influential people, the opportunity of converting people to pacifism.' The COs were mindful of Hunt's considerate behaviour, showing their gratitude by presenting him with a parchment scroll, written in round hand pen.

'As a mark of the high regard and respect in which we, the men who have been employed at Knutsford Works Centre hold you may we ask your acceptance of this address?
    We feel that we speak for all those who have passed through this centre when we say how fully we have appreciated your skilful management of affairs: your unfailing patience; your tact

in preserving harmony among men of such varying tempera-
ments and ideas, and the keen concern which you have always
had for the general welfare of the community committed to
your charge.

We shall not forget these things; and in presenting you with
this small token of our esteem, we should like, if we may, to
wish both for yourself and family many years of happiness and
prosperity.'

In May, 1918, there was great 'rejoicing in the neighbourhood' of
Knutsford because conscientious objectors with good conduct were
released for employment or sent to Dartmoor.

The mailbag group at Knutsford April 23, 1918
(John Adams is 5th left back row)

Knutsford
COs tribute

Later, at Wakefield Work Centre, COs were again exposed to brutal attacks and thefts from elements of the local population, encouraged in their antagonism by a hostile and irresponsible press. It was alleged that up to three hundred conscientious objectors had rioted at Wakefield in May, 1918, but the reality was rather different: they were actually being hounded by local residents, provoked into violent action after their anti-pacifist views were whipped up by the rhetoric of an antagonistic local press. Amid such a tense atmosphere, John Adams heard, in April, of the death at the Battle of Hazebrouck of his eighteen year-old cousin, William Adams. William was the third family member to die, one of the one hundred and twenty servicemen from Briton Ferry who were killed in action or went missing in World War One.

Release

John Adams was not released until early 1919. He returned to his parents' new home at Ruskin Street in Briton Ferry. The street was one of recently-built terraces that also housed half a dozen neighbours who had done military service. Next door lived John Colwill, who served in the Somerset Light Infantry. Three doors away, at number nine, lived Dai Tudor; his brother, Bertie, had been prosecuted under the Defence of the Realm Act. Four doors away lived Robert Diver, late of the Royal Engineers, and at twenty one lived Ben Thomas, a Royal Naval man who had served on *HMS Paluca*.

Dil Thomas, another local conscientious objector, came to live opposite at number fourteen in the early 1920s and, later, became Mayor of Neath. At number 19 lived Emanuel Hayward, late of 8 Battalion of the Yorkshire Regiment. Finally, less than 150 metres away, at 45 Ruskin Street, lived J. Ivan Griffiths. Not only was Griffiths to become John Adams' workmate at the Gwalia Tin Works, he was a former member of the Monmouthshire Regiment who had served in France.

Potentially, such backgrounds and personal histories may have inflamed a delicate situation as far as everyday relationships between former soldiers and objectors were concerned. The situation was not confined solely to Ruskin Street: it was replicated at Shelone Road, for example. It was delicate because of the proximity of objectors to former combatants and it was inflammatory because there had been fears of discharged objectors taking up work which discharged combatants believed should rightfully be theirs. Nevertheless, John Adams, and others like him, seem to have resumed work in the Gwalia Tin Works and elsewhere on amicable terms. In his case, this was possibly because of his father and Joe Branch's influence. Few examples of resentment and rancour between those of opposing views can be found occurring in the aftermath of the War.

John's fiancée, Mary Gethin, had corresponded with him while he had been in custody. They married in 1922 and produced a daughter, but the marriage was destined to be brief, failing after a disappointingly short time. John Adams remained a member of the PPU and subscribed to *Peace News* until his death in 1962.

Bolsheviks: A cartoon by John Adams (Courtesy Cheryl Clement)

William James Ball (1900–)

James Ball was an Ynysymaerdy-born iron-founder's son who lived
in 8 Middleton Street. He was amongst the youngest and last of the
World War One conscientious objectors from Briton Ferry, being
eighteen years of age when he was court-martialled. He went
through the appeal procedure with another eighteen year-old, Cyril
James Phillips. His father, John Bull, was an ILP committeeman.

At Neath Magistrates on 29 September, 1918, he was fined 40
shillings, then held, to be handed to a military escort. A court
martial followed at Cardiff on 11 October, exactly one month before
the Armistice was agreed. For Ball, the Armistice meant nothing
because those objectors who had just reached eighteen, or had been
in prison or work camp for less than twenty months, would be the
last to be released. In fact the last objector was not released until
August, 1919, and sentences for two years' hard labour were still
being meted out until May, 1919. In later life Ball lived at 76
Meadow Road, Neath, with his wife Mary Catherine, whom he
predeceased.

Arthur Emlyn Davies (1899–1980)

Davies was another of the town's young conscientious objectors. He
and his twin brother, John, were born early in 1899. They lived with
their mother, a dressmaker, and widowed grandmother at 36
Regent Street West throughout their school days at Vernon Place. It
was always a populous and busy home because his grandmother
alone contributed nine children to the demanding household. At the
time Arthur Emlyn was eligible for conscription he had been
working for almost four years in a local metal works. His religious
affiliation was Baptist.

Arthur Emlyn was arrested, along with John H. Pearson of
Shelone Road, on 12 July and court-martialled at Cardiff District
Court Martial on 20 July, 1918, at which he received a sentence of
six months' hard labour. At the Central Tribunal at Wormwood
Scrubs on 18 September, the Tribunal wrote for references for him
and, despite his Baptist faith, he was adjudged on 10 October to be

'unconvincing' and was classified as a Class B objector. The classification was made 'On the grounds that it is expedient in the national interests that the man should, instead of being employed in military service, be engaged in other work in which he wishes to be engaged.'

Being classified thus enabled Davies to continue his normal occupation on the grounds that it comprised work of national importance, but he chose not to do so, thereby rendering him an Absolutist at eighteen years of age. Accordingly, he was assigned to Pembroke Dock work camp on 7 January and from there was referred to Carmarthen Civil Prison on 9 January, 1919, where he was committed to one year's hard labour. He received a temporary discharge on 3 July, before his sentence was finally remitted on 7 July, 1919, some seven months after the Armistice. He married Martha M Howells in 1925.

Two years' hard labour was the most severe sentence on the statute book, other than death by hanging, or ordinary life imprisonment. The sentence of two years' hard labour given by the military courts had never been given in the civilian courts to the most heinous of criminals. This harsh sentence was reduced to a standard sentence of 112 days hard labour, after which the objector would be re-arrested for failing to comply with military discipline and sentenced to a further 112 days. Some objectors received six such sentences consecutively. This ploy was known as the 'cat and mouse procedure', a tactic that was initially employed in an attempt to quell suffragette agitation. After a while the authorities realised that such serial sentencing was futile and was failing in its aim of breaking the objectors' resistance; this slowly-dawning realisation led to the authorities eventually accepting that the full two-year sentences must be allowed to stand.

So what sort of conditions would a prisoner like Emlyn Davies experience?

The typical dimensions of an inmate's cell were scarcely spacious – most measured less than fourteen feet by seven feet. During the first month of incarceration the prisoner carried out his allotted work in isolation in his cell. For the first fourteen nights during which he was incarcerated, the prisoner was required to sleep on a wooden plank; food was minimal and basic. After fourteen nights he might expect to receive a mattress.

Such deprivations came at a high price: in all there were seventy-three deaths of resisters. Ten conscientious objectors died in prison; twenty-four died in work camps in the Home Office scheme; six in military custody, and a further six shortly following their release from custody. The conscientious objectors' information bureau reported thirty-one inmates as having 'lost their reason'– and even official figures described twenty COs as 'insane'.

Daniel Thomas Davies (1886–1962)

Daniel Thomas Davies was the unmarried brother of William Meyrick Davies, who was also a conscientious objector. They lived at 48 Church Street in Briton Ferry. He was a member of the NCF and a Baptist. The *Herald of Wales* reported on 10 March, 1917, that Daniel Davies aged 31, grocery manager, was arrested and fined 40 shillings at Neath Magistrates on 7 March, 1917, as an absentee and remanded to await escort with Richard Gethin (29), and John Adams (22). They were escorted to Kinmel Camp via Cardiff Barracks, deemed absentees from HM Forces.

Davies was assigned to 58 Training Battalion at Kinmel on 16 March. He was court-martialled there for refusing to sign military papers and moved to Wakefield. On 28.April, the Central Tribunal at Wormwood Scrubs classified him as a Class A conscientious objector and he was sentenced to two years' hard labour. He chose to work under the Brace System and spent from 19 March to 7 May at Wakefield Civil Prison. It is probable that he was one of a group of conscientious objectors that was transferred to Dartmoor, victims of hounding by local residents and who had been falsely accused of rioting by an antagonistic Yorkshire press in May, 1918. On 10 January, 1918, Davies was transferred to Talgarth Work Centre.

He enjoyed both an affinity with, and proximity to, Jerusalem Church, because the grocery store which eventually bore his name, *Dan T. Davies Ltd*, lay next door to the Church of which he was a congregant. That Davies was successful in running such a business indicates a significant degree of communal tolerance as well as some individual empathy. David Cleaver was of the opinion that such an attitude was also evident elsewhere: 'What is particularly noteworthy is that Gorseinon COs were never ostracised by the community as a whole ... the inhabitants were simply not prepared to castigate members of the community simply because they were pacifists.' Davies was a member of the town's ILP committee in the 1920s. When Davies married Lilian of Brynawel, Cwrt Sart, in Neath's Orchard Place Baptist Church, it was the Rev Rees Powell of Jerusalem Church who officiated.

Dan T. Davies Ltd grocery store, Neath Road, Briton Ferry *(Delfryn John)*
The store is next to Jerusalem Church

Robert J Davies (1895–)

Robert Davies is another of whom it has not been possible to reveal more information. The NCF recorded him living at Sea View Cottage in Baglan and his occupation as a tinplate bundler. *The Herald of Wales*[44] described him as a platelayer. Either is a possibility. Presumably, on the basis of his occupation, he worked in one of the local Briton Ferry tinplate works, such as Baglan Bay. Nonetheless, at Neath Magistrates Court in October 1916 he 'considered himself as doing work of national importance' who was a greater asset at work than out of the army'. Nevertheless, he was fined forty shillings for desertion and awaited a military escort to barracks.

---

[44] 28 October 1917

William Meyrick Davies (1887–1957)

William Davies, Dan T. Davies' younger brother, was a Baptist, and an ILP and NCF member. He was also Treasurer of the Briton Ferry Hardie Memorial Fund. Originally a tin-worker, he later found employment as a railway shunter where he became involved in resistance in two notable ways.

William Meyrick Davies

His first involvement was during his employment on the Great Western Railway (GWR), when his prosecution under the Defence of the Realm Act became a *cause célèbre*. Quite simply, the concern, which was raised in Parliament at one o' clock in the morning, was that the Military Service Act was being used for the purpose of prejudicing workers in labour disputes. This issue had acquired added resonance and had become 'a question on which the whole interests of the working people are concerned and a matter on which we had the clearest and most definite pledges from Ministers when the Bill was passing through Parliament'.

What were the circumstances that made this case worthy of a late-night question in parliament? It started when Davies and Garnet Waters were tried at Briton Ferry police court, in May 1916, for an offence concerning the distribution of leaflets. Such an action was deemed to impede the recruitment of volunteers, and both men were imprisoned, having been sentenced to one month's hard labour. Upon release, Davies was dismissed by the GWR but Waters' employer adopted a contrary position and allowed him to continue work. The case was raised in the House of Commons by Mr James H. Thomas, MP for Derby, President of the National Union of Railwaymen (NUR). Labour Voice/Llais Llafur reported that: 'the company could not honestly certify that he was indispensable to the working of the railway. If, however the man joined the colours, he

(Mr James Mason) imagined the company would consider favourably the question of taking him back into their employ after the war was over'.

To secure his employment became a matter of principle for the NUR. It was also a matter of principle for Davies; despite his resistance to conscription and war, which would take him to prison, he did not want to support the war – even indirectly – by following his employment.

His second act of resistance was to apply for exemption from conscription – despite the fact that he might be granted it anyway – on the basis of 'essential employment'. Davies appeared before the court at Neath on 16 April 1917 and followed the same well-beaten path as other Briton Ferry conscientious objectors. On 6 April 1917, on the grounds that he was an absentee, he was taken to join 58 Training Battalion at Kinmel and on the twenty-fourth he appeared before a court-martial. His sentence was two years' hard labour, later commuted to 112 days by the Central Tribunal. There he was classified as a Class A conscientious objector and offered to join the Brace Scheme. This sentence was served at Princetown Work Centre on Dartmoor from 28 April until 12 July. He joined Army Reserve W on 7 July, but his time in Dartmoor was problematic and unpleasant and he required medical treatment, records of which can be seen today in the doctors' log in the prison museum.

It was not until 8 March, 1919, that the South Wales Weekly Post announced that: 'The GWR have re-instated head shunter William Davies in his former position at Briton Ferry'. It was a victory – of sorts. A year later, Davies married Violet Poley of Mount Pleasant, Neath Road and continued as a member of Briton Ferry's ILP committee into the 1920s.

Edgar Elias (1899–1923)

Elias was one of the first of Briton Ferry's resisters to attend a tribunal. He was exempted from combatant duties only, and is the only Briton Ferry conscientious objector known to do non-combatant service. He was born in Llanelli, the son of a tinplate mill manager who moved to Briton Ferry to live at 9 Gower Street and work as a carpenter. His application for exemption was heard at a tribunal at Briton Ferry on 8 May, 1916. As a result, on 6 July, he was posted with 2 Western Group at Cardiff, before a further transfer the following day to 3 Western Group. Possessed of useful carpentry skills, there would be a range of situations in which these might be put to good use, whether in British Army depots, or in France or Belgium. Some NCC objectors who were posted overseas and refused orders which they considered to have a combatant purpose were treated harshly. Possibly this was because such treatment was easier to perpetrate, and less easy to detect, far from home. Some were tied to stakes each day and/or placed in leg irons within the range of shell fire.

One can only speculate whether Elias chose non-combatant service as the only realistic alternative to prison because the Home Office scheme had not yet become available. On the other hand, the NCF, as a result of their early experience of the tribunal processes, and the role of the NCC, decided to offer greater assistance to COs joining the corps for some time thereafter, having concluded that non-combatant service was a positive support for the War.

Elias married Bronwen Gethin in 1923. She was a sister of Richard, another conscientious objector whose other sister, Mary, married John Adams. When these marriages took place after the war, the Gethin family incorporated three former conscientious objectors.

Ernest Gething (1896–1961)

Ernest was the oldest child amongst the five sons and four daughters of William and Susannah Gething of 5 Regent Street. Over the years, during which the family later lived at 62 Neath Road, his father was an ironworks labourer and crane driver. After Gething left the family home to live at Teifi House, Cwrt Sart, he became a dockers' trade unionist and member of both the ILP and the NCF. He was refused exemption from conscription, applying on philosophical and political grounds, at a Local Tribunal at Briton Ferry on 20 April, 1916, and again at the Appeal Tribunal on 6 May.

He was then directed to Kinmel Camp to join 60 TRB where he was court- martialled on 11 July, receiving two years' hard labour, which was to be served at Caernarfon Prison. However, he was able to flee during his transfer there. After his arrest he was fined at Neath Police Court on 13 September as an absentee from the forces. He was taken to Cardiff Barracks where he was held in the cells for two days and escorted back to Kinmel to join 60 TRB. He was court martialled again on 27 September and received a further sentence of two years' hard labour. At the Central Tribunal at Wormwood Scrubs on 11 October, he was deemed to be a genuine Class A objector and was offered to be held under the Brace Committee regime. He refused to undertake this alternative work and his refusal resulted in him being sent to Caernarfon Civil Prison.

By 19 October he was in Wakefield Work Centre, before being transferred to Dartmoor on 29 March, 1917. Private Ernest Gething had escaped around 24 May and was free until his re-arrest on 16 June, 1917, along with Private Hwyrnos B Jones. Gething was re-committed to Dartmoor. The daily ration for those undertaking hard labour at Dartmoor – twenty-two ounces of bread and two pints of porridge – was, respectively, halved and quartered. Conditions were deliberately worsened: in an attempt to undermine the inmates' unity, camp authorities reduced the pay rate (for nine and a half hours' hard labour) from eight to four pence per day for those they considered troublesome. On the other hand, in a blatant attempt to 'divide and conquer', inmates identified as compliant were offered quasi-supervisory rôles and paid three times as much as their trouble-making brethren.

Such discriminatory and arbitrarily punitive treatment probably provided the motivation for Gething's and Hwyrnos Jones' initial abscondment from Kinmel Camp; it was reported that 'because they did not agree with the conditions imposed . . . (they) did not return'. James Henry Howard, a prison visitor to Kinmel, known as the 'pugnacious pacifist', had reported 'savage ill-treatment by the guards'. *The South Wales Weekly Post*[45] described them as 'Refractory Briton Ferry COs'.

Following the Armistice, absolutists were concentrated at Wakefield and detained there, or taken to their previous prison prior to release. By 1919 Gething, the Absolutist and fugitive, had served two sentences for two years, including four months under the Brace Committee/Home Office Scheme. Gething later lived at 29 Howell Street, Neath, and died in 1961.

Non Combatant Corps members at work on a military road

[45] 23 June 1917

Richard Gethin (1887–1967)

Richard Gethin was born in Clydach. He was one of ten children born to Eleanor and Richard Gethin, senior, of 10 Mansel Street, Briton Ferry. His father was a roll turner and Richard junior was a behinder in Gwalia tinworks and was one of a number of the conscientious objectors who attended Jerusalem English Baptist Church.

Gethin was fined 40 shillings at Neath on Wednesday 7 March, 1917, and remanded as an absentee from HM Forces to await escort with John Adams and Daniel C. Davies of Briton Ferry[46]. He was immediately taken to Kinmel and put before a Court Martial on 16 March. His sentence was two years' hard labour, commuted to 112 days. Further refusal to obey military orders, and continued application for conscientious exemption, saw him appear before the Central Tribunal at Wormwood Scrubs on 28 April. He was transferred to the Home Office Scheme and Army Reserve W on 4 May.

The Central Tribunal had considered him to be a genuine conscientious objector Class A, for referral to work under the Brace Committee's Home Office Scheme. From March to May 1917 he was assigned to Wakefield prison, before moving to Talgarth Work camp on 8 January, 1918. Richard was present when his youngest sister, Mary, married John Adams at Neath Registry Office in August 1924.

Bransby Griffiths (1889–1972)

Bransby was the son of Thomas and Jane Griffiths. Bransby, like his tin shearer father, was born in Morriston, but, by 1900, the bilingual family were in Briton Ferry, living at 87 Hunter Street with his parents, grandmother and two schoolgirl sisters. Bransby followed his father, both as a tinplate worker and as a congregant of the Congregational Church in Ritson Street.

Twenty-eight year old Griffiths was arrested on 27 November, 1916, and two days later, on the Monday, appeared before Neath County Justices with six others. They claimed they were 'drawn from certified occupations, and are therefore not deserters'[47].

---

[46] *Herald of Wales*, 10 March 1917

Within the week, after his despatch to Kinmel's 60 Training Reserve, he was court-martialled and sentenced to two years' hard labour, subsequently commuted to 112 days, by the Central Tribunal at Wormwood Scrubs in December 1916. He was considered to be a genuine conscientious objector, Class A, and was referred to the Brace Committee.

His whereabouts thereafter are unknown for the rest of the war period, but, in the Autumn of 1919, Bransby Griffiths is believed to have married Bronwen Llewelyn. He died in 1972.

The central Military Tribunal at Wormwood Scrubs on 27 December had adjudged Griffiths to be genuine in his beliefs; consequently they categorised him as a Class A (genuine) objector and assigned him to the supervision of the Brace Committee. He was taken to Wandsworth Civil Prison where he was detained from 23 January until 6 March, 1917. Thereafter, he was known to be carrying out work of national importance at Penderyn Waterworks – a Home Office Work Centre.

A Military Service Tribunal in progress

47 *Herald of Wales*, 18 November 1916

Brynley Griffiths (1888–1974)

Brynley was the Welsh-speaking son of John and Caroline Griffiths of Glanyrafon Road, Pontardulais. He was educated at Gowerton Grammar School and Carmarthen College. At twenty-three years of age he lodged at the home of the Davies family in Penalltau Road, Ystrad Mynach. They were teachers of art and Brynley was a student teacher. The Pearce Register entry suggests that he was sacked by the Glamorgan Education Committee for his conscientious objection. The Pelham Committee recommended him to take up work in a Controlled Establishment. He did this work of national importance at Crai Reservoir, but was reported as being 'home this weekend', in early May, 1917, with William and Ivor John and Thomas Thomas[48].

But he refused this work and was arrested along with others to be brought before the Neath Magistrates on the 13 November, 1917. In 1926 he moved to Crynant, Neath, to work as a teacher and later on as a headmaster, retiring in 1952. He was also a President of the Welsh Divisional Council of the Independent Labour Party (ILP). Whilst a member of the ILP he was a tutor at the Party's summer and weekend schools and also lectured for the National Council of Labour Colleges. When the ILP disbanded, he joined the Labour Party. Tillie, his wife, was a Suffragist. Brynley was a major figure in the Independent Labour Party in Wales and they were visited by James Maxton, Professor C. E. M. Joad, Sylvia Pankhurst and, most famously, the revolutionary writer C. L. R. James who completed his book *Black Jacobins* in their library in the late 1930s. (The Griffiths family left their library to the South Wales Miners' Federation).

Brynley was a director of the Briton Ferry and District Co-operative Society from the 1940s to the 1960s. In 1942 he suffered an attack of pneumonia and, as a result, his eyesight began to fail and over time steadily worsened. He suffered from scleritis and was on the blind register. An operation on his left eye was carried out in 1952 in Cardiff. It was successful but his eyesight on the whole was still poor. In 1956, aged 65, he went to the Soviet Union in the hope that the famous Russian eye specialist, Professor Filatov, would be

---

[48] *Merthyr Pioneer* 5 May 1917

able to help restore his sight. Filatov had developed a technique of transplanting corneas from corpses to the eyes of living people[49]. He was treated at the Filatov Institute, Odessa, over four months in 1956-1957. He was examined by the professor who unfortunately died before he could carry out the operation, so the treatment was continued by other Russian eye specialists. Griffiths was the first British patient at the Institute and the last patient of Professor Filatov. The operation was successful.

Brynley Griffiths died in 1974 aged 86.

The Conchie by Arthur W. Gay (*Museum of Peace, Bradford*)

---

[49] The visit was partly organised by the South Wales Miners' leaders of the National Union of Mineworkers, Will Paynter and D. D. Evans

Garfield James (1889–)

The records of the No-conscription Fellowship record that a G. James of Briton Ferry was arrested as an absentee on 26 January 1917, in similar fashion to several other Briton Ferry conscientious objectors. It is believed that James was twenty-eight years old Garfield James of 28 Water Street. He was born at Pontypool and was employed as an ironworker in Briton Ferry. As such he may have been exempted as the result of an application by his employer. That no such exemption was accepted, had it indeed been applied for, then it may well be the case that James was an Absolutist. It may also be the case that there is a very interesting tale to be told about this man and his life.

Sidney Jenkins (1897–)

Sidney Jenkins, of 27 Ruskin Street, was a steelworker. He may be the only example of a Briton Ferry objector whose application for exemption on conscientious grounds was granted absolutely, but was quashed at appeal. The circumstances that suggest Jenkins was that objector are: that a CO, employed as a furnace man, was successful in achieving absolute exemption at the local tribunal in Briton Ferry. The case for exemption was reviewed at Neath Tribunal in April 1916 at the request of the military authorities.

However, it seems that it was a tribunal member – John Powlesland, a trade union official from Swansea – whose influence may have swayed the case. Nothing was reported of the military representative, Lieutenant Buchanan, who had requested the review. Powlesland had questioned the appellant about his membership of the NCF to which the appellant responded by saying that: 'You do not seem to understand the movement'. Powlesland retorted: 'Perhaps you will put me on the right road by and by. I ought to know for I am a member of the ILP, a socialist and a member of Swansea Labour Association'. Powlesland then asked the appellant about Bryce[50]. The appellant said he'd never heard of

---

[50] Lord Bryce wrote about alleged German atrocities in Belgium

Bryce and dismissed the German atrocities as 'piffle in the jingo press'.

The chairman, Ald. J. Hopkin Morgan JP, interjected: And this gentleman has four sons fighting for their country. Powlesland: 'It is a pity they won't take us old chaps. I am ready when they want me.'[51] Powlesland was aged fifty-three. Jenkins was arrested as an absentee 8 August 1916.

Ivor Johns (1893–1956)

Ivor Johns' father, William, was born in Briton Ferry in 1872. He moved to Kidwelly[52] to marry his wife, Emily, and afterwards worked as a furnace man in Kidwelly tinplate works. Ivor, the eldest son in the family, was born in Kidwelly, as were his brother Willie and three sisters. The rest of the family stayed at Alstred Street, Kidwelly when Ivor returned to Briton Ferry to live with his grandparents, Rees and Ann Johns, at 31 Lowther Street. All four of the Johns' children had left their home there, enabling tin worker Ivor to re-establish himself, in his usual employment and in the town. Rees Johns continued to labour in the steelworks into his late sixties.

Following his unsuccessful application and appeal for exemption at local tribunals, Ivor was arrested on 17 November 1916, as an absentee who had failed to report for military duty. Within a week he was sent to join 60 Training Reserve at Kinmel and, within another week he appeared before a court martial. The outcome was a sentence of two years hard labour, commuted to 112 days. He was reported as 'home this weekend', in early May 1917, presumably before being taken to Wandsworth Prison. Was his motive for returning home to meet his girl-friend, or had Ivor Johns made for home having suffered the same experiences at Kinmel as Hwyrnos Jones and Ernest Gething?

---

[51] *Cambria Daily Leader*, 18 April 1916
[52] Kidwelly was an early tinplate manufacturing location

John *Jack* Johns (1886–   )

John *Jack* Johns was the third son of Samuel, and Elizabeth Johns of 13 Osterley Street, and an elder brother of William. John and William were both Baptists, ILP members and tin-workers. By refusing conscription they experienced the military service tribunal process. Jack attended the Local Tribunal at Briton Ferry in March, 1916, and appealed against the decision to refuse his conscientious objection. His appeal was heard at the county Appeal Tribunal which took place in April 1916, but it was again dismissed. After his arrest on 13 November for failing to report for duty, he was

A travel warrant to Kinmel Park
(Allan Colwill)

taken to Cardiff Barracks, pending a date to attend the Central Tribunal at Wormwood Scrubs. On 27 December he was classified as a Class A objector, but initially refused the tribunal's offer to engage with the Home Office Scheme which permitted him the choice of doing alternative work of national importance. Had he so chosen, his decision might have resulted in a return to his former job in the tin works 'On the grounds that it is expedient in the national interests that the man should, instead of being employed in military service, be engaged in other work in which he is habitually engaged.'

On 23 November, after being assigned to 60 Training Reserve Battalion at Kinmel, Johns was court martialled and sentenced to two years' hard labour, commuted to 112 days, at Wormwood Scrubs. His intransigence resulted in him being further transferred to 66 Training Reserve Battalion at Kinmel on 11 July, 1917, from where he was taken to spend the rest of the war in Wandsworth civil prison.

Johns was an absolutist who, had he so wished, could have concealed his objection to conscription and war by sheltering in a reserved occupation: his employer would have made the application on his behalf and it would have stood every chance of succeeding. Instead, he opted for the privations of Kinmel and Wandsworth. Johns made his choice at a time when prison conditions were severely detrimental to the health and welfare of inmates. Inside the camps and jails, cases of influenza and tuberculosis were commonplace and prisoner health was not a top priority. In January, 1917, for example, a Glaswegian prisoner by the name of Peddieston died at Red Roses Camp in Carmarthenshire whilst treating fellow prisoners. Twenty-four year old John Evans of Cardiff later died of tuberculosis, despite being certified as fit for navvy work.

Not too long after the Armistice, on 7 June, 1919, Humphrey Chalmers, Chaplain of Wandsworth Prison, visited Jerusalem Church, Briton Ferry. One can only speculate on the conversations that might have ensued had he met members of his former prison flock such as Jack Johns and his fellow Baptist inmates, Arthur and Tom Thomas. Possibly the Congregationalist inmates would have been present as well: Bryn Griffiths and Edgar Treharne would doubtless have taken the opportunity to re-acquaint themselves with him and perhaps remind him of the harsh and punitive regime that he had overseen at Wandsworth.

However, Jack was soon to marry his wife Florence and to set up their family home at 9 Shelone Terrace. Like several other of Briton Ferry's COs, he became an ILP committeeman in the 1920s.

William Johns (1890–)

William Johns was one of the nine children of Samuel and Elizabeth Johns of 13 Osterley Street. His Devon-born father was a blast furnace worker at Briton Ferry ironworks and William, after leaving Neath Road School, went to work in one of the town's tinplate works in order to help support a large family. Still single, aged 26, he was a Baptist and an ILP member when he applied for exemption from conscription at a Briton Ferry Local Tribunal in March, 1917.

Although the NCF ran tutorials for objectors to 'coach' their responses to predictable questions, few applicants were able to avail themselves of such tutorials and Johns' application was likely to have been refused, regardless of the merits of his case. His county Appeal Tribunal took place a month later; it was, indeed, refused. Thereafter his journey followed the standard procedure designed for dealing with objectors, but in early May, 1917, the *Pioneer* – sarcastically – reported that he was 'home this weekend looking exceedingly well and ruddier than a cherry'.

His home stay proved transient: he was arrested on 13 November and pronounced an absentee by the Magistrates. Along with six colleagues, he claimed that he was an unattested man from a certified occupation. The claim had no effect on Lieutenant W. E. Rees (presiding): Johns followed the well-trodden path to Worm-wood Scrubs for his Central Tribunal hearing on 27 December, where he was classified as a genuine, Class A conscientious objector and was assigned to 60 Training Battalion at Kinmel Park. There he was to serve a sentence of two years' hard labour, remitted to 112 days. The remainder of his wartime CV is unknown. He married in 1920.

Cyntogwawr Tachweddyn Jones (1889–1956)

Cyntogwawr Tachweddyn (CT or Cyn) was the fifth of nine children of Gwilym, a joiner and school caretaker, and Margaret Jones, of 5 Barn Cottages, Shelone Road, Briton Ferry. His forenames are unusual and interesting because they recall, respectively, that he was the fifth child and that he was born in November. He was born in Briton Ferry whereas his eldest brother, George, and sister Mary, were both Carmarthenshire-born, like many others who became residents of the town. They were a tin worker and dressmaker. William, became a joiner like his

Cyn Jones in 1949
(Mrs Caroline Jackson)

170

father, but Briton Ferry-born Cyn continued to work as a tin finisher. He was a Baptist, who like his brothers, George and Hwyrnos Benjamin attended Salem Bible Christian Chapel in Mansel Street. The ninth child of Gwilym and Margaret was their daughter Dorcas, of whom more will be recounted later.

Cyn was escorted with Brynley Griffiths from Neath Magistrates on 14 November, 1916, to Kinmel Park and assigned to 60 Training Reserve Battalion, according to his surviving 'army' papers. At the Central Tribunal at Wormwood Scrubs, on 27 December, Jones was regarded as a genuine conscientious objector Class A. His sentence was two years hard labour, commuted to four months. To date, the remainder of his wartime activities remain unknown, except that he was sent to a Work Centre under the Home Office scheme after Wormwood Scrubs.

CT married Rose Evans in 1920. His neighbour Fred (Frederick H. C. Jenkins), also a tinworks turner, but three years younger, later moved to Birmingham for work. CT and Rose did likewise, but CT died in Birmingham, at the age of 67.

Hwyrnos Benjamin Jones (1892–1972)

Hwyrnos Benjamin Jones (H. B.) was born at dusk . . . and that's what the name Hwyrnos means. H. B. Jones was seventh of the nine children of Gwilym and Margaret and it has jokingly been said that he was so named because his parents had run out of names. His brother, C. T. T. Jones, was also a conscientious objector. The Jones' family home was 5 Barn Cottages, Shelone Road, Briton Ferry. Nearby, at 2 Barn Cottages, lived Arthur E. Thomas, another absolutist conscientious objector.

When conscription was introduced in 1916 he was a twenty-four year old tin finisher, a member of the ILP and NCF and Salem Baptist Chapel. His eldest brother, George, was a deacon at the chapel and a trade union leader in a local tinworks. Jones' first arrest by the police was at Briton Ferry on 15 February 1917. The arrest resulted from his failure to receive exemption at the local or appeal tribunals; subsequently he had failed to report for military service and duly was fined and escorted to Cardiff Barracks the following day. There he was stripped naked with a uniform in the corner of the cell and told that, if he wanted clothes, he should put on the uniform. After further non-compliance he was escorted to Kinmel Camp on 19 February to join 60 Training Reserve Battalion to await his court-martial on the twenty-third. The inevitable result was a sentence of two years' hard labour and a diet, for long periods, of bread and water. It could have been served under the Home Office Scheme at Dartmoor from 19 April 1917, but Jones, as an Absolutist, rejected this possibility.

> Two Conscientious Objectors were dealt with for the second time by the County Justices at Neath on Monday. They were Private Ernest Gethin of Court Sart and Private Hwyrnos Benjamin Jones of Shelone Cottages. Both left Kinmel Park because of the conditions imposed and did not return. They were arrested at Briton Ferry and were on Monday remanded by the Justices to await escort.

Jones was back at Kinmel on the 2 July, this time assigned to 58 Training Reserve Battalion. The upshot was a second court martial and a second sentence of two years' hard labour. By January 1919, Jones had served almost two years and one month in prison. On his release, many months after the Armistice, he looked a changed man, according to family reports, having lost almost half of his body weight.

Jones' entries in the autograph albums are quotations from Dickens and Charles Kingsley. They are undated but were possibly made after he and Ernest Gething had absconded from Kinmel to be at Briton Ferry on the weekend of 16–17 June, 1917. Such insubordinate behaviour would have a predictable outcome: Jones' imprisonment.

William James Lord (1899-1974)

Lord was the son of a Briton Ferry blast-furnace worker who lived at 3 Park Street with his parents and two younger sisters. Lord was arrested in January, 1918, and the *Pioneer* said of him: 'He formerly contributed occasional notes (to this newspaper) and quoted him as saying *I shall stick it*.' He did – and also contributed to a family album with his signature and a quotation from Hamlet, dated 7 April, 1920. No records of Lord's Military Service Tribunals have yet been discovered, but his name can be found as an ILP committee member after the war.

James Mort (1883–1953)

The Mort family lived originally in Tram Road Lane, near to Briton Ferry's ironworks, where Steel Mort was a blast-furnace labourer. His son, Jim Mort, was born across the River Neath at Earlswood Cottage, but the family moved to 64 Rockingham Terrace from where Jim worked as a behinder in one of the town's tinworks.

James Mort was a congregant of Jerusalem Church and a single man when he refused conscription in 1916. Family members[53] have reported that he was the recipient of white feathers. Like others before and after, he followed a familiar path through the tribunal process. He had been arrested in south Wales as a deserter from the 60 Training Battalion Army Reserve based at Kinmel on 30 October and appeared at Neath police court[54] on 13 November, 1916. That appearance led to his being escorted back to Kinmel ten days later for court-martial. The usual sentence of two years' hard labour was duly meted out. The Central Tribunal at Wormwood Scrubs declared him to be a Class A conscientious objector two days after Christmas. He was taken back to Kinmel and categorised as a member of Army reserve class W on 20 February, 1917.

Thereafter we lose sight of his wartime experiences and have to rely on the barest of biographical details. Family members have also reported that, after the war, Jim Mort sold the family home, which by that time was on Neath Road, so that the family could follow socialist principles by living in municipal housing. His younger sister, Edith Mary Mort, was a dressmaker who married Daniel J. Thomas in 1921. Their elder son, Steel, was a German language teacher who became a conscientious objector during World War Two.

---

[53] Alan J. Thomas, Hucknall (2014)
[54] Reported as Thomas Mort in the *Herald of Wales,* 18 November, 1916.

Emlyn Parry (1898–1977)

Emlyn Parry was from 22 Charles Street, Briton Ferry. As a twenty year-old and a Baptist he applied for exemption on 'religious' grounds, but his application was not accepted by the Local, Appeal or Central Tribunals.

On 10 October, 1918, the Central Tribunal considered that Parry was a Class D objector and, as such, not a *Conscientious* Objector: 'On the ground that serious hardship would ensure if the man were called up for Army service, owing to his exceptional financial or business obligations or domestic position.' This meant that he could avoid conscription, but he was an Absolutist who continued to object to the principle of conscription. As a consequence he had to go through the whole 'cat and mouse' procedure. The end result of this was that he was one of the last conscientious objectors to be released from prison. At a court-martial in Cardiff on 6. August, 1918, he received a sentence of six months' hard labour. After a second court martial, which was somewhat bizarrely held after the November Armistice had taken place, Parry was kept at Pembroke Dock Work Centre until 27 January 1919, with a temporary discharge being permitted on 3 July 1919. His sentence was not remitted until 7 July 1919. In these respects, his treatment was similar to that of Morgan Jones of Bargoed. In 1922, Parry married Elizabeth Ann Tudor of 33 Ritson Street, the twenty four-year old daughter of Bert, who had been prosecuted six years earlier under the Defence of the Realm Act for literature distribution.

John H. Pearson (1897–1945)

John Pearson was a foundry worker's son from 10 Shelone Road, one of John and Gwen Pearson's nine children. Little is known of Pearson's early history of conscientious objection until his actual court-martial, as a twenty-one year old, at Shrewsbury in July 1918. It is noteworthy that Pearson's court-martial took place at Shrewsbury, not Kinmel. Unlike most of Briton Ferry's conscientious objectors, who were court-martialled at Kinmel and assigned to the Welsh Regiment's Army Reserve, Pearson was assigned to the reserve for the King's Shropshire Light Infantry. And, unlike in the early years of the war, the regiment to which conscientious objectors were sent often had no connection with the part of the country that they came from. John Pearson married Bronwen M Davies in 1926.

Joseph James Cyril Phillips (1900–1967)

Cyril Phillips was the son of a steel works bricklayer whose home was 4 Grandison Street. He went through the application for exemption and appeals procedure with James Ball, his elder by a few months. They were amongst the youngest and last objectors from Briton Ferry, with them both being little over eighteen years of age when Phillips was court-martialled. The *Merthyr Pioneer* of 5 October, 1918, reported under the heading of 'Briton Ferry Notes-absentees':

> 'Mr James Ball and Cyril James Phillips, two young Briton Ferry men, pleaded guilty at Neath on Friday to being absentees under the Military Service Acts since July. Fines of 40/- were imposed in each case, and the men ordered to be held and handed over to military escorts.'

Their case was heard at Neath Magistrates was on 29 September, 1918, where they received the normal forty shillings fine. Military escorts took them to Cardiff Barracks where they appeared before a court-martial on 11 October. For Phillips, like Ball, the Armistice exactly one month previously did not automatically result in freedom because objectors who had attained the age of eighteen, or had been in prison or work centre for less than twenty months, would be the last to be released. In fact, at the time of the Armistice, around 1500 objectors were still imprisoned, including those still in military custody. The Home Office Scheme was abandoned in July, 1919, when objectors were given a dis-honourable discharge from the army. They were also liable to two years' hard labour if they tried to re-enlist and were to be denied any service pensions, or the right to vote, without first being granted military permission.

Edward Arthur B. Polley
(1884–)

It has not been possible to reveal more information about Mr Polley. It is known that Polley is a name commonly found in London and Essex and that it is not a corrupt version of the name Poley, which is a name found a number of times in Briton Ferry. Indeed Polley was a Londoner, born in Chelsea, who married in 1903 at Fulham. What singles him out somewhat is that he was one of the few married Briton Ferry objectors.

Salem Baptist Chapel in 2015

He was a house painter who had moved to Briton Ferry from Treharris in the Rhondda Valley. He was one of the earliest arrests, being detained on 6 June, 1916. As an absentee from the army he was escorted to the barracks at Cardiff Castle. Readers may have noticed that earlier reference was made to *Private* Gethin and *Private* Hwyrnos Jones. The reason for such a use of rank is that all resisters, who had been denied exemption at tribunals, were still regarded as members of the British Army. This remained the case even after the Home Office Scheme was later introduced which saw resisters being despatched to civil prisons. In those cases they were still deemed to be in an army reserve, known as Class W.

Private Polley's court-martial at Cardiff on June 24 sentenced him to 112 days' hard labour. When he attended the Central Tribunal on 13 July, 1916, he was categorised as a Class A conscientious objector, but he rejected the Home Office Scheme and was held at Cardiff Civil Prison. It is not known what Polley's wife did to make ends meet during the War, but on release many objectors and their families found themselves destitute. A voluntary Joint Board, set up with the objective of assisting objectors and their dependants was established, but the funding needed to provide adequate support was in short supply.

Old Briton Ferry police station[55]
(Briton Ferry Internet and Photographic Technology Club)

Arthur E. Thomas (1895–1953)

Arthur Emlyn Thomas, of 2 Shelone Road, Briton Ferry, was the son of Thomas and Ann Thomas. He had five sisters. His father was a rollerman in a Briton Ferry tin works where young Arthur worked as a labourer. A Baptist, an ILP member, a member of the NCF and a trade unionist, he attended a Military Service Tribunal at Briton Ferry in March, 1917, where his application for exemption from conscription on grounds of conscience was dismissed. Employed at the Gwalia Tin Works, he would likely have received exemption on the grounds of an employer's application, but Arthur refused to countenance any such application. He had been arrested at Neath on 14 November, 1916, and sent to Cardiff Barracks, then to Kinmel on 23 November to join 60 Training Reserve Battalion. As an absentee from the army, he was sentenced to two years' hard labour, commuted to 112 days. At the Central Tribunal at Wormwood Scrubs he was classified as Class D (not genuine) conscientious objector and began to serve his sentence at Wandsworth Prison from 23 January, 1917.

---

[55] The police station was between Jerusalem Baptist and St Clement's Church. Briton Ferry police court was held here

This classification was defined as: 'On the ground that serious hardship would ensure if the man were called up for Army service, owing to his exceptional financial or business obligations or domestic position.'

His sentence was remitted on 24 February so that he could be returned to Kinmel. He arrived there on 26 February but remained sufficiently recalcitrant to be consigned to Caernarfon Prison on 8 March, 1917. In July he was offered the chance to join the Home Office scheme at Blackdown Work Centre. He rejected the offer and by January, 1919, he had served three sentences and had been incarcerated for more than two years.

A few months afterwards, Thomas wrote the following lines in one of the autograph books, perhaps as a reflection on his experiences during the previous few years:

'Truth forever on the scaffold
Wrong forever, on the throne;
Yet that scaffold sways the future,
And behind that dim unknown,
Standeth God within the shadow
Keeping watch above his own'

Eleazor 'Dil' Thomas (1885–1961)

Dil was the youngest child of a coalminer whose death left his mother to care for six young children. At nine years of age, when he lived at Ty'rhalen, Baglan, Dil started work at Baglan Bay Tinplate Works as a bundler who eventually became a rollerman, one of the senior production jobs. He married Elizabeth (Bessie) Rider in St Clement's Church, Briton Ferry, a

Dil Thomas *(Mrs C. Sharkey)*

month before the onset of hostilities. This was still the age of Empire and, for Dil, the age of Keir Hardie, the Independent Labour

Party (ILP) and pacifism. Causes to fight for, as well as against, were many and he espoused quite a few: Home Rule for India and Ireland; abolition of the Truck Acts; decent housing and poor relief. Evidence of his awakened political and spiritual consciousness and the inter-dependence of the two is witnessed by the permanent presence in his home of the Labour Hymn Book.

Dil's was not a lone voice calling in the wilderness: Baglan and Briton Ferry were hot beds of radical thought. He was a regular customer at Gregory's, the barber whose shop could be found on Neath Road. (The significant role of this establishment is given in greater detail in Appendix Nine.) His deep convictions and his readiness to espouse worthwhile political and social causes were an integral part of his life and informed the often difficult choices he made. His outlook on the conflict in Europe was driven by a perception that war was waged on behalf of the upper classes in order to preserve the privileges of a wealthy elite, or to defend empires in order that the imperialist governing class might better exploit their colonies.

Dil could, perhaps, have seen out the War by continuing to work in the tinworks; indeed, idealism apart, he had no need to fight against conscription and had no need to declare publically his beliefs. However, he did not ask his employers to seek exemption for him, even though Bessie had given birth to their two sons in successive years, 1915 and 1916.

Llais Llafur reported on Thomas' activities as a tinplate workers' representative during the War. Food prices had risen substantially in 1915, and, on 4 September:

> 'A meeting was held by over 500 tinplaters at the Public Hall, Briton Ferry, presided over by Mr Eleazor Thomas, Baglan Bay Works, at which the following resolution was passed: That we, as tinplaters, representing Briton Ferry Neath, Aberavon and District, call upon our officials to make a demand of a 15% advance on present rates of wages in consequence of the increased cost of present daily living'.

Thomas was called up in the usual way, applied for exemption in the usual way, and was refused in the usual way, so his

Dartmoor group 1917 – *Dil Thomas is fourth row back and ninth from the left*

disobedience resulted in a court-martial in May, 1917, which sentenced him to two years' hard labour. He spent the first three months in Wormwood Scrubs. The Central Tribunal first considered his case on 6 June, 1917, when it adjourned with a request for references. At the reconvened Tribunal on 23 June, 1917, he was considered to be a genuine Class A conscientious objector. However, he was placed in solitary confinement for the prescribed month for refusing to undertake any work which supported the war effort.

He did this at Princetown Work Centre on Dartmoor. After being transferred there in July, 1917, he worked in the gas boiler house for the duration of the War (possibly about seventeen months in total). During that time fellow objector Henry Firth died whilst required to work on stone duties in the quarry whilst he was ill. During Dil's time in Dartmoor, his third son was born. The annals of Dartmoor have probably never recorded that 'a prisoner once escaped from a working party, travelled home to see his third child, and then returned from 28 Shelone Road, without having been missed.'

During Dil's incarceration and the difficulties it entailed for his wife, Bessie, she decided that the children should quit St Clement's

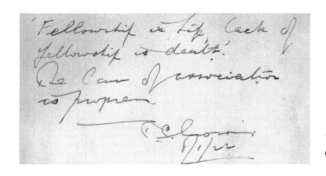

'Dil' Thomas
(Mrs C. Sharkey)

Church and attend Jerusalem. No doubt she may have been influenced to make the decision after hearing that the chief witness in the case that resulted in Garnet Waters and William Davies being sentenced to two years' hard labour, was none other than the incumbent vicar of her church, the Reverend Lloyd.

After the War, the family continued to live in Briton Ferry. The following years were filled with periods of half-time work or full unemployment. Dil took the opportunity of short-time working to begin an education with the Workers Education Association (WEA) and to participate in local politics. He was elected to Neath Town Council in 1932 and council work became his main activity for the next quarter of a century. His mayoralty saw a symbolic change of tradition because he insisted that his 1947 Mayor's procession was to a non-conformist chapel, sympathetic to his socialism and pacifism, namely Jerusalem in Briton Ferry, and not as tradition had previously decreed, to the more staid and 'establishment' St David's Church in Neath.

As Chairman of the Housing Committee, Dil was much concerned about the slum clearance which the War had interrupted. Post-war, a comprehensive house-building programme needed to be organised and financed and there was little inhibition about thinking big and making large-scale plans. There was, indeed, a massive house-building programme which involved the building of the Brynhyfryd council estate in Briton Ferry where he and the family eventually lived – at 14 Ruskin Street.

Dil proved himself unafraid of controversy. His youngest son, Bill, remarked of him that: 'He was a popular and controversial figure, but always at war with the local press who ran a constant vendetta against him.' He was pressurised to stand for Parliament, but was too conscious of his lack of formal education. Despite leaving school at nine, through largely self-education and by making the most of opportunities offered by the likes of the WEA he was a literate, rounded and erudite man. His final letter to his son tells him that he is reading the autobiographies of Gandhi and Nehru. Always a family man, he was very proud of his off-spring and progeny. As his granddaughter fondly recollected in May, 2014:

> 'My own memories of him are very positive. He was one of my heroes, along with my father, Bill Thomas, who became a Conscientious Objector in World War Two. He taught me to recognise trees and flowers. I still have a book of dried leaves we put together when I was about eight. He was very proud of me and believed that equal opportunities was at last possible when I passed the eleven plus, enabling me and others to get the education he had dreamed of and worked for. Socialism was only a few steps away!'

Herbert James Thomas (1894–1973)

Herbert Thomas was the son of David and Mary Elizabeth Thomas of Glan-y-mor Cottage, Baglan. He was a tin worker and one of five children, born with his younger sister in Pennsylvania, USA. Their father had been employed as a steelworker in Brownstown, near Pittsburgh, before returning with the family to Briton Ferry. His father declared him 'British by parentage' on the 1911 census return. However, had Herbert James Thomas not been naturalised after returning to Wales with his family, technically he was not eligible for military service under the 1916 Conscription Acts.

In 1917, 'Friendly Aliens' were given the option of returning to the country of their birth in order to serve, or of becoming subject to British conscription law. A local newspaper reported that Thomas had married 'Saturday last' and had previously been before Neath Court in March, 1916, when his application for exemption had been refused. The report of his marriage is dubious; a date in 1924 is more likely. This time he was, whether married or not, regarded as a deserter and remanded awaiting military escort. His new wife would not, therefore, see him for some time. Herbert was twenty-two years old at the time of his arrest and was the youngest married Briton Ferry conscientious objector.

Ivor Owen Thomas (1898–1982)

Ivor Owen Thomas was born at 3 Hunter Street in Briton Ferry, but later moved to 13 Regent Street, which had previously been the home of his uncle, Ivor H. Thomas. Ivor Owen Thomas was the third child of ten. His father, Benjamin, Ivor H.'s brother, was a roller-man in a tinplate works and a practising Methodist. Regent Street West was close to Vernon Place School which Ivor attended until he left to became a barber's lather boy and, later still, was on the books as a tin worker at Gwalia Tinplate from 1912 to 1919. One wonders whether the barber's shop in which he worked was Gregory's, and whether that was where he accrued his early political education. In between these dates came the little matter of World War One, during which time Ivor objected to conscription on principle and experienced the usual vicissitudes of the tribunal system.

He was court-martialled, for the first time, at Cardiff on 2 August, 1918, and was sentenced to six months' hard labour. The Central Tribunal on 26 September concluded that Thomas was a conscientious objector, Class D: 'On the ground that serious hardship would ensure if the man were called up for Army service, owing to his exceptional financial or business obligations or domestic position.' His second court-martial took place at Pembroke Dock on 15 January, 1919, where he received a further sentence of two years' hard labour, to be served in Carmarthen civil prison. His sentence was not remitted until 7 July, 1919, following a temporary discharge on 3 July.

After finally leaving the Gwalia Tinplate works in 1921 he joined the Great Western Railway (GWR) and, for two years, worked as a tinplate cleaner. This gave him the opportunity to attend the National Labour College in London, after which he worked at the NUR Head Office until 1945 when he successfully fought the parliamentary seat of the Wrekin on behalf of the Labour Party. He was re-elected in 1951, but subsequently lost the seat in 1955, thereafter continuing his career with the NUR and British Rail. He has a road named after him in St George's, Telford.

Tom Tuppeny Thomas (1886–1955)

Tom Thomas was born in Kidwelly, but his family moved to Briton Ferry to live at 42 Regent Street East. From school-leaving age he worked in a Briton Ferry tinplate works and was recorded in the Pearce Register as non-sectarian and an ILP, NCF and Dockers' Union member. His arrest was reported in November 1916, along with Brynley Griffiths, Edgar Treharne, William, Ivor and Jack John, Cyn Jones and James Mort[56].

His application for exemption on the grounds of conscientious objection was dismissed at a Military Service Tribunal at Briton Ferry in March 1917. He was offered, but then refused, to join the Non-combatant Corps at his County Appeal Tribunal. On 3 October, 1917, he married Violet Reynolds by special licence. The Rev. Lloyd Williams officiated. His change of marital status did not prevent his arrest at Briton Ferry on 13 November, followed by a police escort to Cardiff. Thomas made notes of his arrest and his experience at Cardiff. The notes are exactly as he wrote them.

'Therefore the following must of necessity be only a brief account of the different incidents which occurred during my passage through the hands of the military and other authorities.

The morning of my arrest was such a one as would have been looked forward to in early Spring rather than late Autumn and although I had been waiting and expecting every day for the past few months to be called upon to enter into another phase of our fight for freedom I can only express my surprise, when confronted with the police officer, to that received by a person who accidently touched a live electric wire, but after recovering from the shock of the moment one was encouraged to go forward by drawing a simile.

At this particular season, in looking around, it was noticeable

---

[56] *Merthyr Pioneer* 2 December 1916

Tom Thomas back row (R) with fellow tin workers *(Allan Colwill)*

how the trees on the adjacent hillside were shedding its leaves and thereby retaining unto itself the necessary qualities to combat the dark days of winter which threaten its very existence. The breaking of home and other ties where such as this and although it may be assumed or actually believed that in the case of the tree it was fighting for its own particular and selfish self, such was not the case as upon its existence depended the future generation of that particular species.

Another source of encouragement was the sympathetic crowd that so patiently waited outside the police station. I have often heard – and used myself – the words cheer OK. But that morning I felt for the first time what a significant meaning they really conveyed when uttered directly from the heart instead of by a movement of the tongue and lips forming mere words.

It would be as well to mention before passing on to the next stage a question asked us by the local Inspector. e.g. Is it your intention to go quietly or give trouble? The answer to which was so obvious, whatever were our intentions, but we could not help but smile.

At the Police Court our plea was not guilty and I intimated my desire to have the Military Representative placed in the witness box, to call a witness and to question the evidence of the police, in the course of which he stated: Each one admitted being an absentee.

I mentioned a few names and asked him if either of those had made such an admission? To which he replied in the negative, thereby repudiating his previous statements. My next question having been objected to by the Clerk of the court coupled with his refusal to put the Military Representative in the witness box riled me to such an extent that I could not refrain asking them to pass judgement as it was this we were before them for and not to be tried. It was only a few minutes later that I obtained my first view of the prison cell from the inside. Fortunately, we were all placed together and in our short stay of and hour-and-a-half we were singing. We were visited by a police officer and asked if we intended paying our car fare from Briton Ferry as it would only be added to our costs if we didn't. The reply he received was given simultaneously by three or four of the boys to the effect that he had better deduct it out of our army pay. Whether we have earned sufficient army pay to pay that particular part of the cost against us is not very questionable.

The train journey from Neath to Cardiff altogether without incident if I were to exclude the noticeable expression of determination in each feature which became more pronounced as we neared – our then – destination. On our arrival at the Recruiting Office, word was quickly passed around that we were conscientious objectors which immediately drew forth some – but for the adjectives – mild remarks. After having stood in the same place for a few hours they commenced to order us. The first order was to answer our names, which we refused by simply standing still and keeping our mouths closed. The non-combatants had reported to the Officer Commanding our refusal to answer to our names. When we were asked by him to give them, as they could be easily obtained from the local police, he gave a guarantee that whatever we said or did, he would personally be responsible that it would in no way prejudice our position. I therefore – under protest – volunteered the required information so far as I myself was concerned. With the exception of one occasion, all orders where disobeyed in a like manner.

He was reported as 'home this weekend' in early May, 1917, along with Ivor and William Johns and Bryn Griffiths, no doubt awaiting removal to the Central Tribunal. There Tom received a sentence of two years' hard labour, commuted to four months. He spent ten weeks at Wormwood Scrubs before he was taken by train to Kinmel on 23 November to join 60 Training Reserve Battalion and thence to the usual court-martial. Tom wrote a letter to the Briton Ferry branch of the NCF, on behalf of the nine arrested objectors who were taken to Kinmel on 13 and 14 November, in order to reassure their friends and families that all was well and that there had been no submission to military authority.

'It was not till we came here that we realised the debt of gratitude we owe to those who have gone before us and left a highway for us to follow. . . . It is now that we appreciate the value of the NCF which has safely piloted us through channels abounding with rocks.'

Thomas somehow had heard of a report in the Merthyr Pioneer . The newspaper was doubtful about the truth of a rumour which was reported to be circulating in Briton Ferry to the effect that the resisters had lost heart. Thomas referred to the Pioneer article:

'Commenting on an unfounded rumour prevalent in some parts of the town, in which it was freely stated that they had lost heart and submitted. There seems to have got noise about that. We have submitted to be medically examined and have been seen drilling, but if being held by a doctor and sergeant of police while your clothes are ripped off you is submission, then we all submitted.'

Soon afterwards, on 27 December, 1917, he was referred to the Central Appeal Tribunal at Wormwood Scrubs to be classified as a genuine, Class A conscientious objector. His sentence of two years hard labour was later reduced to four months. At Wormwood Scrubs he went on hunger strike from 3 to 8 December, 1917, and was force-fed four times. After transferring to Wandsworth from 1 February to 14 March, 1918, further hunger strikes and forced feeding of inmates took place. Similar activities were reported to have occurred at Newcastle-upon-Tyne.

A combination of hard, manual labour, reduced rations and the food of inadequate quality (as well as being insufficient in quantity) makes one realise that there was little difference between normal prison diet and hunger striking! It is clear from Thomas's writings that he looked forward to leaving prison; the postcard above was pinned up in his cell, with a message to him on the reverse which said *of course you recognise the place in spite of the snow.* Consequently he applied to join the Home Office Scheme, doing work of national importance. He was taken to Princetown work centre on Dartmoor from 31 March, 1918. Not that Princetown was a bed of roses: Cleaver revealed that W. I. Thomas of Gorseinon had written home to say that a 'visiting soldier who had given a nasty bashing to several of the COs last night as they arrived at the settlement. Some ended up in hospital because they did not defend themselves'. The previous month Henry Firth had died there. Officially the COs' death was diabetes, but the truth was otherwise.

The cat-and-mouse system was proving to be a problem for the health of prisoners whose body weight had been reduced to a minimum following their previous sentences. Philip Snowden made many enquiries about specific, emaciated prisoners. One prisoner, who was not a hunger striker, had written to the NCF's Conscientious Objector Information Bureau to describe the stages that prisoners experienced because of the prison diet. At stage one prisoners felt very hungry all day. At the next stage the hunger became more acute with intermittent stomach pains; in turn this was followed by extreme weakness accompanied by nervousness, then constant and very acute pain and sharp abdominal contractions.

It is worth comparing Thomas' account of his committal to custody with that of Tal Mainwaring in Chapter Four. Tom Thomas' account is a personal one in which he reveals his inner thoughts and feelings, whereas the Mainwaring account is a social description of events from a journalist. Together they provide a comprehensive and moving account and understanding of the experiences of a determined conscientious objector.

David Mort was brought up in the same street, as Tom and, as a fellow member of the ILP, became a lifelong colleague of Tom Thomas, even after he had left the town to become MP for Eccles and, later, Swansea East. The reference below, from David Mort MP, is a reflection of this.

Postcard[57] of Briton Ferry incline from
Tom Thomas' prison cell (*Allan Colwill*)

After the war Humphrey Chalmers, the chaplain of Wandsworth
Prison visited Jerusalem Church on 7 June, giving Tom and his
colleagues a chance to meet up once again. In August, 1921, Tom
moved to the newly-built municipal houses on Jack-y-du Road,
Briton Ferry with Violet and their children. He paid ten shillings to
Briton Ferry Urban District Council for the deposit. Later, during the
1920s he availed himself of further education opportunities, for
example, at a TUC weekend course in Swansea in July, 1925. Violet
died in 1932 quite soon after Tom had started working as a
rollerman at Baldwin's tinplate works in Jersey Marine. This meant
he had to take the ferry across the River Neath to get to and from
work. He spent his later working life as a rent collector for Neath
Council's Treasury Department.

Tom's grandson, Allan Colwill, compiled a list of the books Tom
left after his death. The list included a full set of Dickens and
Shakespeare, the 'Complete Self Educator' and many economics and

---

[57] Postcard photographed by Melville Morris, a professional photographer of
8 Mansel Street, Briton Ferry.

politics titles, including biographies of Keir Hardie, Jean Jaurés and Robert Owen. One religious title was included: The 'People's Life of Christ and Lives of the Apostles'. Although the books were in good condition, it was evident that they had not been used just for display.

Leslie James Thompson (1897–1987?)

Leslie James Thompson was the oldest of the five children of Margaret Ann and John Thompson, a roller-man in a Briton Ferry steelworks. The family lived at 19 Vernon Street, near to Garnet Waters, and were Congregationalists. A few years after leaving the local secondary school, Thompson found himself wishing to object to conscription and as a result underwent submission to the customary cycle of human processing experienced by resisters.

After failing in his application for exemption at local and district tribunals on grounds of conscience, and being fined by the magistrates for absence when required to report for Army service, he was escorted to the Cardiff military barracks. The unmarried prisoner appeared at a Court Martial in Cardiff on 12 July, 1917, to receive a prison sentence of 112 days' hard labour. He was detained there several days before being escorted on 17 July to Wakefield Work Centre, where he remained until the 8 October. Thereafter the Central Tribunal at Wormwood Scrubs, on August 30, considered him to be a Class A case.

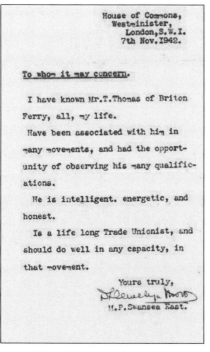

House of Commons,
Westminister,
London, S.W.I.
7th Nov. 1942.

To whom it may concern.

I have known Mr. T. Thomas of Briton Ferry, all, my life.

Have been associated with him in many movements, and had the opportunity of observing his many qualifications.

He is intelligent. energetic, and honest.

Is a life long Trade Unionist, and should do well in any capacity, in that movement.

Yours truly,
D. Llewellyn Mort
M.P. Swansea East.

Reference for Tom Thomas from David Mort MP *(Allan Colwill)*

No doubt he was sent to Wakefield to fill the empty places that had been evacuated after the previous conscientious objector occupants had been brutally attacked and transferred to Dartmoor in order to ensure their safety. A certain James Thompson was a deacon in Jerusalem Church in the 1930s and became a President of west Wales Baptist Association. It is possible that this was the same James Thompson who simply decided to change his place of worship.

Edgar Treharne (1893–1963)

Edgar Treharne was the eldest son of William and Mary Treharne of 40 Shelone Road, Briton Ferry. William was a tinplate worker and son Edgar, at eighteen, was a labourer but already a member of the Steel Smelters Union. A Congregationalist and a conscientious objector, Treharne signed an album at Briton Ferry on 30 September 1916. Shortly afterwards he was arrested, as an absentee, a fact that went unreported reported until 17 November. Within a week of the report he was escorted to Kinmel Camp, as part of 60 Training Reserve, where he was court-martialled on the twenty third. His Central Tribunal hearing was held at Wormwood Scrubs two days after Christmas, but Treharne declined the offer to participate in the Home Office Scheme and received two years' hard labour to be served at Wormwood Scrubs.

Boulton[58] quoted a conscientious objector who was in a similar position to Treharne. On release from Wormwood Scrubs, but awaiting a return for a second prison sentence, he referred to soldiers he met at the railway station: 'The fellows here have a great respect for COs who defy the authorities; they trust us a great deal and admire our stand . . . (they) do not hide their opposition to the continuance of the war.'

As a result of a remission, he was moved to Wandsworth Civil Prison on 23 January, but he had to be taken back to join Kinmel's 58 Training Reserve. He was court-martialled again, as an Absolutist, on 22 March. By January, 1919, he had served two

---

[58] Objection Overruled

The No Conscription Fellowship had a network of prison visitors

sentences and spent more than two years in prison. It is possible that Treharne, too, was reunited with Humphrey Chalmers, the Chaplain of Wandsworth Prison when he visited Jerusalem Church on 7 June. He married Ellen Francis in 1923.

Albert Lewis Walters (1902–1932)

Details that might flesh out the life of the resister, A. L. Walters, are scarce, though we know that he was born at 47 Thomas Street, Briton Ferry, the second oldest son of Morgan and Catherine Walters. His arrest was reported on 5 September, 1916, and he was tried as an absentee for failing to report to serve, or to show exemption from, conscription. He was imprisoned at Caernarfon Civil Prison and is believed to have spent two years in total in prison. Early in 1924 he married Norah Doyle from Green Park, Aberafan. He is buried with Morgan and Catherine Walters in Ynysymaerdy Cemetery.

Samuel Williams

Information relating to Samuel Williams is scant and baldly factual. The Merthyr Pioneer's *Briton Ferry Notes* of 19 May, 1917, report his arrest and describe him as a twenty-eight year old married tinplate worker who lived with his aunt at 10 Glan-y-mor Street, Briton Ferry. We know also that he was a Baptist and that he was court-martialled at Kinmel Camp on 17 May, 1917, and taken to Wormwood Scrubs prison.

Summary – the resisters and their legacy

At the age of arrest, one-third of Briton Ferry's conscientious objectors were less than twenty years of age, and one-fifth were aged thirty or older; the remaining half of those arrested were in their twenties. Only the older resisters were married and almost all, with the exception of the odd shopkeeper, or decorator, were steel or tinplate workers. Most were affiliated to a chapel, but religious affiliation was often not the sole, or even over-riding, motive for objection. For the majority, their objection emerged as a political expression of dissent through membership of the ILP, the NCF or both.

The degree of resistance from the thirty-three Briton Ferry objectors covered the whole spectrum from non-combatant corps to absolutist. Age and marital status did not seem to affect the degree of resistance and the large majority of objectors were to be found on the 'high resistance' end of that spectrum.

Many of the rights that we sometimes take for granted in this country today are, to a significant degree, a legacy of those who fought against conscription and war in World War One. Today the United Nations Commission on Human Rights sees freedom of thought, conscience and religion as a standard to be achieved. The objectors did not always receive the 'fair and public hearings by an independent and impartial tribunal' that the Commission now expects. And some did, originally, suffer degrading treatment.

Nor were their supporters allowed 'freedom of opinion and expression and (the opportunity) to impart information and ideas through any media'. These things had to be fought for. It is to their supporters that we now turn.

Ironworks, Gwalia and Victoria/Villiers Tinplate & Old Steel works from south
(Royal Commission Ancient and Historical Monuments, Wales)

Albion steelworks (foreground), Whitford and Baglan Bay Tinplate works
(middle ground) and town of Briton Ferry (background)
(*Royal Commission Ancient and Historical Monuments, Wales*)

ORGANISATIONAL SUPPORT

From all sedition, privy conspiracy, and rebellion . . .
Good Lord deliver us

The second source of resistance to conscription came from those who supported the conscientious objectors through the offices they held in organisations such as the ILP, the NCF or a chapel. Such support was most evident from those who protested publicly against conscription from a mainly political viewpoint and who were prosecuted under the Defence of the Realm Act. In this respect Joe Branch was a leading supporter; from a religious perspective the Rev Rees Powell exemplified equally strong anti-conscription and anti-war support.

Arthur H. Armstrong (1872–1946)

Arthur H. Armstrong

Arthur Henry Armstrong was born in Cwmbran, the son of a tinplate rollerman and a Buckingham-born mother. It is noteworthy that Armstrong's birthplace was close to two other names famous for their resistance to World War One: Bertrand Russell of Trellech and Clifford Allen[59] of Llantarnam. All three moved from that area in their formative years: in Armstrong's case, to Briton Ferry, where he married his wife, Edith, and settled at 9 Tucker Street and fathered a daughter, Annie May.

---

[59] Allen was a conscientious objector, NCF Chair, imprisoned three times during the war, later ILP Chair. There is no record of him visiting Briton Ferry during the war.

Armstrong was active in Briton Ferry NCF in the rôles of Chair and Secretary at various times. When Garnet Waters was President, in 1916, Armstrong was Secretary. He was also a committee member of Briton Ferry Public Hall from its inception. In September, 1918, he spoke at the Hardie Memorial Meeting, held at the Salem Bible Christian Chapel, on Booker Washington's *Oration on Abraham Lincoln*. Councillor Jo Branch presided and further speeches and a rendering of the *Internationale* were made by George Gethin and Ivor H. Thomas.

Joe Branch (1869–1954)

Joe Branch

Joe Branch was the son of a Cwmafan-born tinman, born at 22 Lowther Street. Jim Adams, and his son John[60], were neighbours at number twenty-four before the Branch family moved to Railway Terrace in 1891[61]. At an early age Joe became a washman/ tin finisher in Vernon Tinplate Works alongside his two elder brothers. He soon became involved in trade unionism at an early age and, by 1903, was a Briton Ferry Urban District councillor and father of Irene Olive Branch. His growing political experience enabled him to go on and chair the council for five years, and, as a result of this, he became an ex-officio magistrate on Neath Magistrates' bench.

He had married Mary Howells in 1897 at Bethel Calvinistic Methodist Church and had set up home initially at 6 Osterley Street, before finally settling at Dulais House in Cwrt Sart. They often

---

[60] Co-defendant in this case and conscientious objector, respectively.
[61] Lowther Street and Railway Terrace were demolished in 1973

received visiting ILP speakers at their home even before Branch became Chair of Briton Ferry ILP. For example, on census night 1911, John Bruce Glasier was a guest. Branch was then Chair of Briton Ferry Urban District Council, an Associate of the NCF (being outside military age), and a founding committee member of Briton Ferry Public Hall. Branch had also been one of the founder members of the Mid-Glamorgan Divisional Labour Party in 1905, until it became part of the Aberafan division. The year 1912 saw him become chair of Briton Ferry ILP and, in 1914, local Secretary of the Dockers' union, being Llanelli based for some ten years.

During World War One Branch was a staunch pacifist and, in 1916, he was prosecuted for handing out anti-war leaflets outside Briton Ferry's Bethel Chapel. (This event is covered in detail later in the section entitled *Sedition on Sunday: support on the streets.*) It is necessary to record here that the pastor of the chapel, the Rev James Llewelyn, and its deacons, gave evidence in court. As a result, after the court case, Branch never again attended Bethel. At Joe Branch's funeral, significantly and appropriately, the Rev Trevor Evans of the pacifist Jerusalem Church officiated.

After his appointment as South Wales District Secretary of the tinplate section of the Transport and General Workers' Union (TGWU), Branch was in close touch with its then General Secretary, Ernest Bevin. Similarly, in his position as Chair, over many years, of Aberafan & District Labour Party, he had regular contact with Ramsay MacDonald, MP for Aberafan and first Labour Prime Minister in 1924. Not surprisingly perhaps, with contacts such as these Branch became a Member of the Court of Governors of the University College of Swansea and attended its first meeting at the Guildhall in May, 1920. No wonder that Len Williams, a fellow ILP member considered him 'a very well-educated man'.

After 1922, when Briton Ferry Urban District Council was merged with Neath, he continued to represent Briton Ferry on the larger body. In 1932–33 he was Mayor and father of the council for several more years. A serious deterioration to his eyesight in 1934 caused him to retire from his TGWU post and his thirty-year long Presidency of Aberafan ILP.

Olive Branch

Olive Irene Branch, daughter of Joe and Mary, was born in 1903. She worked during the school holidays at Chequers, the Labour Party Headquarters and shop, on Neath Road. Despite qualifying as a teacher and working at Cwrt Sart primary school, she contracted tuberculosis at an early age and was sent to South Africa where, it was hoped, the dry climate would improve her health. At the age of twenty-nine, however, after only three months in Johannesburg, she died. As a mark of respect to her father, and, as its construction was taking place at the same time that peace was declared in 1945, Neath Council named a new street after her in Briton Ferry. It is Olive Branch Crescent. The olive branch is a symbol of peace or victory. Irene is the Goddess of Peace.

At the age of 65, Alderman J. O. Branch retired from fully from his temporary post of Tinplate District Secretary. His failing eyesight further deteriorated after his retirement, but he underwent one of the first operations to have cataract removed, enabling him to live a more normal life, such as becoming Vice-President of Neath's Eisteddfod Committee. After the death of his wife, Mary, in 1950, Joe Branch returned to Osterley Street where he died, in December 1954, at 85 years of age.

His contribution to Briton Ferry, as an elected representative of the working man and the working man's family, was enormous; so was his wider contribution to a just society through his trade union and political activities. In this respect, perhaps all his beliefs, and his abilities to apply them, came into clear focus during his pursuit of peace and justice at the 1916 trial of the ten ILP/NCF members. Then, as President of the local branch of the ILP he said:

> 'I thought if the Christian Church would not speak out . . . to call public attention to the barbarities imposed on men . . . then it was the duty of someone else to do it.'

Joe Branch spoke out – for all of us.

George Gethin (1873–1948)

George Gethin was from an iron and steel working family which lived at 33 Regent Street. After his marriage to Margaret Jane in 1895 they lived at 30 Vernon Street. Len Williams, a fellow ILP member, claimed that the strength of the ILP in Briton Ferry was due to its large membership from the Albion Steelworks and the influence of leaders such as Gethin, who worked there, and Joe Branch, who had equal influence in the Gwalia tinplate works. Gethin was also a trustee of Briton Ferry Public Hall from its inception in 1911, along with Arthur Armstrong and Joe Branch as committee members. George Gethin . . . 'was a very famous Labour man in Briton Ferry. He was a kind of Danton of the Labour Movement in the Ferry', said Williams of Briton Ferry ILP's post-war chairman.. Gethin and Branch's socialism and anti-war stance led to some ostracism by other local chapels and the Church. Nevertheless, after his death, aged 74, in November 1948, Wallace Street in Briton Ferry was re-named Gethin Street in remembrance of his life and work. It seems the town had more to thank George Gethin for than Alfred Russell Wallace.

Wallace Street was renamed Gethin Street

Sam Mainwaring, Junior (1878–1943)

A steelworker from a Briton Ferry steelworks brought America's most dangerous woman to south Wales. He was Sam Mainwaring,

Junior, and she was Emma Goldman, whose activities are covered in Chapter Six.

Sam Mainwaring Junior was the nephew of Sam Mainwaring Senior, a well-known anarchist from Neath and a personal friend of William Morris who spent much time in London as an active speakerfor the Socialist League. Sam Junior was born in Swansea in 1878 but moved to Cuthbertson Court, Water Street, Neath, where he lived with his mother, two brothers and two daughters until the age of three.

Tom Mainwaring was Sam's brother and a Swansea Docks blacksmith, and landlord of the Three Mariners pub in the Strand, before he absconded to Pennsylvania. He returned from the USA in 1891 and during his six year stay in Swansea, raised Sam Junior at Morris Lane in St Thomas. Young Sam migrated to South Africa, where he was active in the nascent labour movement before moving both to South America and the USA. There he was active on the western seafront with the Industrial Workers of the World and it was there he met Emma Goldman and Eugene Debs.

He returned to Britain and became a steelworker in the Albion steelworks, Briton Ferry. In 1909, in his early thirties, he was Secretary of Briton Ferry ILP, married Sarah Williams and lived on the Old Road in Briton Ferry.

Sam was believed to be the author of *Neath Notes* in the Merthyr Pioneer. In the June 16 edition of 1916 he described Neath's social and political ethos, implicitly comparing the town with Briton Ferry:

> 'As far as the ancient town and borough of Neath is concerned, to readers of the Pioneer it is not on the map, or in other words is completely out of the scheme of things . . . unfortunately the town is notorious for being the most snobbish and reactionary in the whole of industrial south Wales, and a place where the feudal spirit and atmosphere still exist side by side with some of the worst slums in existence. To alter this condition of things is one of the aims in the life of the writer of these notes, and of those to whom he is connected'.

Sam did not mince his words.

Rev. J. Rees Powell (1862–1932)

The year before Jerusalem Church opened in 1863, Rees Powell was born to Anna and Evan Powell at 30 Nightingale Street, Abercanaid, a community in Merthyr. They had moved to Merthyr from west Wales for Powell to become an ironworks labourer. The family was bilingual, speaking Welsh and English.

Rev. J. Rees Powell [62]

Thirty years later, in 1895, the, as yet, unmarried Powell was ordained as minister of Jerusalem Baptist Church, but his story took on a new dimension after 1903 when he married Elizabeth Mary Jones of Rhymney. They made their home at Glasfryn, in Court Sart Terrace, Briton Ferry, and had two daughters and a son before World War One.

He, with his wife's support, built up the church to become a 'strong, virile church' which became an important influence on the anti-war movement. Under him the church and most of its members took the very uneasy course of making a stand for peace. This sometimes resulted in bitter opposition and hostile abuse, from the time the Rev Herbert Morgan made the first plea for peace at the church. Reverend Powell was even ostracised in his own profession. During the war some young members of the Church joined the army and others simply left the church. Many others did not: some objected to conscription and war and were imprisoned, but gradually, the Powells built up the membership. The range of activities which were hosted at the Church under his authority, and which led to the increase in membership are shown in Appendix Thirteen. No doubt, his chairmanship of the NCF, from Spring, 1916, onwards, had an influence on Church membership.

Powell was not the only pastor in the area who supported the conscientious objector. In nearby Neath, in April 1916, the Rev W Degwel Thomas, of Neath's English Baptist Chapel, gave his support, lauding 'the triumph of the conscientious objector' from the pulpit. Powell was, however, special for the large number of events which he supported or participated in. In a public meeting, as the war was coming to a close, Rev Powell said: 'I thank God that

---

[62] © West Glamorgan Archives

no young man can ever say that I sent him to war'. He remained at the Church until his death in 1932, despite invitations in 1917 for him to return to his old church in Treherbert.

In June 1917 Powell was otherwise engaged; commenting on the King's Economy Proclamation, he said that war economies 'should not start where men only work two or three shifts a week but where creatures such as hounds and racehorses were fed simply for sport.' In his role as Minister, and as chair of the Briton Ferry Council against Conscription, he 'has taken his stand for freedom of conscience and peace by negotiation', reported the *Merthyr Pioneer*.

Powell was scrupulous in his duties and carried out his role as pastor without prejudice against individuals who had fought. For example, on 30 June, 1917, he willingly officiated at the funeral of David Williams, who had been killed in the war.

Strangely neither the church's minute book of 1915, nor the Church's Centenary Booklet[63] says anything significant about the attitude of the Church to pacifism, to war, or the events of World War One, but it did say:

> 'The First War brought its problems of *why* and *wherefore*. While many went to the forces, many also went to prison for conscience sake. It was not an easy period for any, but in all the confusion men knew where the minister stood.'

It was clear where the Rev Powell stood: 'The increased activity of the Labour Party would make for the well-being of the nation as a whole'. Powell said this at a meeting with Minnie Pallister in Briton Ferry, in support of Reverend Herbert Morgan as the ILP candidate for Neath.[64] After the war Powell continued his support for peace by chairing a series of public meetings at the Church under the theme of *Reconstruction*. In 1929 he became chaplain to the Mayor of Neath, who was none other than Dil Thomas, the trade unionist and former conscientious objector.

Perhaps Dil Thomas' granddaughter aptly summarised the incumbency of Rev Powell by saying that 'God was clearly an active member of the Labour Party in Briton Ferry'.

---

[63] *Jerusalem 1859–1959: The Story of 100 years.* (K. Donovan, 2014).
[64] *Cambrian Daily Leader*, 2 December 1918

Ivor H. Thomas (1876–1963)

Ivor Hael Thomas was the son of Elizabeth and Llewelyn Thomas, an iron moulder, of 13 Regent Street West. At fifteen years of age he was an office boy in a tinplate works but by the turn of the century he worked on production as a tinplate finisher. His eldest brother, Ben, was the father of Ivor Owen Thomas. After their marriage the family moved to 65 Rockingham Terrace. Their next door neighbours were Steel and Louisa Mort and their young son, Jim. In due course young Jim became a conscientious objector.

During the War, Ivor, for a period of five years, was Wales's representative on the ILP's National Administrative Council. He had been on the executive of the Dockers' Union for just two years in 1916 when he became the full-time organiser for the newly established National Council for Civil Liberties (NCCL). The Council's work overlapped with that of the NCF, but the NCCL were also against several aspects of the Defence of the Realm Act. He realized,too, that the Military Service Act also threatened civil liberties other than through conscription. Nonetheless, the NCCL was quite prepared to take great issue with the penal conditions imposed on conscientious objectors in Home Office camps.

Thomas was a 'genial and enthusiastic organiser', ensuring, for example that Briton Ferry was well-represented at the NCCL's confer-ences. It is a credit to him that, Briton Ferry's ILP, NCF and Trades and Labour group attended the Cardiff Peace Conference of 1916.

Thomas was a prime mover in Anti-Conscription Sunday, an event held throughout south Wales, on 2 March, 1919, to mark the anniversary of the first Military Service Act. Its purpose was to persuade the Government to redeem its pledge to remove conscrip-tion. In a *Pioneer* article he expressed concern at the efforts being made to militarise children in state schools. He referred to a grue-some publication called *Elements of Military Education* which explained how to kill an already wounded man using a bayonet. Meetings were held throughout south Wales at Aberafan, Amman-ford, Abertillery, Bargoed, Briton Ferry, Swansea, Cardiff, Neath, Kenfig Hill, Cwmafan, Newport Llanelli, Treherbert, Merthyr, Maesteg, Ystradgynlais and elsewhere. The speakers involved included Noah Ablett, John Bromley, Herbert Dunnico, T. Gavan-

Duffy, Vernon Hartshorn MP, H. B. Lees-Smith, Minnie Pallister, Richard Wallhead, James Winstone and Col Joseph Wedgwood. The list of venues and speakers demonstrated Ivor Hael Thomas' influence in south Wales in matters of Civil Liberties.

It was Thomas, along with Henry Davies of Cwmafan, Port Talbot, who took a leading part in the formation of the Aberavon District Labour Party,[65] with Thomas becoming its first secretary. (Davies also became a member of the National Administration Committee of the ILP in the 1920s, and Mayor of Port Talbot in 1924).

Massena Garnet Waters (1883–1960)

Garnet Waters was born at Pilton Green, Gower, the oldest of the seven children, of whom, in 1916, six were of conscription age. Originally a butcher in Porteynon, Garnet moved to Briton Ferry and became a locomotive driver in the Albion Steelworks. At 24 years of age he married Mary Catherine Evans of 10 Vernon Street, later setting up home at Pilton Green House in 2 Gower Street. Two of Garnet's brothers Hubert Victor and Albert George were conscientious objectors. For an unknown reason Garnet, known as 'Massie', wrote his name as 'Waters', whilst his brothers used a double 't'.

Waters was an ILP member and the Chair of Briton Ferry NCF, a role that led to his involvement in the famous legal case with a fellow member of both organisations, William Meyrick Davies, a GWR shunter. The case proved of such seminal importance that it was raised in Parliament. The reason was that the NCF felt that the Military Service Act was being used for the purpose of prejudicing workers in labour disputes. This was 'a question on which the whole interests of the working people are concerned and a matter on which we had the clearest and most definite pledges from Ministers when the Bill was passing through Parliament.'

Thirty-three year-old Waters and William Davies were sentenced by Neath Magistrates to a month's imprisonment with hard labour for distributing a leaflet against recruiting. The court was told that the pair were distributing the leaflets near St Clement's Church on Neath Road, Briton Ferry, when the activity was reported to the

---

[65] *Labour's Who's Who*, Labour Publishing Company, 1927 p. 51

authorities by the Reverend Lloyd, the Vicar of St Clement's Church. The *Merthyr Pioneer* reported the case on 20 May, 1916:

> 'Mr G. Waters, Chair of Briton Ferry NCF and William Davies were summoned last week under the Defence of the Realm Act for distributing pamphlets similar to (those) which formed the grounds for the Cefn prosecution and were sentenced to one month's imprisonment with hard labour. Further, last Thursday, the ILP premises were raided whilst a branch meeting was taking place by Superintendent Ben Evans, Inspector Morris, and three constables. Pamphlets and literature were removed.'

The issue arose because of the differential treatment by their respective employers. Davies was dismissed by the Great Western Railway, but Waters' employer allowed him to continue work after industrial action was threatened by workmates in his support. The case was raised in the House of Commons by Mr James H Thomas, MP for Derby and President of the National Union of Railwaymen. Labour Voice/Llais Llafur reported that: 'the company could not honestly certify that he was indispensable to the working of the railway. If, however the man joined the colours, he (Mr James Mason of the Board of Trade who was responsible for the railways during the war) imagined the company would consider favourably the question of taking him back into their employ after the war was over'.

The imprisonment of Waters and Davies spawned serious consequences in industrial South Wales because of the contrasting treatment they received from their respective employers following their discharge from prison. With the possibility of a national rail strike looming, James Thomas MP said to the House of Commons:

> 'Can you conceive of anything more disastrous than this, that, when the country is engaged in a war such as this, the down tools policy succeeds in one case in winning, while conciliation and all efforts to try to avert a stoppage, fails to succeed in the other?'

Garnet Waters was reinstated following imprisonment, but Davies was not offered re-employment, even though the rail union kept the workforce at work pending talks. The rail union felt strongly that a failure to reinstate Waters would effectively be a double punishment. The issue of their re-employment became a matter of principle because neither man had any intention of concealing their objection to conscription and belligerence by sheltering in reserved occupations. Their resistance meant that they would object to conscription on grounds of conscience anyway. The treatment of Davies caused burning indignation in South Wales and became conflated with actions that were taking place elsewhere in the country. The Lancashire and Yorkshire Railway were particularly culpable in Liverpool: during periods of industrial action, the company were offering work on the railway which would exempt those accepting it from conscription. In this way the company were misusing the exemption provisions of the Military Service Act to support the use of blackleg labour.

Cecil David Watters (1887–1965)

Cecil Watters was born at Pilton Green, Gower, the younger brother of Garnet Waters and brother of Hubert Victor Watters, another CO who worked at Porteynon as a blacksmith. In 1911, after marrying Phoebe Eleanor Edwards the previous year, the couple settled at Maes-y-cwrt Terrace in Port Talbot, where he was a railway signalman, before moving to 6 Elm Road in Briton Ferry. He became an NCF and ILP member, attending the National ILP Conference at Leeds in June, 1917, with Ivor H Thomas and Joe Branch. His daughter, Iris C. G. Watters, attended Brynhyfryd School where she made a diary entry in 1924, quoting Kingsley's *Young and Old*.

The defendants who were charged with sedition
Back: *a* Arthur Armstrong; *b* James Rees; *c*; *d* James Adams; *e*; *f*;
Front: *g*; *h* Joe Branch; *j* William Davies

...ORE DISTRIBUTION PROSECUTIO...

Counsel's Brilliant Defence in Briton Ferry Case

Moral Victory for I.L.Peers.

Mr. Llewelyn Williams, M.P., and the Suppression of th...

Ten prominent Socialists appeared before the Neath City Magistrates on Friday last charged under Regulation 27 of the Defence of the Realm Act with distributing articles likely to cause disaffection and prejudice to his Majesty's subjects. It is the second batch from Briton Ferry, of another of those foolish prosecutions for the Easter distribution of the Everett and Maximilian pamphlets, for which a month previously two local Socialists had been sentenced to a month imprisonment by the same court. The defendants on Friday were Coun. Joseph Branch; Wm. Henry Davies; Bertie Tudor; James Rees; James Adams; Harry Evans; Robert Poley; Thomas John Jeffries; Arthur Henry Armstrong, and Henry John Kyle.

Mr E. L. Thomas was the presiding magistrate, and the prosecution was conducted by Mr Edward Powell—Clerk to the Local Education Authority—whilst Mr Llewelyn Williams K.C., M.P. for Carmarthen Boroughs), barrister-at-law, was for the defence.

All the cases were for alleged offences committed six weeks before the trial.

The first case heard was that of Councillor Joseph Branch, and owing to the brilliant defence put in by counsel for the accused, it ended in what Socialists can only only regard as a moral victory. On the decision in this case, all the others were decided.

...speech for the prosecution, Mr

Between April 20 and May 12, wa... repetition of this alleged offence?—...

Are you taking any action against... It is under consideration.

Do you suggest that Mr Branch h... to do with the distribution of leaflet... lets since the alleged offence?—I d... that he has, but he is Chairman o... mittee of the Socialist Party in B...

At all events, you have not hea... Branch was personally concerned... buting any leaflets?—I have not.

Before April 30 had there been a... tion instituted against anybody in... for distributing these two leaflets... complain of?—No.

In answer to a further question,... intendent said that the police had... sons for distributing these leaflets... 30, but he could not say whether... was one who was warned.

Mr Llewelyn Williams: Did you... those pamphlets on the premises... raided them on May 11?—After co... list, the Stipendiary said he could... of them named.

Mr Powell: You found ten thou... other?—Yes.

William Jenkins said that at 7-30... April 30, he and his wife were lea... Chapel, Briton Ferry, when he saw... —whom he believed was a membe...

The *Merthyr Pioneer* report on the Briton Ferry case *(National Library of Wales)*

SEDITION ON SUNDAY: support on the streets

The third source of resistance to conscription came from those who individually and publicly supported the activities of the conscientious objectors. In Briton Ferry the ten men who were charged with sedition are examples of such support. With Councillor Joe Branch as principal defendant, he and nine others were charged with distributing seditious pamphlets at Neath Magistrates trial on 9 June, 1916. Prior to this, it should be noted, press offences during the war had been dealt with under Court-Martial, and not civil, jurisdiction. The other accused were:

- James Adams, aged 45, tinworker, of 3 Ruskin Street
- Arthur Henry Armstrong, aged 43, of Tucker Street
- William Henry Davies, aged 18, of 10 Charles Street[66]
- Harry Evans, aged 21, of 24 Osterley Street
- Thomas John Jefferies, aged 25, steelworker, of 32 Ynysymaerdy Road
- Henry John Kyte, aged 41, steelworker, of Hardie House, 41 Victoria Street
- Robert Poley, aged 29, steelworks crane driver, of 8 Mansel Street
- James Rees, moulder of Glan yr Allt, Victoria Street
- Bertie Tudor, aged 25, steelworker, of 33 Ritson Street

Joe Branch stated at the trial that he had handed out *Everett* and *Maximilian* leaflets to the congregation as they left Bethel Chapel on Sunday 30 April. He was fined £50 and bound over to keep the peace for twelve months. The other defendants, who pleaded guilty, were similarly bound over for the sum of £25. Costs of £1 and one shilling were given against each of the other defendants and witness costs were divided amongst them. The police told the court that when they raided the ILP premises on Neath Road on 11 May, they had found ten thousand leaflets there. The *Pioneer* headed its report 'Counsel's Brilliant Defence in the Briton Ferry case'.

The 'brilliant defence' was based on three principal arguments. Firstly, as put forward in the Merthyr case, that the leaflets were

---

[66] Now Bethel Street

factual and, rather than discouraging people from becoming conscripts, the leaflets merely pointed out the penalties that would be incurred by those who resisted conscription. The second argument was that the *Maximilian* leaflet portrayed Christ as a conscientious objector and that to ban its distribution would, effectively, be banning the Bible. Thirdly, if the purpose of imprisonment was a deterrence and not punishment, then imprisonment was not appropriate since no leaflets had been distributed since the 30 April.

There were similar occurrences elsewhere, with NCF branch officials in Liverpool, Penrith, Abercynon and Merthyr being fined for distributing leaflets that 'prejudiced recruiting'. Soon afterwards the majority of the NCF National Committee were arraigned on a similar charge for publishing a leaflet on conscription called *Repeal the Act*. Following pressure on the Home Secretary from Conservative backbench MPs to do something, the Home Secretary, Herbert Samuel, said on 10 May he was powerless to act but eager to suppress any illegal action. Public advocacy of repeal was perfectly legal, but much of the NCF's publicity was claimed to be direct incitement to defy the Defence of the Realm Act. The eight National Committee members were charged at the Mansion House, London, on 17 May where they asserted their right to publicise the Fellowship's pacifist views. Their appeal was rejected and each was fined £100.

In the meantime, another major prosecution under DoRA was causing concern to the NCF. In Lancashire a young teacher called Ernest Everett objected to conscription on socialist grounds, but was denied the chance at St Helens appeal tribunal to call for witnesses in his defence. Just like the Dan Griffiths case in Llanelli and Jimmy Edmunds' case in Cardiff, the Tribunal Chair wrote to Everett's employers asking for him to be dismissed as a teacher. Everett was handed over to the army to be court-martialled at Kinmel on 10 April and given the savage sentence of two years' hard labour, subsequently commuted to 112 days.

The NCF produced a factual account of the case in the *Everett* leaflet, but worse was to follow because of another case at Cefn, near Merthyr on 12 May. Two young objectors, who had distributed the leaflet, were tried by a magistrate who had been the military representative at their tribunal. When they were given a month's hard labour and fined, Bertrand Russell decided it was time to reveal himself as author of the leaflet. Russell's defence was that the effect of the leaflet was simply to inform civilians that if they chose to become conscientious objectors they would get two years' hard labour. The court could hardly object to information to discourage soldiers to resist discipline!

James Adams – one of the 'Briton Ferry Ten'

The Crown Advocate in all the London prosecutions (known as the Mansion House trial) under DoRA was Archibald Bodkin. In one case he unfortunately remarked that 'war would become impossible if all men were to have the view that war was wrong'. The NCF made a poster of the phrase, which made its case for them. The authorities were enraged and asked Bodkin to prosecute the author of the words on poster. The NCF's *Tribunal* newspaper suggested Bodkin must therefore prosecute himself.

Bodkin must prosecute himself (*Emily Johns/Peace News*)

People may be surprised that the accused in the Briton Ferry case were represented at the trial by Llewelyn Williams KC, barrister-at-law and MP for Carmarthen Boroughs. Even barristers sympathetic to clients' causes are expensive, but Briton Ferry ILP branch was the largest in Wales and successful at fund raising. Its response to an appeal for extra funds – *the special effort fund,* which was launched after the court cases, in February 1918, raised £57 7s 3d. This was the highest sum of any branch except Leicester, which raised £87 14s 6d. Its closest competitor, in membership and funding in Wales was nearby Cwmavon, which raised £12.

People may be surprised, too, that in both the *Briton Ferry Ten* and the *Waters/Davies* 'sedition' cases, the defendants were reported to the authorities by clergymen.

All the individuals who were engaged in both events were manual workers. Robert Poley, for example, was one of the six children of a widowed mother. He was a steelworks crane driver, and neighbour of conscientious objector Richard Gethin. They were not just protesting against an abstract concept: conscription for them was about their neighbours, friends and workmates.

Chapter Six:
Women against war

'Being in prison with like-minded COs might have been the easier part'. (Bessie Thomas – Conscientious Objector's wife)

The Women's Peace Crusade was the first truly popular campaign in Britain to link feminism with anti-militarism. Its central demand was a 'people's peace'; that is, an end to the war without annexing territories or enforcing crushing indemnity repayments. The movement had 123 branches across the UK from Aberdeen to Ystradgynlais, including Briton Ferry and Port Talbot. The Briton Ferry branch was launched at Jerusalem Church in September, 1917, with Ethel Snowden as guest speaker and Mrs Rees Powell being elected Chair of the Briton Ferry committee.

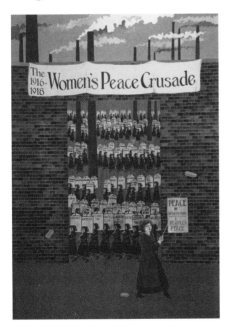

Women's Peace Crusade (*Emily Johns/Peace News*)

Each branch of the Peace Crusade is represented by a banner-carrying protester, including Port Talbot and Briton Ferry representatives

Mrs Powell presided at the launch after being denied the use of the town's Public Hall by its committee. Gwen Jefferies, committee member, recited *Mothers of England* and Mrs Snowden spoke of 'the sufferings of the women in this country during the last three years (which) have been terrible'. She was adamant that a dictated peace after military victory would only sow the seeds of revenge. A collection raised £3 18s 6d, literature sales were £1 5s 6d and 'all badges were sold'.

The Crusade faced repression, mob violence and a massive government campaign against it. In Nelson, 1200 Crusaders were met by a 15,000 mob of patriots who bayed for blood and hurled clinkers at the Crusaders. This is in contrast with the National War Aims Committee, officially a non-governmental organisation, which was almost wholly funded by the government. It flooded the country with pro-war propaganda to encourage such 'patriotism' as repression and mob violence.

Nonetheless the women of Briton Ferry continued with their campaign throughout the war: Sylvia Pankhurst visited Jerusalem Church in February, 1918, and Charlotte Despard, too. They did not succeed in persuading the politicians to negotiate an end to the war, but, as events were to show in the 1920s and 1930s, however, they turned out to be right when they had said that punitive war reparations would lead to further trouble.

Women and the No Conscription Fellowship

Catherine E. Marshall
(*Spartacus Education*)

Women were extensively involved in the NCF, as mothers, wives, girl-friends and friends of the men who had to face hostility from family and neighbours. They were also involved as workers in the organisation itself, especially as male members were being increasingly imprisoned. The brilliant administration of the NCF, which tracked the whereabouts of all its members and their experiences, was most efficient. It enabled information on the treatment of conscientious objectors to reach Parliament and the public via MPs like Philip

Violet Tillard
suffragette, nurse,
pacifist, supporter of
conscientious objectors

Snowden. It was in the capacity of its Parliamentary Secretary, and later Acting Honorary Secretary, that Catherine E. Marshall demonstrated her admirable organisational skills.

Her colleague, Violet Tillard, acted as Secretary General from 1914-1916. She was sentenced to 61 days imprisonment for failing to tell the police who the NCF's printers were. Ada Salter, Gladys Rinder and Joan Beauchamp were jailed twice and Lydia and Edith Smith of the Press Department were sentenced to six months for not submitting a leaflet to the censors before printing it.

CATHERINE MARSHALL
VIOLET TILLARD
JOAN BEAUCHAMP
LYDIA SMITH

Anti-war activists, editors and publishers
of the No-Conscription Fellowship
1915-1920

Ada Salter – member ILP, Women's Labour League, Women's International League of Peace and Freedom

Four NCF women (*Emily Johns/Peace News*)

Dorcas Butler, née Jones (1894-1980)

Dorcas Jones was one of the local supporters of peace who signed the autograph albums referred to in Chapter Two. Her inscription in the album simply reads: 'Love rules his kingdom without a sword.' Dorcas Gwendoline Jones was born to Gwilym and Margaret Jones of Barn Cottages, Shelone, Briton Ferry. She was a sister of Cyn and Hwyrnos, both of whom were

Dorcas Butler
(Mrs Caroline Jackson)

conscientious objectors, and George, a trade unionist and chapel deacon at Salem Chapel. Even though her two brothers endured a terrible time in prison in World War One, Dorcas actually married a conscripted soldier, Dick Butler, who served in the Somme. He considered the war so wasteful of human life and a purposeless error. Doubtless that view engendered Dorcas' desire for a world at peace and one which would fulfil women's hopes for fairness.

After attending Brynhyfryd Primary School in Briton Ferry, Dorcas proudly helped to clean it as a family activity on Friday evenings. This led to her working, for a while, as a 16-year-old domestic for the Howards, a steel working family living at Rose-mount on Shelone Road. At the end of the war 20-year-old Dorcas married the now-discharged soldier, and cricket-loving, Dick Butler. Thereafter, he supported her in her endeavours for sisterhood, peace and prosperity.

Dorcas was invited as one of twelve members of the British National Assembly of Women to visit Russia in 1952 for four weeks as a guest of the Soviet Women's Anti-Fascist Committee, no doubt because of the strong trade union and peace links the Jones family had.

> 'Being just an ordinary housewife, I still can't understand why I was fortunate enough to be chosen as a represen-tative from Wales to visit the Soviet Union last August along with eleven other members of the National Assembly of Women . . . since my return I am more convinced than ever

that the people in the USSR are MOST anxious for Peace
and Goodwill amongst the nations of the earth and are
really doing all in their power to try and convey their
messages of Peace to the World. . . .'

The journey to Russia was overland, via Brussels and Prague. At
Prague Dorcas met the Mayor of Lidice – the town which the Nazis
razed and killed every adult male and fifty-two women and children
as a reprisal for the assassination of the Nazi Governor, Heydrich.
My brothers and I borrowed the book about the assassination from
Briton Ferry Library – we found the story fascinating. At long last
we have an idea who may have requested the book for the library's
shelves.

British Women's Delegation Press Conference, Moscow, August and September
1952 (*Mrs Caroline Jackson*)
Front row (left to right): Mrs Mattison, Mrs Mason, Miss Harrison, Mrs Jones,
Anna Karavayeva, Mrs Carling, Mrs Petrova.
Standing: Mrs Butler, Mrs Drongin, Mrs Bagshaw, Mrs Howley, Mrs Wing,
Mrs Yanchuk

The group had dinner with Nina Popova, in her role as member of the World Peace Council, Chairwoman of the Committee of Soviet Women and a member of the Supreme Soviet of the Communist Party of the Soviet Union.

Councillor Bagshaw of Sowerby Bridge reported[67] that the delegation visited Stalingrad, Sochi and the Republic of Moldavia where they saw schools, nurseries, hospitals churches, collective farms and textile and tractor factories. In Stalingrad, she said, 'people were more serious...with lots still living in wartime dugouts.' Dorcas Butler elaborated in her handwritten notes:

> 'We travelled down Peace Street in Stalingrad . . . I met a lady who lost her husband, baby and home on the same day during the siege of Stalingrad, but fortunately her baby son was found alive six hours later and brought to her by one of the artillery soldiers. She told me that is why she belongs to the World Peace Movement, so that he may not see any more war and with it all its horrors. Stalingrad has been razed to the ground three times since 1917.'

British National Assembly of Women

Her grand-niece still keeps the set of Russian dolls that Dorcas brought back for her. Dorcas' daughter, now in her nineties and still living in Briton Ferry, recently gave her niece all the information from that trip, including the photographs taken by Soviet journalists. The British National Assembly of Women still works for full social, economic, legal, political and cultural independence and equality for women irrespective of age, race, religion, philosophical belief, sexual orientation or nationality-aims which can only be realised in a world at peace. 'In the struggle against racism, fascism and imperialism we will work with all women and other progressive organisations that share these aims.'

---

[67] Halifax Weekly Courier and Guardian, September 1952

Charlotte Despard (1844–1939)

Charlotte Despard was the Edinburgh-born sister of John French, the commander-in chief of the British Expeditionary Force. When her husband died in 1890, she decided to dedicate the rest of her life to helping the poor and so moved to Wandsworth to live with the people she intended to assist. There she funded and staffed a health clinic, as well as organizing youth and working men's clubs, and a soup kitchen for the local unemployed.

In 1894, Despard was elected as a Poor Law Guardian in Lambeth. Charlotte became friendly with George Lansbury and, for the next few years, was involved in the campaign to reform the Poor Law system. She joined the Social Democratic Federation and later the Independent Labour Party, getting to know Margaret Bondfield, the trade union leader and Keir Hardie, the new leader of the Labour Party.

Despard became a member of the National Union of Women's Suffrage Societies (NUWSS). However, in 1906, frustrated by their lack of success, she joined the Women's Social and Political Union (WSPU), a militant organisation established by Emmeline Pankhurst and her three daughters. Their main objective was to gain, not universal suffrage, (i.e. the vote for *all* women and men over a certain age), but votes for women, on the same criteria as men. This would have meant winning the vote, not for all women but, for those who could meet the property qualification. As one critic pointed out, it was not 'votes for women', but 'votes for ladies'.

In 1907 she was twice imprisoned in Holloway Prison. However, like other leading members of the WSPU, she began to question the leadership of Emmeline and Christabel Pankhurst who were making decisions without consulting members. Emmeline Pankhurst told members that she intended to run the WSPU without interference. Mrs Despard, who did not like this idea, dealt with it quietly, affirming her belief in democratic equality, and was convinced that it must be maintained at all costs. Mrs. Pankhurst challenged all who did not accept their leadership to resign from the Union that she had founded, and to form their own.

As a result of this speech, Despard, and over seventy other members of the WSPU, left to form the Women's Freedom League

A meeting of the WSPU (left to right) Christabel Pankhurst, Jessie Kenney, Nellie Martel, Emmeline Pankhurst and Charlotte Despard. (*Wikipedia*)

(WFL). Like the WSPU, this was a militant organisation which was prepared the break the law, but non-violent. As a result, over one hundred of their members were sent to prison after being arrested on demonstrations or refusing to pay taxes. Despite its militancy, the WFL was a completely non-violent organisation and opposed the WSPU campaign of vandalism against private and commercial property. The WFL were especially critical of the WSPU's arson campaign.

From 1908 onwards Charlotte Despard made several visits to the industrial towns of south Wales. Swansea, Llanelli, Aberdare, Barry, Caldicot, Merthyr, Penygraig and Briton Ferry welcomed her. Despard argued that:

> 'Fundamentally all social and political questions are economic. With equal wages, the male worker would no longer fear that his female colleague might put him out of a job, and 'men and women will unite to effect a complete transformation to the industrial environment. . . . A woman needs economic independence to live as an equal with her husband. It is indeed deplorable that the work of the wife and mother is not rewarded. I hope that the time will come when it is illegal for this strenuous form of industry to be unremunerated.'

Despard met Gandhi and was influenced by his theory of 'passive resistance'. As the leading figure of the WFL, Despard urged members not to pay taxes and to boycott the 1911 Census.[68] Like most members of the Women's Freedom League, she was a pacifist. During the First World War she refused to become involved in the British Army's recruitment campaign, even though her brother was General Sir John French, Chief of Staff of the British Army and commander of the British Expeditionary Force which was sent to Europe in August 1914. Her sister, Catherine Harley, supported the war and served in the Scottish Women's Hospital in France. Briton Ferry was one of her later visits, where on 17 February 1918 she attended Jerusalem Church for a function under the banner of the Women's Peace Crusade.

Despard argued that the British government was not doing enough to bring an end to the war and supported the campaign of the Women's Peace Council for a negotiated peace. After the passing of the Qualification of Women Act in 1918, she became the Labour Party candidate for Battersea. However, in the euphoria of Britain's victory, her anti-war views were very unpopular and like most other pacifist candidates, who stood in the election, she was defeated. She was also a supporter of Irish Home Rule, and the Friends of Soviet Russia organisation.

Katharine Glasier (1867-1950)

Katharine Glasier was born Katharine St John Conway into a Congregationalist family in north-east London. After attending Newnham College Cambridge, a college which did not award degrees to women, she taught at Redland College, Bristol. There she joined the Fabians and Socialist Societies. In 1893 she became a founder member of the ILP, and the only woman elected to its first national administrative council. She also married John Bruce Glasier that year.

In May, 1914, she was at Ystradgynlais. Her topic, when speaking at the New Cinema, was *The Cry of the Children*. This was an attack

---

[68] 'Women do not count; neither shall they be counted'.

on the so-called 'half-time' system in which children still had to work several hours a day at ten years of age when strong, able bodied men were unemployed. In her plea she pointed out that these were the same men that were refusing women the vote. The local branch of the ILP enlisted eight new members that night as a result of her speech. Just before Christmas the following year, she was at the Picture Palace, in nearby Seven Sisters, speaking on *The Road to Peace on Earth*. This

Katharine Glasier
(*Wikipedia*)

event was followed by a *Patriotic Presentation*, two days later, at which Mrs Davies, the local infant school head mistress, spoke from the platform and claimed that she was not allowed to speak after Katharine Glasier's speech two days earlier. This provoked a letter to *Labour Voice* from Samuel Lloyd, the Chair of the peace meeting to say that the opportunity was offered but was not taken up. Perhaps 1916 was the opportune time for Katharine Glasier to take over the editorship of the *Labour Leader* from Fenner Brockway. She had certainly discovered the flavour of a south Wales community.

She visited Briton Ferry after her husband's death on 18 May 1924. Her inscription, above, reads: 'Inscribed in the love of comrades in the year of the first Labour government in Britain'. She campaigned for the introduction of pit-head baths in Britain and for the Save the Children Fund and also became ILP's national organiser until 1931. She bequeathed her former home at Earby in Lancashire for use as a Youth Hostel.

inscribed in the love of comrades, in the first year of the first Labour Government in Britain

Katharine Bruce Glasier.

May 18. 1924

Emma Goldman (1869–1940)

It was Sam Mainwaring, a Briton Ferry
steelworker at the Albion Works, who
brought Emma Goldman to Briton
Ferry.

Emma Goldman

> 'I welcomed the Welsh crowds
> and their enthusiasm. The
> difficulty was not the indifference
> of the workers, but their dreadful
> poverty. . . . If I could at least
> enter their lives, share in their
> struggles, show them that
> anarchism alone has the key that
> can transform society and secure
> their well-being. . . .' [69]

During Dr Hywel Francis' maiden speech as MP in the House of
Commons on 25 June, 2001, he spoke of the internationalist values
in his new constituency:

> 'The internationalist values are best expressed by the old ILP
> centre at Briton Ferry by such remarkable speakers as
> Emma Goldman, James Maxton and C. L. R. James, who
> completed his masterpiece *Black Jacobins* in our locality in
> 1938.'

He repeated the message in an address to Swansea Bay Racial
Equality Council in July, 2001, when he said that 'the Russian-
American revolutionary (Goldman) often came to Briton Ferry, as
did C. L. R. James'.

Emma Goldman was deeply committed to the ideal of absolute
freedom of expression, sexual freedom, birth control, equality and
independence for women, radical education, union organisation and
workers' rights. She fought against inequality, repression and

---

[69] Emma Goldman, Living My Life

exploitation. Many of these ideas were unpopular in the USA and she was often harassed or arrested while lecturing. She attracted the enmity of several powerful political and economic interests. Goldman was regarded by the FBI as 'the most dangerous woman in America'. She had migrated to New York from Lithuania where she became a writer and lecturer on anarchist philosophy, women's rights and social issues. There she organised the No Conscription League. 'We oppose conscription because we are internationalists, anti-militarists and opposed to all wars waged by capitalist governments'.

Goldman was imprisoned several times, including a two year sentence in 1917 for resistance against the draft. With her lover and lifelong friend Alex Berkman, she was charged with the attempted assassination of the industrialist and 'philanthropist' Henry Clay Frick, 'the most hated man in America'. Frick was manager of Homestead Steelworks in Pittsburgh during the notorious Homestead steel strike, in which ten people were killed and sixty wounded, and during which martial law was introduced.

In 1901, President McKinley's assassin, Leon Czolgosz, said he had been inspired by Goldman. As a result Goldman was charged with planning McKinley's assassination and Czolgosz was executed. It is piquant to recall that it was McKinley's import tariffs a decade earlier which had seriously threatened Briton Ferry's tinplate industry. The connection was, surely, coincidental.

Emma Goldman's itinerary of speaking dates during her stay in the UK shows that the most extensively toured area was the south Wales coalfield in 1925. Goldman came to Britain in 1921 and married James Colton in order to get British citizenship. He was an Amman Valley miner and working class intellectual who attended meetings at the White House in Ammanford. It was a marriage of convenience which made front page news in the New York Times:

'Cupid was armed with a coal pick when he dug his way into the heart of Emma Goldman. James Colton, a miner living here, is the man whom the Anarchist leader chose after spurning marriage for forty years. Colton won't say much at present about the romance.'

At one of the Neath meetings organised by the Trades and Labour Council 'her husband was present and passed Emma Goldman on the stairway. They greeted each other cordially with a raised hand and a friendly wave but then proceeded on their respective ways'[70]. When in Neath she stayed with the Nefts, a Polish Jewish family owning a dental practice at 19 London Road, Neath. In 1925 she spoke at a meeting in Gwaun-cae-Gurwen. *The Amman Valley Chronicle* recorded that the audience agreed to: 'protest against the conspiracy of silence and boycott of Emma Goldman's exposure of the Russian dictatorship by the British Labour press and pledges itself to do all in its power to combat the said conspiracy.'

Emma was well aware of the difficult position she was putting herself in and the effect that exposing the reality of the Bolshevik regime:

> 'You can well imagine the time I had and how rotten I felt that I had to take away the last ray of hope from the unfortunate Welsh slaves in regard to the 'Heaven' in Russia. There is no doubt, we who have taken a stand against the Dictatorship are in a rotten position since we are compelled to tell the same tale reiterated by the reactionary press.'[71]

Goldman continued to be hounded by the FBI, and returned to the USA only once before she eventually died in Toronto. The documentary film *Emma Goldman: The Anarchist Guest* had its Canadian release in 2000 but the film was not released in the USA until 2003, then with the title *Emma Goldman: An exceedingly dangerous woman*. Emma Goldman is still one of the world's most celebrated radicals, despite the fact she has been dead for over seventy years. Beyond her ideological contribution to libertarian socialism her work on contraception, abortion and the rejection of marriage laid the foundations for greater freedoms for countless women and men.

---

[70] Leonard Williams, Neath Antiquarian Society
[71] Quoted in *Emma Goldman in Wales*: Fowler, Tom

Minnie Pallister (1885–1960)

THE ORANGE-BOX

MINNIE PALLISTER

Minnie Pallister began life in Brynmawr when her father, a Methodist minister received preferment there. She was an excellent piano player and elocutionist and she was a teacher by profession. At the University College of south Wales and Monmouthshire she gained a double first, studying social and economic questions and doing much fieldwork with local families.

In June, 1914, Pallister was elected President of Monmouthshire ILP, the first woman to hold such a position in Wales. In this role she also spoke at events throughout south Wales. After speaking at the Athenaeum Hall in Llanelli, the *Llanelli Star* described her as 'Wales' Great Woman Orator'. Later she became ILP organiser for South Wales.

Pallister was concerned about the welfare of children and not only encouraged women to use their vote, but to vote ILP, so that the party's policies for child welfare could be put in place. She linked this subject to her anti-conscription stance in a speech at the Olympic Rink, Merthyr, when she said: 'the government is irresponsible for children to the age of eighteen and then steps in and claims them as their own'.

In her travels around Wales thirty-two year old Minnie Pallister spoke at peace meetings held under the auspices of Jerusalem English Baptist Church in Briton Ferry in February, 1916 and 1917. The meeting on 23 December, 1917, was also attended by three police officers and a police reporter. She spoke of a Stockport conscientious objector called Butler who died in November, 1917, after he contracted tuberculosis on his third confinement in

Y.M.C.A. HALL, AMMANFORD.

CASEY & DOLLY

Will give their famous

Lecture Recital:
" Music and the People,"

At the above place on

THURSDAY NEXT, Dec. 7th.

Doors open at 7; to commence 7.30.

Admission - 1/- and 6d.

Don't miss this Musical Treat.

Music and the People:
Advert for a Lecture
Recital

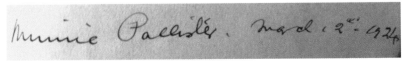

Preston prison. His mother's request for relief on health grounds had been refused by the Home Office. The entry she inscribed in my uncle's album in Briton Ferry was quoted from William Morris:

'Then that which the worker winneth
    Shall then be big indeed
Nor shall half he reaped for nothing
    By him that sowed the seed'.

Pallister was also at Neath on 10 August, speaking in the open air on Cimla Common, but the rain, or was it the police presence that resulted in a small crowd? At Briton Ferry in December 1918, at a meeting to support Reverend Herbert Morgan as ILP candidate for Neath, she was supported by another large crowd. She returned to Briton Ferry on 12 March, 1924, no doubt taking advantage of the occasion to promote her recently written book: *The Orangebox: thoughts of a Socialist Propagandist*.

Pallister was sufficiently accomplished as a pianist to accompany the well-known violinist, known as Casey, on his ILP-supporting 'lecture recitals' around south Wales when Dolly, his regular pianist, was not available. Casey suggested a national tour together 'to present a new common foundation for an international brother-hood'. The *Amman Valley Chronicle* reported that 'a serious truth lies in his remarks', perhaps regarding him as the equivalent of today's Rory Bremner. Pallister also composed an election battle song[72] for Ramsay MacDonald's campaign in the Aberafan constituency. It was to the tune of *Men of Harlech*:

'Ramsay, Ramsay. Shout it.
    Don't be shy about it.
Labour's day is bound to come,
    We cannot do without it.
On then Labour, on to glory
    'Twill be told in song and story,
How we fought at Aberafan
    On Election day'.

---

[72] Hanson, as before

Emmeline Pankhurst (1858–1928)

Emmeline Pankhurst was a political activist and leader of the British suffragette movement. The movement was of crucial significance in gaining women the right to vote. She came from a Manchester family which had a tradition of radical politics and her husband, Richard Pankhurst, was a radical Liberal lawyer and ILP member. They had three daughters, whose stances – at different times – overlapped with, or differed from, those of their mother. It is

Emmeline Pankhurst (*Daily Mirror*)

important to understand this, particularly in order to appreciate Emmeline and Sylvia's positions with regards the war.

In 1895 Emmeline stood, unsuccessfully, as an ILP candidate for Gorton. By 1903 her daughter, Christabel, had persuaded her to help in the foundation of the WPSU, an organisation whose members were known as 'suffragettes'. They would fight for votes for women and this was sometimes by violent means. Sylvia also joined the cause which included window-smashing, demonstrations, arson and hunger strikes. Emmeline was arrested six times by 1913 under the *Cat and Mouse Act*; an act which allowed prisoners to be temporarily discharged for ill-health, but then to be imprisoned again until they weakened and eventually gave up. (The same technique that was used on many conscientious objectors).

Emmeline Pankhurst (*Daily Mirror*)

During an early visit to Briton Ferry under the auspices of the ILP in November 1905, Emmeline Pankhurst spoke of *Socialism for Women* at Bethel Chapel, but in 1908 she spent six weeks in prison for her activities. As time went on and war came, she began to see that it would be support for the war, rather than Socialism for Women or demonstrations, that would best secure her aims. On 10 August 1914 all imprisoned suffragettes were released.

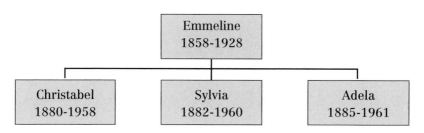

Hence, suffragette militancy ceased in July, 1915, after Christabel's last demonstration (which involved 30,000 suffragettes). However, by this time Emmeline and Christabel's position had caused their estrangement from Adela and Sylvia. After that the cry from the WPSU became pro-War: 'we demand the right to serve'. The underlying thinking was that if women were seen to be helping the war effort it was only fair that being granted the vote would soon follow. Sadly both Emmeline and Christabel were leading figures in the 'white feather' movement to encourage men to volunteer for the front lines.

Emmeline's visit to Briton Ferry on 24 October 1915 was under the auspices of the WSPU. On a Friday evening, at the English Congregational Chapel in Ritson Street she stated that her purpose now was to 'aid the country's war effort'. She spoke of 'her previous visits to the town in another movement'. This was a reference to her earlier advocacy of *Socialism for Women* under the ILP banner. She now asked the women of the town to do 'useful work for soldiers if they could not do it for munitions.' Her position had changed dramatically from 1914, for she now asked: 'What is the use of fighting for a vote if we haven't got a country to vote in?'

Emmeline and Christabel both visited Russia in an attempt to persuade those in power not to accept Germany's peace conditions in 1917. At that time Emmeline severed her connections with the ILP. Prime Minister David Lloyd George, in praising Pankhurst and the Women's Party, said: 'They have fought the Bolshevist and Pacifist element with great skill, tenacity, and courage'.

In February 1918 Emmeline made a 'long expected visit' to Briton Ferry and – according to *Labour Voice* – even attacked the town's strikers. At a public meeting she not only advocated the formation of a branch of the Women's Party at Briton Ferry; she also castigated the ASE Union[73] whose bricklayer members had recently returned to work after a two week strike which had hampered munitions production. Pankhurst told her audience that if they were 'to carry out their policy of down tools there were thousands of women ready to take their place'. So, an interesting volte face on the part of one who had thirty years earlier supported the Match Girls strike!

Possibly due to her vociferous support for the war, in 1926, Emmeline was adopted as Conservative parliamentary candidate for Whitechapel, but she never actually stood as a candidate and died in 1928. This was just eighteen days before the Representation of the People Act gave women over twenty-one equal voting rights with men.

Sylvia Pankhurst (1882-1960)

Sylvia Pankhurst was a friend of Keir Hardie, and a writer and artist who linked socialism with women's rights. She was, clearly, not the first of the Pankhursts to visit Briton Ferry. Her mother, Emmeline, had already made a speech at Bethel Chapel in 1905 in support of women's suffrage. The following year Sylvia, with her parents, joined the Women's Socialist Political Union (WSPU) in order to get working class women into the struggle for the vote. The WSPU were independent of any political party but Pankhurst wished them to align with the ILP.

In 1913 (after her visit to Briton Ferry on 5 January) she was arrested three times and went on hunger strike. She broke with the WSPU in 1914 in order to form the Women's Suffrage Federation.

On 10 August 1914 the Government released all suffragettes from prison, but the Federation organised against war and some of its members hid COs from the police. As her mother supported conscription, Sylvia set up cost-price restaurants to feed the hungry and defended the rights of soldiers' wives to have proper

---

[73] It became the AEU engineering union, which eventually became part of today's Unite Union

Sylvia Pankhurst

allowances. When she visited Briton Ferry on 23 July 1916, in order
to support the ILP's pacifist stance, she was already a substantial
national figure in opposition to the war, whereas her mother and
sisters similarly, were national figures in support of it. Sylvia
continued to visit south Wales during the war. She and Adela left
the WPSU 1919 but Sylvia remained involved in left wing politics for
the rest of her life.

Sylvia Pankhurst

	Attitude to war	WPSU	Attitude to conscription	Relationship with ILP
Emmeline Estranged from Adela & Sylvia by 1914	It changed; whereas she saw the Boer War as Imperialist she supported the World War especially through the harsh programme of the Women's Party after 1917.	Co-founder 1903 Imprisoned Hunger striker	Demanded military conscription of men and the industrial conscription of women	John Bruce Glasier of the ILP was against supporting her suffragist efforts (1903)
Christabel Estranged from Adela & Sylvia by 1914	Supported World War especially through the harsh programme of the Women's Party after 1917	Co-founder and organising secretary Imprisoned Hunger striker	Demanded military conscription of men and the industrial conscription of women	John Bruce Glasier of the ILP was against supporting her (1903) Christabel did not want to affiliate with political parties
Sylvia	Supported the ILP's pacifist stance	Left the WPSU in 1910 due to increased violence		Wanted the WSPU to align with the ILP
Adela		Left WPSU in 1910 due to increased violence. Supported Sylvia		

Relationships amongst the Pankhursts

Elizabeth M Powell (née Jones)
(1873–1947)

Eira Mary Powell

Elizabeth Powell was not quite so well-known
as her husband, the Rev Rees Powell, whom
she married in 1903. Her role in relation to
her husband's was rather like that between
the Snowdens. Whilst Mrs Snowden supported
Mr Snowden's work, she was also an activist in her own right.
Likewise, whilst Mrs Powell supported her husband, she was
eminent in her own right. Her eminence arose from what she did as
a resident of Briton Ferry, as a Women's ILP, chapel member and
peace campaigner, whilst more celebrated female speakers such as
the Pankhursts, Swanwick and Snowden achieved their eminence
elsewhere.

Powell (née Jones) was born in Rhymney. She was the daughter of
Salem Church's first minister and, when she married Rees Powell, a
link between the two churches was strengthened. The link was one
that continued until the 1950's with Salem members, such as its
General Secretary George Jones, contributing much value to
Jerusalem's 'Conscription and Reconstruction' and other lectures.
When Mrs Powell was elected Chair of the Briton Ferry Peace
Crusade Committee in September, 1917, she was already a more
than capable chair person, able to attract such eminent speakers as
Charlotte Despard. She also demonstrated that she herself could
speak from a wide repertoire of interests: in September 1918, for
example, with Ethel Snowden at Jerusalem Church on the subject of
No Annexation and no Indemnity. In January of that year she had
already spoken to remind the authorities that the war was over and
that it was pointless to continue the punishment of conscientious
objectors. 'The audience was regaled with a feast of reason and
flow of soul.'[74] During the seventy-five minutes of her speech, she
covered many aspects of the war and its legacy, referring to the
pernicious influence of 'the armchair patriots and the likely effects
of war weariness'. In April, she considered the legacy that
conscientious objectors would create in terms of prison reform.

---

[74] *Pioneer*, 12 January 1918

Rees Powell's successor, the Rev Trevor Evans, said of Mrs Powell: 'This was a dual ministry, for Rees Powell was greatly assisted by his gifted wife'. Her third child, Eira Mary continued her work at Jerusalem and was Head Teacher of Cwrt Sart Secondary Modern School in the 1950s.

Maude Royden (1876–1956)

Maude Royden

Dr Maude Royden was born at Mossley Hill, near Liverpool, but it was while she was at Oxford University that she developed an interest in alleviating poverty and returned to Liverpool to work in a women's settlement. She became the University extension department's first female lecturer. That was her start in public speaking. She became increasingly interested in women's rights and joined the National Union of Women's Suffrage, becoming one of its chief speakers and editor of its newspaper, *The Common Cause*. She was a strong supporter of the NCF and because of it came into conflict with Millicent Fawcett and others in the NUWSS who supported the war.

At the end of 1914 Royden became Secretary of the Fellowship of Reconciliation, but in February 1915 she resigned as editor of *Common Cause* and joined the Women's League for Peace and Freedom. Her involvement in the organisation and the Church League for Women's suffrage led her to campaign for a priesthood of women. By 1918 she was offered a preaching post at the Congregational church in Holborn where she spoke on the League of Nations and Christianity. The Bishop of London rebuked her for this.

A visit she paid to Briton Ferry in January 1918, representing the National Union of Womens' Suffrage, was to speak at one of the Thursday meetings held at Jerusalem Church as part of the Church's peace meetings programme. She joined the Labour Party in 1922 and spoke all over the world on similar themes. In the late

1920s she supported Radclyffe Hall, the author of *The Well of Loneliness*, a book about lesbianism which the press campaigned to ban. The publisher agreed to withdraw the book and the magistrates ordered that all copies be destroyed. In 1935 Maude Royden joined the PPU but renounced pacifism in order to fight the evils of Nazi Germany.

Ethel Snowden (1881–1951)

Ethel Snowden

Ethel Snowden, from a middle-class background in Harrogate, Yorkshire, became a Christian Socialist through a radical preacher after being influenced by a speech of his entitled 'Can a Man be a Christian on £1 a week?' She is described by Philip Snowden's biographer as a 'woman of strong will and striking good looks'. She initially promoted temperance and teetotalism in the slums of Liverpool after which she aligned with the Fabian Society and later the Independent Labour Party, earning an income by lecturing in Britain and abroad. It was rare for someone of Ethel's background to be a socialist, but she was one of the leading campaigners for women's suffrage before the First World War, then founding the Women's Peace Crusade to oppose the war and call for a negotiated peace. After a visit to the Soviet Union she developed a strong criticism of its system, which made her unpopular when relayed to the left-wing in Britain.

She married the prominent Labour Party politician and future Chancellor of the Exchequer, Philip Snowden in 1903. Ethel Snowden first lectured in south Wales in 1905 on socialism and women's suffrage, but she never endorsed the violent tactics of the suffragettes.

After 1906 Snowden became increasingly active in supporting women's suffrage, being one of the national speakers for the National Union of Women's Suffrage Societies; she decried the concentration on such things as dresses, jewels and cake recipes and wrote a book called *The Woman Socialist*. It advocated state control of marriage, joint title by women to the housekeeping money, and a state salary for mothers; she also wanted housekeeping organised collectively in each street and declared that under socialism women would have 'no need to paint face and tint hair.'

By 1914 she was speaking at two hundred public meetings a year on the subject of women's suffrage, and temporarily resigned from the Independent Labour Party in order that her political allegiance did not cause problems with her campaigning on the matter.

On 25 September, 1916, she visited Briton Ferry with her husband, even though she was of sufficient stature as a pacifist figure to visit in her own right. On 3 December she addressed a meeting of over one thousand at the Public Hall, calling on the Government to open up peace negotiations in response to a motion moved by Henry Davies for a 'lasting and honourable peace'.[75]

A year later, in September 1917, Snowden was the principal guest at the launch of the Briton Ferry branch of the Women's Peace Crusade in Jerusalem Church. She had become the organiser and principal speaker for the Crusade, estimating that she had addressed half a million people in the previous year of the war. Her husband supported her ideals and was often present at suffragette and other public meetings such as these.

At the end of the war, Snowden was elected to the National Executive Committee of the Labour Party in its Women's Section. This position made her a very prominent figure within the left-wing movements and led to a great deal of foreign travel, including a joint TUC-Labour Party delegation to Russia in early 1920 which was sent to be an impartial inquiry into the Bolshevik Revolution. After her return she published a book to reveal her own findings. Although she liked Lenin her general reaction was profoundly critical declaring that 'we want power, but we do not want a revolution', and stated that 'I oppose Bolshevism because it is not Socialism, it is not democracy and it is not Christianity', and likened working conditions to slavery.

---

[75] *Pioneer* 9 December 1917

In 1926 she became one of the first BBC Governors. When in 1937 she attended the rally at Nuremburg as a reporter but said of Hitler: 'I would not hesitate to accept his word'.

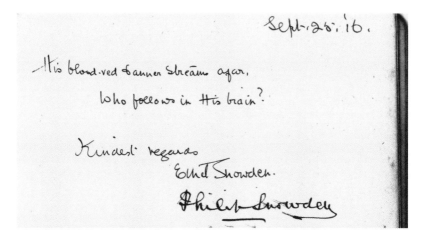

Helena Swanwick (1864-1939)

Ethel Helena Swanwick

At school Helena Swanwick had been deeply influenced by John Stuart Mill's ideas after reading his work *On the subjection of women*. She rebelled against her parents' views on the role of women and complained about the way she was treated by her mother. 'A boy might be a person but not a girl.' In 1882 Helena's father refused to pay the fees for her to attend Girton College, Cambridge but she had a sympathetic godmother who financed her studies. By 1885 she had been appointed lecturer in psychology at Westfield College.

She married in 1888 and set up home in Manchester where she became a close friend of the Manchester Guardian editor, C. P. Scott, and his wife. Over the next few years she wrote articles and reviewed books for the paper and also did voluntary work in a girls' club. This brought her into contact with trade unions, and the Independent Labour Party. During this period she met Emmeline Pankhurst and her daughters and, in 1905, joined the National Union of Women's Suffrage. By 1908 she was travelling over the whole country and addressed one hundred and fifty meetings annually. The following year she became editor of the NUWSS's weekly journal, *The Common Cause,* and visited south Wales branches of the NUWSS. As a pacifist, she was a strong opponent of the Women's Social & Political Union and also disapproved of what she believed was the anti-male stance taken by its leading members, Emmeline and Christabel Pankhurst.

When, in 1912, Millicent Fawcett tried to persuade Swanwick to be less critical of the Women's Social and Political Union, she resigned her post as editor in order to write a book *The Future of the Women's Movement,* (published in 1913) in which she was able to express her own views on the best way to achieve universal suffrage.

In July 1914 the NUWSS argued that Asquith's government should do everything possible to avoid a European war, but two days afterwards the British government actually declared war. Millicent Fawcett announced that it would be suspending all political activity until the conflict was over. Although the NUWSS supported the war effort, it did not follow the WSPU strategy of becoming involved in persuading young men to join the armed forces. Eventually Swanwick resigned from the NUWSS over its policy on the war.

The founders of the UDC produced a manifesto and invited people to support it. Over the next few weeks several other leading figures joined the organisation. In January 1915 a hundred British women pacifists published a Christmas 'open letter' to the women of Germany and Austria; its signatories included Helena Swanwick, Margaret Bondfield, Maude Royden and Sylvia Pankhurst. 'Do not let us forget our very anguish unites us, that we are passing together through the same experiences of pain and grief. We pray you to believe that come what may we hold to our faith in peace and goodwill between nations'.

However, Millicent Fawcett attacked the peace efforts, arguing that it should continue until the German armies had been driven out of France and Belgium: Most of the officers of the NUWSS and ten members of its National Executive resigned, including Catherine Marshall, and Maude Royden, the editor of the *The Common Cause*.

In April 1915 a suffragist in Holland invited suffrage members all over the world to an International Congress of Women at the Hague where they women formed the Women's International League for Peace and Freedom. Although Helena Swanwick had been banned by the government for attending, she soon joined the organisation and later became its chairman, its aim was to harness feminism to the peace movement; and throughout the First World War she continued campaigning for a negotiated peace and the establishment of an international peace-keeping organization.

On October 21 1916, she spoke at Briton Ferry at the invitation of the Briton Ferry Council for Civil Liberties. The meeting, yet another in a packed hall, started with the hymn *O Beautiful My Country*. That, the Chairman, Dai Mort, said in his opening remarks that it would no doubt surprise a great many people, people 'by whom we are looked on as unpatriotic'. Swanwick expressed her pleasure that such interest was being taken by the women of Briton Ferry: her main theme was motivated by anxiety that the Defence of the Realm Act, meant the effective annulment of Habeas Corpus. She condemned as monstrous the treatment being meted out by the authorities to conscientious objectors and said that such treatment in no way helped in the successful prosecution of the war. She also advanced her opinion that:

> 'You cannot wage war in a democratic spirit, but only in the spirit of an absolutist', and continued, saying that 'Behind the veil of secrecy (of Military Service Acts) there lay hid a far deeper motive, and if the worker is not wide awake he will discover he has placed in the hands of his employer a very powerful weapon'.

During this Briton Ferry visit, she was highly critical, and fearful of, proposals being made for a post-war economic boycott of Germany. Later her fears were justified. In 1919 she criticised the terms under which the League of Nations was established, partly because the League was to use of force and economic sanctions, and partly because it was committed to supporting the Versailles settlement, which she regarded from the outset as 'an unjust and unstable peace'.

In 1924 she became editor of Foreign Affairs, the journal of the Union of Democratic Control and wrote for the feminist journal, *Time and Tide*. In November, 1927, she wrote:

> 'It is my conviction that most men have not a notion how immensely better the world could be made for them, by the full co-operation of women. But that's another story'.

Helena Swanwick was active in the League of Nations Union and was a member of the British Empire delegation to the League of Nations in 1929. Depressed by poor health and the growth of fascism in Europe in 1939, after the outbreak of the Second World War she committed suicide.

Elizabeth (Bessie) Thomas (1891–1950)

Bessie Thomas
(*Mrs C Sharkey*)

Readers may well wonder why Bessie Thomas is included in this story. Compared with the other women depicted – Pallister and Pankhurst, Snowden and Swanwick – she was unknown but that, however, is precisely the point. For, whilst the other's experiences were expressed on public platforms, (rather in the manner of today's celebrities it must be said), Bessie's 'modus operandi' was to suffer in silence. Silence, though, in a metaphorical sense only: Bessie was voluble, articulate and with strong convictions but just did not have the opportunity that middle-class women had for expressing herself on public platforms.

The third child of George Ryder and Mary Ann Chenhall, Bessie was born at Llantwit Fardre, near Pontypridd, where the family lived in Rickard Street, close to the workhouse, the railway line and the Smallpox hospital. George was described variously as an itinerant concertina musician, a general labourer and as registered blind. They were not affluent and there were no family resources to fall back on in times of hardship. When her future husband and she met, Bessie was a nurse at Margam Isolation Hospital, which was located 'well up one of the mountains'. Her son, Bill Thomas, later said he 'doubted that she had received any training but her medical knowledge was quite extensive for that time'.

Dil Thomas, Bill's father, was unusual for, unlike most of the other Briton Ferry conscientious objectors, he was married, Bessie had become his wife in July 1914. No doubt she well understood Dil's attitude to war and to conscription, for both loomed ever closer between 1914 and 1916. One speculates what she, a mother of two young babies, foresaw of what lay ahead?

Thirty years old in May 1917, Dil was a senior trade union representative, quite capable of assessing what awaited him. Again, one can only imagine what the conversations between husband and wife can have been like and no doubt he must have confided some of his fears and expectations to Bessie, but surely not all? He was in the older age group of Briton Ferry conscientious objectors when he was court-martialled at Kinmel Camp. That was when life became especially hard for her, for after three months in Wormwood Scrubs, the first of which he had spent in solitary confinement, Dil was transferred to the even more inaccessible Dartmoor. Bessie visited Dartmoor on one occasion with her two small boys, then under three years old. Her youngest son, Bill, born in 1920, wrote:

'There was snow at Princetown and six hours to wait for a train. She walked down the street (at Princetown) while the locals shouted abuse and slammed doors. Being within the prison with like-minded CO's might have been the easier part'.

Their third son, Ramsay, was born on 1 December 1917, whilst Dil was still in Dartmoor. His younger brother, Bill, wrote:

'It was many years later we realised that the real hero was my mother who had to cope with three young babies single handed, never knowing where the next meal was coming from. As usual it is the women that suffer in these situations (so) my mother had to go into lodgings with a friend, Mrs Waters, in Water Street.' [76]

Bessie decided that the children should in future attend Jerusalem Church rather than their wanted Anglican one, St Clement's. She regarded the latter's Vicar Lloyd's behaviour, (as the chief witness in the case that saw fellow ILP members Garnet Waters and William Davies receive a prison sentence for distributing anti-war leaflets), as unethical. Moreover, she felt that she would receive better support from Jerusalem Baptist Church with its strong tradition of support for pacifist beliefs. Whether Bessie herself had any specific *Christian* beliefs is uncertain, but what is known is that she felt war to be wrong. Some indication of her independence of thought however, was her being a keen member of a society that supported cremation. Consequently her family went to some trouble to ensure her wishes were adhered to when she died in April 1950.

As a footnote to this, it is interesting that Cyril, the couple's eldest son, went to Spain in order to fight against Franco's fascists in the Spanish Civil War, but youngest son, Bill, born in 1920, became the youngest deacon in Jerusalem Baptist Church and thus continued the family's tradition of resistance to war. As in so many families, the tradition of conscientious objection and resistance to war was continued. In World War Two Ramsay was granted CO status without conditions. Robert William (Bill) became the youngest Deacon at the Jerusalem Baptist Chapel, became a CO and was sent to do customary 'directed labour' work, farming and with the Forestry Commission. Only Cyril broke the family tradition. After his anti-fascist stint in Spain he eventually joined the Royal Navy, in which he served for the duration of the war. As in so many families, the differences in opinion never caused a rift between them.

---

[76] Later renamed as Ormond Street

Sybil Thorndike (1882-1976)

Sybil Thorndike

Many people today will have only vague ideas of the significance of the name Sybil Thorndike but those having clearer knowledge will almost certainly ask: 'why is one of the last century's greatest actresses included in this book about the peace movement in Briton Ferry and what was she doing there?' The answer is that Thorndike was not only one of the last century's great actresses, but she was also a pacifist and a Peace Pledge Union member. It was in this capacity that she gave readings to support the No Conscription Fellowship and the PPU's cause at the Thursday meetings held at Jerusalem Church, Briton Ferry. Indeed, during World War One she had toured many Welsh mining villages to give those causes her support, despite her growing status as a Shakespearean actress at the Old Vic.

In the pre-war suffragette years Thorndike promoted votes for women, going on to found Equity, the actor and actresses' union. Ironically it was later discovered that her name had featured on the list of Britons who were to be arrested by the Nazis in the event of their invasion of Britain.

Sybil Thorndike's peace appeal to women electors

243

Theodora Wilson Wilson (1865–1941)

The fourth child of a Westmoreland JP and a bible publisher, Theodora Wilson Wilson spent two years studying music in Germany. She was a radical, a supporter of women's suffrage, a pacifist, a Labour Party member and Quaker who also served on the general Committee of the Fellowship of Reconciliation from 1915–22. In the course of her life she wrote sixty books and many stories. They were simple stories,

Theodora Wilson Wilson

directed at casual readers and she was thus able to make a unique contribution to FoR propaganda. She was the author of *The Last Weapon: a Vision*, which set out the FoR view with regards war. 18,000 copies were seized on the basis that it was dangerous and subversive. She did not wish it to demonise the enemy but urged readers to look for positive deeds, and not words, to lead to the Kingdom of God.

The *Pioneer* reported that Miss Wilson Wilson visited Jerusalem Church on 6 December, 1917 where she described the raid which had been made, on the premises of *The Christian Peace Crusader*, edited by a conscientious objector called Wilfred Wellock, from Nelson, before he was imprisoned. Theodora was editor until 1919. She said two large wagons were needed to carry away 'the pernicious literature'[77] and told how her private flat was also ransacked and money was taken. This particular peace meeting at Jerusalem was said to be *magnificent* and the best attended of the series. *'Christ was not behind the British guns nor the German guns, but stood between them'*. As an NCF member she was appointed to a caretaker committee to carry on the NCF's work after its dissolution. She joined with James Maxton, John Langdon-Davies and others on the Committee to Oppose Military Training in Schools. In 1921 she helped establish the *No More War* movement.

---

[77] It is important to remember that the Defence of the Realm Act insisted that every leaflet dealing with war or advocating peace should bear the names and addresses of its author and printer showing that it had passed the inspection of the Official Press Bureau.

THE CONTRIBUTION OF WOMEN TO PEACE AND UNIVERSAL SUFFRAGE

The contribution of the women who visited Briton Ferry in the interests of such causes resulted from the evolution of complicated events and interests rather than any deliberately planned strategy. It is nevertheless possible to explain something of the connections between the events and those involved. Some, such as Sybil Thorndike, had specific and limited interests whilst others, Despard and Royden for instance, pursued a wider range of concerns. The broad spectrum of interests included military and industrial conscription, peace, pacifism, socialism and universal suffrage.

Consideration of each individual's interests shown in the table of organisations below indicates the extent to which they overlapped and were mutually sustaining, or how interests sometimes conflicted. As examples we see how Despard's goals were to achieve suffrage and peace through sexual equality and socialism. Goldman was committed to freedom of expression, sexual freedom, birth control, equality and independence for women, radical education, union organisation and workers' rights. Glasier, by becoming a woman founder of the ILP, asserted women's rights through socialism. Pallister was a socialist who stood against military conscription and for the rights of mothers and children.

Emmeline and Christabel Pankhurst moved from viewing socialism as the vehicle to achieve women's suffrage to supporting war and female industrial conscription as the way to achieve it. Sylvia and Adela Pankhurst saw the way to the achievement of women's suffrage being through socialism. Royden covered the full gamut of interests, being anti-military conscription through her support for the NCF; internationalism through the FoR and women's suffrage through NUWSS. Snowden was an early Pacifist and advocate of women's suffrage and her membership of the Women's Peace Crusade combined both pacifism and women's suffrage. She occupied the opposite end of the spectrum from Emmeline and Christabel Pankhurst. Swanwick's interests were much wider in civil liberties in general and democratic control for peace. Thorndike's agenda was straightforward: support for peace. Wilson opposed censorship.

Collectively their activities had a lasting effect on both universal suffrage and how the people were represented. For example, in 1918, after the Parliament (Qualification of Women) Act enabled the Countess de Markievicz to become the first woman to be returned to the House of Commons, fewer than 1% of MPs were women. After the 2015 general election, the figure stood at approximately 30% of the 650 MPs.

	ILP	NCF	PPU	NCCL	NUWSS	UDC	WFL	WPC	WPSU	FoR
Despard	•				•		•	•	•	
Glasier	•									
Goldman		•		•						
Pallister	•									
Pankhurst A									•	
Pankhurst C									•	
Pankhurst E									•	
Pankhurst S									•	
Royden		•			•		•			
Snowden	•							•		
Swanwick				•	•	•				
Thorndike		•	•							
Wilson	•									•

Chapter Seven
So what?

'The notion that Second World War was finer and nobler than the first is highly dubious.' (G. Wheatcroft)

Now is the time to ask ourselves whether the objectors were right to resist, and if so should there be an apology for their physical mistreatment and injustices suffered. It is also time to ask whether their resistance has implications for today's world? At the beginning of this book the question was asked whether the opposition to war in Briton Ferry led to a lasting 'community consciousness' going beyond pacifism? Was there a radical philosophical thread in the town which stood for human rights across the board? To what extent was the town a place which advocated women's and universal suffrage, equality of opportunity, justice, freedom of expression, racial and religious toleration and world peace? Was Briton Ferry aberrant in its tolerance of the war resisters?

Politics

It has become clear that Briton Ferry's cohort of objectors was a combination of religious and political war resisters, which mainly expressed its dissent through an alliance of the ILP, the NCF and the chapels. The strength of this cohort's wartime support through the ILP was still very evident in the 1919 municipal elections. The first two successful candidates were ILP with the Discharged Soldiers and Sailors candidates making up the rear in the polls, after local industrialist, M. G. Roberts.

Despite the well-recognised fact that the political and religious motivations for resisting war were not always separable, it is still possible to distinguish various threads of interest within the general dissent. That these interests continued after the war was over is clear from the themes of lectures and general preoccupations of the town's eminent visitors.

Universal suffrage

During the first decade of the 20th century visits from such as Emmeline Pankhurst, Keir Hardie and Ethel Snowden demonstrated the townspeople's interests in women's and universal suffrage.

Freedom of expression

The issue of freedom of expression came later, in 1916, as a result of the Defence of the Realm Act. The subjects covered by speakers such as Gilbert Cannan, Tom Mann, Dick Wallhead, Theodora Wilson-Wilson and Bertrand Russell exemplify the town's interest in, and fight for, freedom of expression and in particular their support for the cause of the 'Briton Ferry Ten' and the 'Waters/Davies' case.

Racial tolerance, anti-colonialism and imperialism

Another interest within this political-religious cohort was the desire for racial tolerance, emanating indirectly from the visit of Bipin Chandra Pal and the later work of E. D. Morel to combat exploitation in the European colonies. The town's resisters, like Dil Thomas, followed Brockway and Sorensen's interest in the lives of Gandhi and Nehru. The much later visits of C. L. R. James, Paul Robeson and George Padmore was a further manifestation of this position; one that showed that the town had a vision which was more positive than anti-war and much more international than anyone would expect from a small Welsh town.

Welsh nationalism

During World War One Welsh nationalism was not an issue in Briton Ferry, despite the fact that bilingualism was still reasonably strong; but elsewhere, for the first time ever, George Lloyd of Wrexham and Robert J. Evans of Brymbo, were prosecuted for their refusal to join the armed forces on the grounds of their Welsh nationalist beliefs.

World peace

The fact that the town attracted such formidable names as Norman Angell, E. D. Morel, Charles Trevelyan and Herbert Dunnico during the war period was an indication that sections of the populace were, through their visitors' ideas, also considering the implications of the post-war settlement for world peace. This interest maintained for another half a century.

Should Briton Ferry apologise for its treatment of COs?

The question has been raised whether Briton Ferry's religious organisations should apologise for its attitude to conscientious objectors, who sometimes suffered harrowing and brutal treatment by refusing to go to war. At its AGM in Bridgend, in June 2014, the Union of Welsh Independent Churches, which represents four hundred and thirty Welsh churches and chapels, apologised for its role in backing World War One recruitment. 'There are contemporary accounts in the newspapers of full chapels being addressed by politicians and by ministers encouraging people to go out and fight', reported Cemlyn Davies of BBC Wales. Gavin Matthews of Swansea University has referred to Lloyd George's friend, the Rev. John Williams of Brynsiencyn, who portrayed the war as one to protect the rights of small nations and 'accepted the honorary rank of Colonel and began preaching sermons in uniform from the pulpits of Wales'.

Matthews went further, saying that Welsh chapels responded to the war in very different ways.

> 'Two Baptist chapels in Briton Ferry illustrate the point. One, Rehoboth, preached the message of a just war, and has ninety-nine names on its roll of honour. Another, Jerusalem, just down the road, was known by its detractors as the "Kaiser's Temple", being strongly anti-war: it hosted anti-conscription meetings. There was a plurality of attitudes to the war, in other words.'

But do the two Baptist chapels in Briton Ferry illustrate the point? They only do so partly. There was also plurality of attitudes *within* them. Jerusalem had members who enlisted and Rehoboth possibly had members who objected. The records held by the NCF and the Pearce Register do not differentiate between the two denominations, English and Welsh.

Matthews' ninety nine names were those from Rehoboth who served, not the number killed.The town lost 120 killed. The town also had thirty three known conscientious objectors, many of whom were Baptists of both English and Welsh varieties. There is as much evidence for Jerusalem's 'anti-war' position as there is of Rehoboth's 'just war' stance, but it is undeniable that Rehoboth lost twelve of its members in military service.

The Rev Rees Powell, minister of Jerusalem Church, seems to have been made of better stuff than the aforementioned Rev John Williams. But Powell was exceptional, too, both within Briton Ferry and more generally. The stance of the present Church in Wales, and in Briton Ferry particularly, may still be considered to have an apology to make. In a secular age it is easy to underestimate the social and moral role and influence of the churches and chapels at the time of the First World War. One assumes that influence was always intended to be good and, by today's standards, sometimes it was not. However, for some of the town's twenty chapels and churches, with Jerusalem as the outstanding example, the mass 2014 apology was unnecessary.

Was Briton Ferry aberrant?

As a result of Cyril Pearce's work, *Comrades in Conscience*, Huddersfield's experience in the Great War could have been regarded as eccentric and untypical of other communities, because the community was tolerant of opposition to war. In terms of population, Briton Ferry was twelve times smaller than Huddersfield and had a smaller range of religious and political organisations. Both towns were predominantly nonconformist, with Briton Ferry having four times more places of worship per head. Some disruption of meetings was experienced in both towns, but these were minor incidents when compared with the large number of events held. Pearce showed that Huddersfield's resistance was not from isolated individuals, but was from the whole community. Nor was Briton Ferry's resistance eccentric and merely from individuals. The coherence of support resulted from objectors' affiliations, which were almost exclusively with the NCF. In this comparison of two communities, I feel that the most striking statistic emerging is that, as a proportion of the population eligible for conscription, there were four times the number of conscientious objectors in Briton Ferry than in Huddersfield. In summary, as a result of this additional, local, study of Briton Ferry, the question that must now be asked is: what will be discovered about the degree of resistance and the amount of tolerance for the war resisters when further local studies are carried out?

Between the wars

In Briton Ferry the educational events associated with pacifism, politics and religion continued, even if on a reduced scale after the war. The election results for Briton Ferry in April, 1919, perhaps provided the townspeople's judgement on the war.[78] The two anti-conscription Labour candidates topped the poll and were elected. So, too were a Conservative candidate, M. G. Roberts, and John Hayes, representing the Discharged Soldiers and Sailors. James Thomas, an Independent and Chair of Briton Ferry's military service tribunal was not elected, nor was L. Watts, the Liberal.

On a bigger picture, the Welsh Council of the League of Nations was established in 1922 with substantial financial support of David Davies, Llandinam, the industrialist and philanthropist. The aim of the League was to secure co-operation between the nations of the world. In 1937 the Welsh National Pacifist Society was established with G. M. Ll. Davies as president (a World War One objector) and Gwynfor Evans (a World War Two objector and Plaid Cymru founder) as secretary.

[78] G. Gethin (Labour) 1329; D. L. Mort (Labour) 1123; M. G. Roberts (Conservative) 803; John Hayes (D. S. & S.) 762; James Thomas (Independent) 716; L. Watts (Liberal) 393

World War Two and afterwards

Briton Ferry's tradition of conscientious objection continued into World War Two, with Steel Thomas, Bill Thomas, Ramsay Thomas, Ewart Adams and Vernon Martin being among the objectors. On this wider front 2,920 conscientious objectors were recorded in Wales during the Second World War, four times the estimated number for World War One. On 10 December 1948 the General Assembly of the United Nations adopted and proclaimed the Universal Declaration of Human Rights. The European Convention, which became one of the great legal instruments of the 20th century, holding forty-seven European governments to account, including our own, through the 1998 Human Rights Act is now threatened with an inferior replacement. The rights and protections offered to individuals against governmental excesses, including freedom of expression, fair trials and prohibition of torture are now endangered.[79]

The twenty-first century

Today many organisations are commemorating the centenary of World War One by holding events of different kinds. Schools are among the organisations doing this. Their commemoration activities will take many different forms so it is worth considering what some of them are doing.

As part of the *Wales Remembers 1914–1918* project, fourteen pupils from years 7 to 10 at Cwrt Sart Community Comprehensive School in Briton Ferry were due to research the county archive in Swansea, to find out the impact and effects (of the war) on local people and report back to the rest of the pupils. They were also to research the records of the 72 Briton Ferry men awarded honours during World War One and also the 1911 census to create a context.

---

[79] The Human Rights Act is embedded in the devolution arrangements for Scotland and Wales and in Northern Ireland's law through the Good Friday agreement. (Michael Sands, QC)

Research may also have included working with the local war memorial committee as well as local residents. The aim was to produce a database, blog, resources for associated primary school for use in transition work and a school mural. This was in order to help pupils to gain greater understanding of the impact of the war. Dyffryn Comprehensive School in Port Talbot and Llangatwg Community School in Neath, along with a dozen other Welsh schools were planning to do similar work.

At this point we must return to Matthews who points out that

> 'In England, money is given to schools to take children to visit the World War One battlefields. In Wales, there are initiatives to encourage children to find out about the men who joined up, and how their communities were affected by their going. That's quite a different emphasis.'

Whilst he is right to point out that World War One remembrance is devolved, he is wrong to claim 'that remembrance is more a matter of community in Wales than it is elsewhere in Britain'. Has he forgotten that Scotland is in Britain, and is also devolved? Has he forgotten that England is geographically closer to France than Wales or Scotland and it is, therefore more likely that its schools will visit the battlefields ?

Scotland's *Experiences of War* Project, described below, uses a more balanced community methodology for commemoration which includes a study of opposition to the war. The National Library of Scotland has produced a Higher History resource for schools in the form of a case study called *Conscientious Objectors in the First World War*. It was aimed at supporting the study of the domestic impact of war, society and culture through critical thinking and research skills using archive resources.

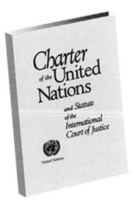

Matthews also believes that, while many historians have focused on the stories of Welsh conscientious objectors, for him, this is 'more than their numbers warrant'. Yet, in 2011, the case of the sixteen Richmond conscientious objectors from World War One came up in evidence before the European Court of Human Rights,[80] which led Boulton to comment:

> 'In retrospect the most enduring achievement of World War One war resisters of all nations was that they, more than any other group, may be said to have kick-started the movement for international recognition not only for the rights of conscience but, as a logical sequence the wider field of human rights.'

Is Matthews really suggesting that the quality of an argument is less important than the numbers involved in it?

Press freedom and freedom of expression

The UN Declaration states: 'Everyone has the right to freedom of opinion and expression, this right includes freedom to hold opinions without interference and impart information and ideas through any media regardless of frontiers'.

In 1985 the British Government tried to stop the publication of MI5 Officer Peter Wright's publication of *Spycatcher*. More recently privacy injunctions have been used by people like the BBC's Andrew Marr and footballer Ryan Giggs to stop the publication of personal information. The manner by which information has been obtained, by phone hacking and the paparazzi for example, is another story in itself. Nevertheless, in 2013 the Guardian newspaper was subjected to *prior restraint* and property destruction by GCHQ of documents relating to PRISM,[81] the US National Security Agency and Edward Snowden.

On 12 December 2014 the chief constable of Greater Manchester, Sir Peter Fahy, expressed concern about the need for 'academics

---

[80] In the judgement in *Bayatyon v Armenia*.

[81] PRISM is a clandestine global data surveillance programme under which the USA's National Security Agency (NSA) collects internet communications of foreign nationals from major US internet companies such as Google. Its existence was leaked by NSA contractor Edward Snowden who warned that data collection was far greater than the public knew.

(regarding extremist speakers on campuses) and civil society to decide where the balance line fell between free speech and extremism. If these issues are left to securocrats then there is a danger of a drift to a police state . . . the securocrat says we do not want to be in the space of policing thought or the police defining what is extremism.'

Not a lot different, perhaps, from *The Early Conscientious Objector: a story for Easter 1916* and the *Everett* circulars, for which Joe Branch and nine others, including my grandfather, were charged with contraventions of the Defence of the Realm Act for distributing the two pamphlets in Briton Ferry.

Were Briton Ferry's conscientious objectors right? *Good* wars and *bad* wars?

Geoffrey Wheatcroft of the *Guardian* compared the general view of World War One and World War Two *(9 December 2014)*: 'In crude terms we have come to think of them as the Bad War and the Good War.' He brushed aside the validity of this concept by pointing out that the significant difference between them was in the nature of the casualties: in World War One most of the 18 million or so who died were uniformed, whereas in World War Two, of 70 million who died, 50 million were civilians.

He continued by arguing that . . . 'the notion that the Second World War was finer and nobler than the first is highly dubious in itself since it sanitises so much, such as the slaughter of civilians by allied bombing. As a consequence . . . it has led us to an easier acceptance of liberal interventionism based on the assumption that we in the west are alone virtuous and able to distinguish political right from wrong.' Some historians now see the 1941–45 era as a time of two wars, both of which were straight imperialist conflicts of the old World War One pattern. Neither had noble motivations: Germany and Russia were effectively in a land war for mastery of east Europe, and the USA and Japan were engaged in a sea war for mastery of the western Pacific.

In the 1914–18 war, twenty-two sitting MPs were killed in action and eighty five sons of MPs, including those of Asquith and Bonar

Law were lost. Some were volunteers and others were conscripts. Finally, Wheatcroft points out that in the 2003 Iraq War, 'no minister or journalist would dream of volunteering. The days are gone when our politicians were prepared to die in the wars which they had begun.'

Ken Donovan expressed regret, when writing of Briton Ferry[82] that such events as these, as the author has described, and which are very much an intrinsic part of the town's history and culture, may have been lost. That is nearly, but happily not entirely, so. Whether simply through the erosions of time, accident, or deliberate suppression, what is recorded here is all but absent from the accepted historical narrative. Hence, the bravery of my three great uncles, who probably died in vain, no more than matches that of my father, my uncle and many of their neighbours and friends, who resisted the propaganda and sheep-like orthodoxy and thought it out for themselves. That all that bravery and richness needs discovery, recovery and proper recording, is my motivation and reason for researching and writing this.

---

[82] In Praise of a Much Loved Community (2014)

Appendix One
Timeline of key dates affecting conscription

Date	Event
1914	
4 August	Outbreak of World War One
September	Friends Ambulance Unit (FAU) set up in France
November	The No-Conscription Fellowship established
1915	
August	Compulsory registration of men and women up to age 65 (Derby reviewed the census)
September	Results of census showed that almost five million men of military age were not in the forces
11 October	Introduction of the Derby Scheme – men were given the chance to enlist voluntarily or to 'attest' with an obligation to come if called up later on
November	First National Convention of the No-Conscription Fellowship
1916	
2 March	Compulsory conscription in Britain for all single men and childless widowers aged 18–41 years (Military Service Act 1916)
March	Creation of Non-Combatant Corps (NCC)
June	Compulsory conscription extended to all married men aged 18–41 years
August	Introduction of Home Office Scheme – work camps
1918	
November	Armistice signed; recruiting under the Military Service Act suspended
1919	
August	The last conscientious objector (CO) released from prison
November	Final Convention of the No-Conscription Fellowship held; NCF disbanded
1920	
January	Last of the men demobilised from the NCC
1921	Majority of tribunal records destroyed

Appendix Two
Abbreviations

ASE	Amalgamated Society of Engineers
CO	Conscientious objector
CND	Campaign for nuclear disarmament
CPGB	Communist Party of Great Britain
DoRA	Defence of the Realm Act
FAU	Friends' Ambulance Unit
FoR	Fellowship of Reconciliation
ILP	Independent Labour Party
ITF	International Transport Federation
NCAC	National Council against Conscription
NCCL	National Council for Civil Liberties
NCF	No Conscription Fellowship
NUR	National Union of Railwaymen
NUWSS	National Union of Women's Suffrage
MSA	Military Service Act
NATO	North Atlantic Treaty Organisation
PPU	Peace Pledge Union
SDF	Social Democratic Federation
TUC	Trades Union Congress
UDC	Union of Democratic Control
WEA	Workers' Educational Association
WFL	Women's Freedom League
WPC	Women's Peace Crusade
WSPU	Women's Social and Political Union

Appendix Three
Reasons for exclusion from military service by a Tribunal

Category	Reason for application being accepted
A	On the grounds that it is expedient in the national interests that the man should, instead of being employed in military service, be engaged in other work in which he is habitually engaged.
B	On the grounds that it is expedient in the national interests that the man should, instead of being employed in military service, be engaged in other work in which he wishes to be engaged.
C	If he is being educated or trained for any work, on the ground that it is expedient in the national interests that, instead of being employed in military service, he should continue to be so educated or trained
D	On the ground that serious hardship would ensure if the man were called up for Army service, owing to his exceptional financial or business obligations or domestic position.
E	On the ground of ill-health or infirmity.
F	On the ground of a conscientious objection to the undertaking of combatant service.
G	On the ground that the principal and usual occupation of the man is one of those included in the list of occupations certified by Government Departments for exemption.

Appendix Four
John Wellington's tribunal at Port Talbot

We can gain the flavour of tribunal proceedings from John Wellington's application for exemption from military service on religious grounds.

When asked if he would undertake non-combatant service by the President and Mayor, Mr Percy Jacobs, he said: 'Noncombatant service is part of the military machine. I am prepared to do anything to bring the war to an end. I am fighting for these aims now in the church.'

The Chairman: 'Is there anything you can suggest to bring this about?'

Appellant: 'I want you to respond to the dictates of my conscience. I feel that I cannot kill on any account I am serving the Christ who stood alone in the garden of Gethsemane. To take life I cannot.'

The Chairman: 'I quite appreciate your views; but we have an unpleasant duty to perform. I would rather any job in the world than to judge between consciences.'

Wellington was recommended for non-combatant service. He refused this as an unacceptable type of exemption and was referred to the Glamorgan Appeal Tribunal. Mr F. W. Gibbins of Neath presided, with Lieutenant Buchanan as Military Representative. He again rejected the recommendation. This meant he was deemed to be enlisted and liable to prosecution for desertion. The next step was police arrest and escort to the recruiting office and police station prior to charges being put at Port Talbot Magistrates' Court on 23 May. He was fined forty shillings, regarded as a deserter and awaited an escort.

He was transferred to Kinmel Camp and, following further refusal to wear a uniform, was sentenced to two years' hard labour at a Court-Martial on 20th June.

He lodged an appeal to the Central Tribunal.

Appendix Five
The appeal tribunal [83]

[83] Ref: Cymru 1914 newspaper/4001351/0/ART5: *Pioneer* Saturday 27 May 1914

Appendix Six
The final appeal at the Central Tribunal

Central Tribunal
Queen Anne's Chambers
Westminster SW

2nd May 1916

Local Tribunal

Subject: Appeal re...............

Sir

I am desired by the Central Tribunal to state that before deciding this appeal from the decision of the Appeal Tribunal for Glamorgan......they will be prepared to consider any further representations you may wish to make, provided they are submitted in writing within five days of the date of this letter.

The Appeal Tribunal state:
The man desired to have absolute exemption. He said non-combatant service would not meet his wishes and refused the same. He said he could not do anything connected with war of any kind. He referred to the Local government Board's circular of 23 March 1916.
The Appeal Tribunal, having had the appellant before, them exempted him from combatant service only, as they thought that the exemption would meet his case. This was also the decision of the local Tribunal.
The appellant's version of the Tribunal's opinion as to their powers is not correct.
The Central Tribunal will be glad to receive replies to the questions on the annexed schedule.

Yours faithfully

(Signed) J. W. Rending
for Central Tribunal

Appendix Seven
Tribunal outcomes

1. Exempt from all military service
   a) Absolutely conditionally or temporary
   b) From combatant service only: conditional on being engaged in work of national importance

2. Exempt from combatant service only
   a) Service in the non-combatant corps
   b) Refusal to serve and court-martial

3. Refused exemption by the tribunal

4. Others
   a) Conditional exemption by the Army Council
   b) Did not apply for exemption on grounds of conscientious objection
   c) Miscellaneous

Appendix Eight
Definitions and tribunal jargon

From the *Concise Oxford English Dictionary* etc

Pacifism	The doctrine that the abolition of war or violence is desirable and possible; the support of arbitration in international disputes
Militarism	The prevalence of military spirit or ideals as a valid policy for foreign affairs; undue influence of the generals on government
Conscientious objector	One who for reasons of conscience objects to military service, etc
The Cat and Mouse Act	The proper name for this 1913 Act of Parliament was the Prisoners (Temporary Discharge for Ill-Health) Act. When a suffragette (or, later, a conscientious objector) was sent to prison, it was assumed that she or he might go on hunger strike to cause problems for the authorities. The Act let prisoners get weaker until they had to be released from prison. On release they were unlikely to protest until they regained their strength. At that point they would be re-arrested and the cycle might start all over again.
Army Order X and Home Office Scheme	Army order X of 25 May 1917 enabled COs to be sent to the nearest public civil prison and have their case reviewed by (HOS) the Brace Committee, and if genuine, would be released from military prison to do work of national importance in a civil prison or work camp under the Home Office Scheme. The order was not retroactive and this left hundreds of objectors in military prisons or guardrooms.
Brace Committee	Brace was an Under-secretary at the Home Office whose Committee on the Employment of Conscientious Objectors ran the Scheme. It created Work Centres throughout the country in under-used prisons or as countryside work camps. It was aimed at avoiding the brutality that COs had experienced from the army or prison. Those who took part are sometimes known as schemers, but were paid by the police and many regarded themselves as political prisoners. The Schemers and the Absolutists bore the brunt of the persecution.

Reserve Class W	The Schemers moved from the army to the HOS by being transferred to Army Reserve Class W. The Home Office Scheme was civilian controlled and the men were paid by the police The NCF said that this meant COs so classified were still part of the military machine and liable to recall. COs were based in used prisons, asylums and workhouses and worked outdoors or indoors depending on the location. Typical outdoor work was timber cutting, road making; drain-laying; rail maintenance and agriculture. Indoor work was often mailbag fabrication; brush and basket making and rope-making.
Pelham Committee and Work of National Importance	A Board of Trade appointed committee whose purpose was to advise Military Service Tribunals on the types of work that were alternative to military service but were of national importance. Such work included agriculture, forestry, food supply, shipping, transport, mining, education and public utility services. As a result, in Huddersfield, for example, two thirds of COs stayed where they were to do this work and did not go to prison or work camps. This situation does not seem to have been the case at Briton Ferry, however.
Alternativists	Alternativists were those who were prepared to accept work of national importance which was clearly non-military to them. For example the FAU or FSC. The ILP and the NCF did not discourage acceptance of this.
Absolutist	The Military Service Act allowed for absolute exemption but tribunals were reluctant to grant absolute exemption from military service for reasons of conscience. It is not absolute exemption that made one an absolutist but one's absolute refusal to support the war effort directly or indirectly. Usually this was on religious grounds (such as Christadelphians or Quakers) or political grounds (such as Marxists). In fact most objectors to conscription received absolute exemption for reasons other than conscience, such as ill-health. Some conscientious objectors who suffered ill health were exempted for health reasons rather than conscience.
Non-combatant corps	The corps was formed in March, 1916, and existed until January, 1920. It was an army unit for COs and subject to military discipline. Its members would not be required to fight or take life. The NCF and the Quakers repudiated this compromise arrangement, considering it to be part of the military machine.
FAU	The Friends Ambulance Unit (FAU) was set up in France in September 1914 by a group of young Quakers; most of its 1200 members were pacifists.

Appendix Nine
Bill Gregory's story

W. H. (Bill) Gregory was a barber on Neath Road, Briton Ferry, who recalled his political memories to Hywel Francis and Richard Lewis of Swansea University. Bill Gregory studied with the WEA (Workers' Educational Association) and later became Head of Extra Mural Studies at Cardiff University.

Francis, Hywel: Were you still in the barber's shop then?

Lewis, Richard: Still working in the barber's shop, the other educational influence of tremendous importance to me, apart from the library in the town, was the fact that my uncle who ran the barber's shop was a member of the ILP and the barber's shop really was like a political centre. And it made a tremendous impact on me, the kind of politics that the WEA represented because during the war years, a large number of people from Briton Ferry went into the CO movement. And I believe I don't know whether my figure is right, I've heard it said that ninety people were in jail at one time. This may be an exaggeration, but a large number of chaps from Briton Ferry went to jail and in the barber's shop of course, when they were on the run, they would come there some times and have a haircut before the shop opened. On one occasion for example, when a chap by the name of Tom Thomas, Tommy Tupp'any he was known as in Briton Ferry, was on the run, his brother came to my uncle and asked him if he could cut his hair one morning, say, about quarter to nine before the shop opened. And I remember my uncle pulling the window of the barber's shop half way down, taking the tools off the table and putting the table close to the window on a chair, so that if Sergeant Williams came in, Tom could make a dash for it through the window. It didn't come to that but that was the atmosphere. Then people used to come into Briton Ferry to lecture and it was a common thing for the little boys then to go on a Sunday night after the chapel was over to go then up to the Public Hall to listen to the speeches. What they were listening to of course was the heckling and the struggle that went on when men were shouting at each other and so on. But the very best talent used to come there. The first political speaker I ever heard, for example, was Keir Hardie. He came there, I think it was 1913. Then when war was declared, or it could have been 1914, just after war was declared. Then when the war was on say a year or two years, then people used to drift in and they went and stayed with people like George Gethin and Jo Branch who were the local leaders of the Labour Party.

Lewis, Richard: The kind of people that used to come down, I was thinking of one man's name, Professor {Northcote} from Liverpool University.[84] He had lost his job there because of his attitude towards the war. He came down and spent quite a long time with us, giving lectures in the local Liberty Hall on the life of the bee taking us up the mountain with Harry Davies, Cwm Afan, the Miners' leader, to study the local geology, and as a little boy I used to go with them. Then we used to go into the Crown Park in the afternoons, on Sunday afternoons, and listen to the local speakers coming there. These men like Walter Newbold used to come down.

Francis, Hywel: These classes, these lectures, were they organised by the ILP or . . . ?

Lewis, Richard: These classes were organised by the ILP, but it's part of the atmosphere into which adult education fits. By the time the extramural department in Swansea was formed somewhere between 1920 and 1924, there was already a very large educational influence at work in the form of this political influence. And it wasn't just straight forward propaganda. Due to the accident of War all sorts of highly educated people moved through the area. You know you would be listening in the barber's shop when I was a boy, I'd be listening in the barber's shop to tremendous arguments over our attitude and the attitude of the Germans toward North Africa, for example, when the British fleet or the German fleet threatened to go to [Agadir] wasn't it, in 1912. This type of thing was continually being fought over and as a little boy I'd be listening to all this, and I suppose gathering something on the way.

---

[84] The *Pioneer*, 19 May 1917, reported that Professor Henry F Northcote, FLS, visited under the ILP's auspices. The topic he addressed was astronomy, but the ILP group also visited a local Roman encampment

Appendix Ten
Prisons and work centres

The places listed were used for Absolutist and Home Office Scheme Conscientious objectors. Briton Ferry men were definitely held in those in **bold** print and may have been held in others, whether or not they are listed here.

Aberdeen, Dyce; Aldershot;
Ballachulish; Bedford – Howbury; Birmingham – Winson Green; **Blackdown**; Brandon, Suffolk; Brockenhurst; Broxburn;
Caernarvon; **Cardiff**; Carlisle; **Carmarthen**; Red Roses; Canterbury; Chelsea: Clipstone, **Crai**.
Dartford; **Dartmoor, Princetown**; Denton; Ditton Priors; Dublin, Mountjoy;
East Harling, Norfolk; Exeter;
Glasgow, Barlinnie; Glasgow, Calton; Garboldisham, Norfolk; Gloucester; Grimsby;
Haverhill, Keddington; Hereford; Hornchurch; Hull;
Inverness; Ipswich;
Knutsford;
Leeds; Leicester; Lincoln; Llanddeusant; Llanon; Loch Awe; Lyme Regis; Lyndhurst;
Maidstone; Maxton;
Newcastle; Newhaven
Parkhurst Camp – Salisbury Plain; **Pembroke Dock**; **Penderyn**; **Pentonville**; Plymouth, Mutley; Preston;
Rathdrum, Co Wicklow; Rhinefields; **Rhyl, Kinmel**; Richmond; Rugeley;
Salisbury; Santon-Downham, Suffolk; Parkhurst; Seaford; Shrewsbury; Sunk Island; Strangeways; Sutton; Swansea;
Talgarth; Tumble; Usk;
Wakefield; Walton; Warwick; **Wandsworth**; Weston-super-Mare; Winchester; **Wormwood Scrubs**; Wrexham – Park Hall.

Appendix Eleven
Dietary for male convicts

DIETARY FOR MALE CONVICTS IN CONVICT PRISONS.

MEALS.	DIET C. For MALE Convicts undergoing separate confinement.	DIET D. For MALE Convicts after period of separate confinement when engaged in ordinary Industrial Employment. Convicts engaged on certain Forms of Industrial Employment may, on the recommendation of the Medical Officer, receive in addition ½ oz. of butter or margarine daily for breakfast and 2 oz. cheese on Wednesday and Friday for supper.	DIET E. For MALE Convicts after period of separate confinement when employed at specially prescribed forms of Labour.
Breakfast..	Daily:— Bread .... 8 oz. Porridge .... 1 pint	Daily:— Bread .... 8 oz. Gruel, sweetened with ½ oz. sugar ...... 1 pint	Daily:— Bread .... 8 oz. Butter or Margarine§ ½ „ Porridge .... 1 pint
Dinner..	Sunday:— Bread .... 6 oz. Potatoes .... 12 „ Cooked meat preserved by heat ...... } 5 „ Monday:— Bread .... 6 oz. Potatoes .... 12 „ Beans .... 12 „ Fat Bacon.......... 2 „ Tuesday:— Bread .... 6 oz. Potatoes .... 12 „ Soup .... 1 pint Wednesday:— Bread .... 6 oz. Potatoes .... 12 „ Suet Pudding ...... 12 „ Thursday:— Bread .... 6 oz. Potatoes .... 12 „ Cooked Beef, without bone .... } 5 „ Friday:— Bread .... 6 oz. Potatoes .... 12 „ Soup .... 1 pint Saturday:— Bread .... 6 oz. Potatoes .... 12 „ Suet Pudding ...... 12 „	Sunday:— Bread .... 8 oz. Potatoes .... 12 „ Cooked meat preserved by heat ...... } 5 „ Monday:— Bread .... 8 oz. Potatoes .... 12 „ Beans .... 12 „ Fat Bacon.......... 2 „ Tuesday:— Bread .... 8 oz. Potatoes .... 12 „ Cooked Mutton, without bone } 5 „ Wednesday:— Bread .... 8 oz. Potatoes .... 12 „ Pea Soup (Pork).... 1 pint Thursday:— Bread .... 8 oz. Potatoes .... 12 „ Cooked Beef, without bone .... } 5 „ Friday:— Bread .... 8 oz. Potatoes .... 12 „ Vegetable Soup (Beef) 1 pint Saturday:— Bread .... 8 oz. Potatoes .... 12 „ Suet Pudding ...... 12 „	Sunday:— Bread .... 8 oz. Potatoes .... 16 „ Cooked meat preserved by heat ...... } 6 „ Monday:— Bread .... 8 oz. Potatoes .... 16 „ Beans .... 12 „ Fat Bacon.......... 2 „ Tuesday:— Bread .... 8 oz. Potatoes .... 16 „ Cooked Mutton, without bone } 6 „ Wednesday:— Bread .... 8 oz. Potatoes .... 16 „ Pea Soup (Pork).... 1 pint Thursday:— Bread .... 8 oz. Potatoes .... 16 „ Cooked Beef, without bone ...... } 6 „ Friday:— Bread .... 8 oz. Potatoes .... 16 „ Vegetable Soup (Beef) 1 pint Saturday:— Bread .... 8 oz. Potatoes .... 16 „ Suet Pudding ...... 16 „
Supper....	Daily:— Bread .... 8 oz. Cocoa .... 1 pint	Daily:— Bread .... 8 oz. Cocoa.............. 1 pint	Daily:— Bread .... 12 oz. Cocoa.............. 1 pint Wednesday and Friday:— Cheese .... 2 oz.

A convict on attaining the third stage may have one pint of tea and 2 oz. additional bread in lieu of gruel or porridge for breakfast.

§ Butter or margarine to be given for six months in the year, October to March (inclusive). During the remaining months, April to September (inclusive), milk, ¼ pint for each convict, to be substituted for butter or margarine, and to be given in the form of milk porridge.

(Carys Lewis: London School of Economics:
Swords into Ploughshares Project)

Appendix Twelve
Bibliography

Author	Year	Title	Publisher
Adams, Philip	2014	A Most Industrious Town: Briton Ferry and its people 1814-2014	Ludlow: Philip Adams
Boulton, David	2014	Objection overruled	Friends Historical Society
Davies, David, J. P.	1870	Rhyd-y-Brython: History of Briton Ferry	Port Talbot: N. Harris.
Cleaver, D.	1984	Conscientious objection in the Swansea area	Glamorgan History Society
Ellsworth-Jones, Will	2013	We will not Fight: the Untold Story of World War One's Conscientious Objectors	Aurum
FoR, Pax Christi, PPU et al	2013	FoR, Pax Christi, PPU et al	FoR, Pax Christi, PPU et al
Griffin, Nicholas	2001	Selected letters of Bertrand Russell – the Public Years 1914–1970	Routledge
Griffiths, Robert H.	2014	The Story of Kinmel Park Military Training Camp 1914–1918	Pwllheli: Llygad Gwalch
Hansen, J. Ivor	1968	Portrait of a Welsh Town	MacDonald
Jerusalem Baptist Church	1959	Jerusalem English Baptist Church, 1859–1959: The Story of 100 years	Briton Ferry: Jerusalem Baptist Church,
Jerusalem Baptist Church	1937	Centenary of the Baptist Cause in Briton Ferry 1837-1937	Briton Ferry: Jerusalem Baptist Church
John, Ken	1986	Sam Mainwaring and the autonomist tradition	Llafur, Aberystwyth
Matthews, Gethin	2014	The Sacred Cause of Liberty and Freedom (*How the Great War was viewed in Wales*)	Planet, Aberystwyth
O'Brien, Anthony Mor	1987	Conchie: Emrys Hughes and the First World War	National Library of Wales, Aberystwyth

Author	Year	Title	Publisher
Morgan, Kevin	2008	Emma Goldman in south Wales	Llafur, Swansea
Pearce, Cyril	2014	Comrades in Conscience	Francis Boutle, London
Rees, Dylan	1987	Morgan Jones, Educationalist and Labour Politician	National Library of Wales, Aberystwyth
Taylor, A. J. P.	1965	English History 1914–1945	Oxford University Press
Williams, Leonard	1977	Emma Goldman – Associations with Neath	Neath Antiquarian Society

Appendix Thirteen
Chronology of visits to Briton Ferry and matters covered

The numbers in brackets indicate the running total of each persons visits.

Date	Speaker	Subject	Venue/notes
1903			
July 11	Keir Hardie (1)	*On Religion*	Villiers Recreation Ground
1905			
	Keir Hardie (2)		
November 11	Emmeline Pankhurst (1)	*Socialism for Women (ILP)*	Bethel Chapel
1906			
May 26	Philip Snowden (1)	*The importance of trade union membership*	Assembly Rooms
May 26	Ethel Snowden (1)	*Object & Policies of the ILP*	Rehoboth Chapel
May 27	Ethel Snowden (2)	*The work of the labour party*	Zion *(sic)* Zoar Chapel
1910			
June 20	Ben Tillett	*My recent visit to Australia*	Rehoboth
1911			
January 8	Ernest Bevin (1)		
March 5	Bipin Chandra Pal	*Indian Independence*	
April 2	J. Bruce Glasier (1)	*The progress of socialism*	
November	Philip Snowden (2)	*Socialism*	
1912			
January 21	George Lansbury (1)		

Date	Speaker	Subject	Venue/notes
1912 continued			
November 3	Fenner Brockway (1)		
1913			
January 5	Sylvia Pankhurst (1)		
1914			
	Rev. H. Dunnico (1)	Church Jubilee Service	Jerusalem Church
1915			
May 28	J. T. W. Newbold (1)		
June 19	Morgan Jones (Chair)	Formation of a south Wales Branch of the NCF	
October 24	Emmeline Pankhurst (2)	*Aid the country's war effort.* Under the WSPU's auspices	English Congregational Chapel
1916			
January 16	Richard Wallhead (1)	E. C. Hutchinson (Chair)	Public Hall
March 5	Herbert Dunnico (2)	*Dare to be a Daniel*	Jerusalem Church
March 12	J. Ramsay MacDonald (1)		
March	W. C. Anderson (1)		
March 16	J. Ramsay MacDonald (2)		
April 15	Thomas Richardson Bob Williams; Gilbert Cannan	*Censorship Resolution against extension of Military Service Act*	Jerusalem Church
May 16	George Jones; Chris Way; Rev. R. Powell	Trades Council Vote on conscription	
May 16	C. P. Trevelyan (1)	*Avoidance of War*	Public Hall
June 5	E. D. Morel (1)	*German Internment Camps-the truth*	
July 2	Bertrand Russell (1)	NCF Meeting Harry Davies Cwmafan (Chair)	
July 15-16	Richard Wallhead (2)	*Peace Negotiations*	

Date	Speaker	Subject	Venue/notes
1916 continued			
July 23	Sylvia Pankhurst (3)		
August 31	Rev. T. E. Nicholas		Jerusalem
September 2		Women's ILP meeting	
September 5	E. D. Morel (2)		
September 7	B. N. Langdon-Davies (1)		
September 25	Ethel Snowden (3)		
September 25	Philip Snowden (3)		
October 7	Tal Mainwaring; Harry Davies (Cwmafan); Henry Davies (Taibach)	NCF Social with M. Watters Presiding and J. Rees Powell in attendance. *An inspiration to all.* Ivor Thomas and Arthur Henry Armstrong also present	Briton Ferry Minor Public Hall
October 21	Helena L. M. Swanwick (London) (1)	*Military Service Acts mean withdrawal of Habeas Corpus.* Briton Ferry Council for Civil Liberties; D. L. Mort in Chair	Indoors
November 12	Charles Roden Buxton (1)	*Peace by Negotiation*	
December 3	Ethel Snowden (4)	Motion by Henry Davies for *Peace*	Public Hall 1000+attendance
December 15	C. P. Trevelyan (2)	*Civil Liberties*	Public Hall no longer available
1917			
January 28	Norman Angell (1)		
June 1	A Conscientious objector from Wormwood Scrubs	*The Gift of Power*	Jerusalem Christian Endeavour
June 3	Harry Davies (Cwmavon); D. J. Morgan (Swansea Blind Institute); Joe Branch (Chair)	*Favours, privileges & rights – a celebration of the Russian Revolution*	Crown Park as Public Hall no longer available for Public Meetings

Date	Speaker	Subject	Venue/notes
1917 continued			
June 3	Rev. Rees Powell	*King's Economy Proclamation*	Jerusalem Church
August 4/5	Philip Morrell M. P. (Burnley); George Gethin; Joe Branch; D. L. Mort	*Council for Workers and Soldiers: Principles of the Revolution*	Crown Park
August 9	Rev. Herbert Morgan (Bristol)	*Peace Day – the futility of war*	Jerusalem Church
August 31	Rev. T. E. Nicholas *(Pioneer Editor)*	The first time a church had invited him to speak about peace. Rev. Nicholas regretted the *Church's impotence when war broke out*	Jerusalem Church
September 1	Robert Williams (2) D. L. Mort (Chair)	Smillie is *no office seeker and beyond the influence of gold*	Crown Park
September 19	Arthur Henry Armstrong	Hardie Memorial Lecture: *Oration on Abraham Lincoln*	Bible Christian Chapel, Mansel Street
September 20	Dr. Rawlings J. P. (Swansea)	*The Church's Impotence in preventing war*	Jerusalem Church
September 22	Ethel Snowden (5) Mrs Powell (Chair)	*No annexation & no indemnity*	Jerusalem Church
October 6	Dr Walsh (London) (1) J. Branch (Chair)	Hardie Memorial Lecture: *The Public Hall & a number of other chapels had refused to host the event.*	Jerusalem Church
October 31	Rev. J. Morgan Jones (Merthyr)	Public Peace Meeting: *Man is more precious than fine gold.* The best attended meeting since inauguration despite refusal by billing company to post bills	Jerusalem Church Rev. Rees Powell Presiding
November 14	C. R. Buxton (2)		Jerusalem George Jones
November 21	Rev. Ronald Fraser (Liverpool)		

Date	Speaker	Subject	Venue/notes
1917 continued			
November 22	Rev. George Neighbour (Mountain Ash)	Neighbour's son, George John, was a Class A conscientious objector	His son had been at Talgarth, Knutsford and Liverpool prison on a punishment diet
December 6	Theodora Wilson-Wilson (1)	*The raid on the Crusader's premises.*	Jerusalem
December	James Maxton (1)		
December 28	Richard Wallhead (3)		
December	Minnie Pallister (1)	Butler of Stockport: *the World's debt to the Conscientious Objector*	
1918			
January 3	Mrs Rees Powell	*The legacy of Conscientious Objectors for prison reform. My criticism of armchair patriots*	Jerusalem Church
January 4	Rev. E. K. Jones (Cefnmawr) Rev. D. Wyre Lewis (Rhos)	*Pacifists are now better understood. Liberty of speech War weariness might end the war, but not bring lasting peace.*	Jerusalem Church
February 16	George Lansbury		Neath
February 17	Charlotte Despard	*Women's Peace Crusade*	Jerusalem Church
February 23	G. H. Paton	*War aims of the Government* Under the auspices of the National War Propaganda Movement	Near the Dock Hotel (Open Air)
February 23	Emmeline Pankhurst (3)	*The Women's Party* Women's Peace Crusade event	Public Meeting at Jerusalem
March 9	Bob Williams (3)	Welcome sign of toleration (after ILP ban for previous 18 months)	Public Hall (Ivor Thomas)
March 16	Richard Wallhead (4)	*Prison experiences*	Public Hall
March 21	Rev. Herbert Morgan (Bristol)	*Reconciliation*	

Date	Speaker	Subject	Venue/notes
1918 continued			
March 25	Rev. H. H. Hughes (Bangor) Rev. W. J. Rees (Alltwen)	*Reconciliation as the means to end the war's chaos*	Jerusalem Church
April 1	Mrs Powell	*The war is over; conscription is no longer a military necessity*	Jerusalem Church Chair: Mrs White
April 7	Rev. Llew Boyer (Pontardawe)		
April	Herbert Morgan		
April 24	Rev. W. J. Rees (Alltwen)		
April	Herbert Dunnico (3)	Every seat taken	Jerusalem Church
May 23	Rev. J. Puleston Jones (Pwllheli-The blind preacher)	*War is one of interests not of ideals*	Jerusalem Church
June 29	J. B. Houston MA	*Secret treaties & their effect on housing*	ILP Ivor Thomas
September 30	Joe Branch; George Gethin; Ivor H. Thomas	*Hardie Memorial Meeting*	Bible Christian Chapel, Mansel Street
October	J. Bruce Glasier (2) Ivor H. Thomas	*The present situation*	Bible Christian Chapel, Mansel Street
October 29	Rev. George Neighbour (Mountain Ash)		Jerusalem Church
December 14	Morgan Jones (2)		
December	Minnie Pallister (2)	*Support for Rev. Herbert Morgan, ILP candidate for Neath*	
1919			
January 18	Rev. D. J. Davies (Ogmore Vale)	*Reconstruction – first of a series*	Jerusalem Church *Rev Powell (Presiding)*
January 19	Dan Griffiths	*Experiences as a CO*	Ivor H. Thomas Presiding
March 9	Charles Matthews (Port Talbot)	ILP Meeting: *Education and Housing*	E. C. Hutchinson (Chair)

Date	Speaker	Subject	Venue/notes
1919 continued			
April	Morgan Jones (3)	UDC visit	Ivor H. Thomas Presiding
May 3	Mr Kneeshaw (1) (Birmingham)	UDC meeting	Ivor H. Thomas Presiding
June 7	Humphrey Chalmers (Chaplain of Wandsworth Prison) & A. Rosina Davies (Treorchy)	*Prison Reform*	Jerusalem Church
July 7	Robert Smillie (1)		
July 20	J. E. Edmunds (Cardiff) (1)		
July	J. Langdon Davies		
November 15	Herbert Dunnico (4)	*The Church & the new age*	Jerusalem Church
December 6	Rev. David Hughes (ex-servicemen's union)	*Comrades of War & Peace*	Kindly lent by Jerusalem Church *due to prohibitive price of the Public Hall*
December 12	J. E. Edmunds (Cardiff) (2)	*Education & Democracy*	
1920			
19 November	J. N. Graham Peace		
29 November	Benjamin G. Harriman		
1921			
February 20	George Lansbury (2)		Briton Ferry
May 29	Reginald Sorensen (1)		
June 3	Emrys Hughes		
1922			
January 18	Fenner Brockway (1)		
February 20	Richard Wallhead (5)		
June 4	Robert Smillie (2)		
December 18	Ben F. Wilson, Berkeley, California		

Date	Speaker	Subject	Venue/notes
1923			
June 26	Jimmy Edmunds (3)		
1924			
January 23	Hugh Dalton (1)		
March 12	Minnie Pallister (3)	*The Orange Box; thoughts of a socialist propagandist*	
May 18	Katherine Glasier (1)		

Other visitors to Neath/Aberafan constituencies
Their activities and future roles

	Clement Attlee	Later, Prime Minister	
	Margaret Bonfield	Britain's first woman cabinet minister. Women's rights activist	
	C. T. Cramp	General Secretary of the National Union of Railwaymen and Chair of the Labour Party	
	Arthur Henderson	Later, Leader of the Labour Party, Leader of the Opposition	
	J. H. Thomas	President of TUC and IFTU (1920–24) and General Secretary of the National Union of Railwaymen	
1925			
March-April & Autumn	Emma Goldman		
Later dates			
	C. L. James		
	Tom Mann		
	Paul Robeson		

Appendix Fourteen
COs' motivations in Briton Ferry and Huddersfield: a comparison

Motivation	Huddersfield Population 107,821 18,864 eligible Places of worship 70	Briton Ferry Population 8,456 1,836 eligible Places of worship 20
Socialists		
BSP	15	
Fabian	1	
ILP	7	6
SSS	7	
Socialists	15	3
Sub Total	**45**	**9**
Religious		
Anglican	1	
Christadelphian	18	
Congregationalist	1	2
Methodist	1	3
Primitive Methodist	1	
Quaker	13	
Wesleyan	3	
Roman Catholic	2	
Baptist		6
Religious	2	
Sub Total	**42**	**11**

Motivation	Huddersfield Population 107,821 18,864 eligible Places of worship 70	Briton Ferry Population 8,456 1,836 eligible Places of worship 20
Other		
FoR	1	
NCF	7	8
UDC	1	
Moral and ethical	1	
Sub Total	10	8
Not Known		
	18	5
TOTAL	**115**	**33**

**Rate of conscientious objectors per thousand of population
eligible for conscription**

Huddersfield 6.26   Briton Ferry 19.06

Appendix Fifteen
Fetters and Roses Dinner

An informal dinner was given at the House of Commons on 9 January 1924 for the 19 MPs and others who had been imprisoned for political or religious reasons during World War One. The MPs were past MPs, at the time of the dinner or in the future. The dinner was held two weeks before Baldwin resigned and Ramsay MacDonald became Prime Minister. Forty six people are in the photograph. The table below lists those present, including the general reason for their imprisonment. Those in **bold** visited Briton Ferry.

House of Commons dinner on 9 January 1924
(Parliament and Constitution Centre)

James Maxton (2nd left back row); Dick Wallhead (2nd left front row);

Name	Constituency	Reason for imprisonment/affiliation
Ayles, Walter Henry	Bristol North; Southall; Hayes & Harlington	Conscientious objector; NCF
Davies, Rev George Maitland Lloyd	University of Wales	Conscientious objector; FoR
Diamond, Charles	North Monaghan	Incitement to outrage
Dukes, Charles	Warrington	Conscientious objector
Gould, Barbara	Hendon North	Suffragist
Haycock, Alex Wilkinson	Salford West	Conscientious objector: Defence of the Realm violation
Hudson, James Hindle	Ealing North	Conscientious objector; NCF; UDC
John, William	Rhondda West	Riot: Tonypandy strike
Jones, Morgan	Caerphilly	Conscientious objector; UDC Defence of the Realm violation
Kirkwood, David	Dumbarton East	ILP: Defence of the Realm violation
Lawrence, Susan	Poplar	Contempt of court: withholding rates
Lupton, Arnold	Sleaford	Defence of the Realm violation
March, Samuel	South Poplar	Contempt of court: withholding rates
Maxton, James	Glasgow Bridgeton	Conscientious objector; Defence of the Realm violation
Morel, E. D.	Dundee	Defence of the Realm violation; UDC
Muir	Glasgow Maryhill	Defence of the Realm violation
Pethick-Lawrence, Frederick William	Leicester West; Edinburgh East	UDC; conspiracy with WSPU

Name	Constituency	Reason for imprisonment/affiliation
Pethick-Lawrence, Frederick William	Leicester West; Edinburgh East	UDC; conspiracy with WSPU
Scurr, John	Stepney	Contempt of court: withholding rates; pacifist and supporter of Conscientious objectors
Shinwell, Emanuel	Linlithgow; Seaham; Easington	
Wallhead, Richard Collingham	Merthyr	Defence of the Realm violation
Non-elected candidates		
Albery, Wyndham		
Evans, Dorothy		
Foan, Gilbert		
Hunter, E. E.		
Merell, Robert O.		
Millwood, Philip		
Pethick-Lawrence, Emmeline		
Pritchard, Rev A. G.		
Russell, Hon Bertrand		
Russell, Mrs Dora		
Scott-Duckers, James		
Others		
Archdale, Helen		
Barret, Cornelius		Quaker Sentenced to death
Norman, C. H.		
Rhondda, Viscount (Margaret Haig Thomas)		WSPU; Usk jail
Sharp, Evelyn		WSPU; suffragist

Acknowledgements

Some time ago I determined to discover whether (and, if so, why) my family had included both serving soldiers and conscientious objectors during World War One. Like so much research, however, it took on a life of its own and failed to find answers to the seminal question but succeeded instead in emerging as a rather different book, entitled *A Most Industrious Town: Briton Ferry and its people 1814–2014*. It outlined two hundred years' history of the town of my birth. However I rapidly realised that there was still much to research and write about the town's attitude to World War One, particularly regarding the resistance to the War and the support in the town for peace. What you now have in this book is the result.

Many organisations (but especially the people who work within them) deserve thanks for helping to bring this project to fruition. Two special digital information projects, run by the National Library of Wales (*Cymru 1914 and Welsh Newspapers on line*) provided an invaluable resource. The West Glamorgan Archives, Neath Antiquarian Society, and Neath-Port Talbot Libraries were also called upon. Briton Ferry's phoenix-like, and now thriving, Community Resource Centre all greatly assisted me in my research. The Royal Commission for Ancient and Historical Monuments Wales Library also sourced for me a number of rare photographs.

The Peace Pledge Union and *Peace News* provided much essential background information. Jan Melichar of the Peace Pledge Union kick-started a journey that allowed me to 'change lenses', by directing me from national data collection to that of individual and family experiences, by way of the Sharkey family of Liverpool. They not only provided invaluable family information on Dil Thomas but also introduced me to Cyril Pearce of Huddersfield, whose knowledge and achievements are so deservedly well-known. He offered me access to the *Pearce Register of Conscientious Objectors* and was also instrumental in leading me to Aled Eurig, whose current doctoral studies on *Conscientious Objectors in Wales*, enabled a pooling and validation of data.

A Most Industrious Town contained a chapter headed *Politicians and Pacifists*. For encouraging me to extend this venture, I must thank Dr. Hywel Francis MP, whose knowledge of both those topics has revealed itself during the course of my own research. After reading the same chapter, a number of readers contacted me with information which has become central to this book. One of them, Cheryl Clement – literally – handed me the third album of evidence during the launch of the *Briton Ferry and its People* book. Her donation was crucial in that it allowed me to verify what I suspected already: that the people and events in Briton Ferry during the era under consideration were nationally important. In similar fashion Philip Mort, by providing further evidence from a fourth album, added yet further significant information. Caroline Jackson (born in Briton Ferry but a long-time resident of the Peak District) later entrusted me with her family archives enabling me to acquire much fascinating information on the conscientious objector brothers, C. T. T. and H. B. Jones, and their sister, Dorcas. Similarly, Allan Colwill of Malvern generously opened up his grandfather's (Tom Thomas) diaries and library. Through a chance conversation with Andrew Dewar in Termes d'Armagnac, France, I was able to trace Dai Mainwaring to Cornwall. Consequently I am indebted to Dai for his personal memories of his grandfather, Tal. What Dai did not know of Tal, Allen Blethyn (and his amazing *Taibach and District Group of All Things Historical*) did. Another chance conversation at Termes d'Armagnac between guests at Marciac Jazz Festival, just as this book was about to be printed, resulted in the revelation that James Rees (see pages 145, 208) was the grandfather of Gareth Rees. Gareth recalled the family tale of his grandfather having to stand on Neath Road 'with one foot on the pavement and the other in the gutter to avoid an obstruction charge, during the distribution of anti-conscription leaflets.' Alan Thomas of Nottingham and his brothers also provided family background about his great uncle, Jim Mort, and added what they could to currently unpublished information.

Locally, Ken Donovan's knowledge and documents of Briton

Ferry's politics and religious bodies, especially of Jerusalem Church, proved a valuable resource. Audrey and Brian Minty deserve profuse thanks for providing me with contacts at the Resource Centre – and elsewhere – in Briton Ferry. They may not realise just how much they have done to make possible the present publication. I would like also to express my thanks to Anita Phillips of Mike's Newsagents, Briton Ferry, whose extensive network of contacts in her town has opened doors and eased my journey in making this work known.

Prior to publication, a series of presentations was held in Briton Ferry Resource Centre to publicise the contents of this book and, hopefully, to elicit further information. This yielded important information on the trial of the 'Briton Ferry ten' from Mrs Euronwy Rees and her brother, Malcolm Hill, niece and nephew of Joe Branch and holders of much fascinating information about Briton Ferry. Although some of the ten names have yet to be linked to the nine faces in the photograph of the ten accused, there is no longer any question that the photograph is of the 'ten'.

At this time I was fortunate, too, to be introduced to Dr Harold Lewis of the International Transport Federation. His contribution from their archives was to yield information of inestimable value.

Martin Davies encouraged me to plunder his well-stocked vault, filled with information about Briton Ferry and its personalities. Philip and Paul Ware's help with fieldwork in the area also contributed in progressing the project, whilst Steffan Newton and colleagues from Neath-Port Talbot Council proved assiduous in their searches of the town's cemetery records.

That this work ever started is due to my Bristolian elder brother, Hugh: he insisted that there was a very important, but largely lost, story; that it needed telling, and that it must to be told in a particular way that would do justice to the people and events in Briton Ferry. My Northumbrian younger brother, Andrew, gave me the wherewithal to tell it, (both by digitising family albums and other papers and also by offering sound advice in researching and presenting the story within the necessary context). He, in collaboration with Angus McKie, provided creative expertise, and a number of suggestions that have found their way into this publication.

The design, layout and pre-press work owes much to the

experience of John Fleming, a man who has succeeded in bridging the digital divide by marrying techniques he acquired as a former hot-metal printer with his current expertise in electronic publishing.

For her patience and wise counsel, in the face of my insistence that this *must* see the light of day, I offer my partner, Dr. Sylvia Duffy, my profuse apologies and recognition for her understanding and her patience during a difficult time.

Everyone I have mentioned above has reiterated that their respective contribution is serving a clear purpose. Obviously all felt that *Not in Our Name* had a place awaiting it on the shelves of Briton Ferry Resource Centre. They were anxious, too, that it should reach a much wider audience, so that present and future generations will be better able to discuss and learn the implications of what really went on a century ago. By considering the philosophical, political and social undercurrents that pulled and pushed individuals and families hither and thither on a tide of war, the domestic consequences of 'a shot heard around the world', in Briton Ferry and elsewhere, can become more comprehensible.

Philip Adams
Ludlow
August 2015